Contents

Preface

I have been very gratified by the continuing success and popularity of this book since it first appeared. However, I felt that a new edition of the book was needed to take account of changes in policy and practice. In particular, this edition includes material that addresses the new professional standards for qualified teacher status and beyond, and better addresses the needs of those undertaking masters-level work as part of their initial teacher training programme. Whilst the thrust of the book remains the same, some sections have been polished further and other sections have been substantially rewritten. The revised text has taken particular account of developments in personalised learning, the use of ICT, interactive teaching, classroom dialogue, inclusion, assessment for learning, evidence-based classroom practice, the *Every Child Matters* agenda, and the teaching methods underpinning the National Strategies.

Effective Tea

Theory and Practice

Third Edition

Chris Kyriacou

OXFORD

UNIVERSITY PRESS

OXFORD
UNIVERSITY PRESS

Great Clarendon Street, Oxford, OX2 6DP, United Kingdom

Oxford University Press is a department of the University of Oxford.
It furthers the University's objective of excellence in research, scholarship,
and education by publishing worldwide. Oxford is a registered trade mark of
Oxford University Press in the UK and in certain other countries

First published by Stanley Thornes (Publishers) Ltd in 1997
Second edition published by Nelson Thornes Ltd in 2009
This edition published by Oxford University Press in 2014

British Library Cataloguing in Publication Data
Data available

978-1-4085-0423-9

10 9 8 7 6

Printed in Great Britain by CPI Group (UK) Ltd., Croydon CR0 4YY

Acknowledgements

Page make-up: Pantek Arts Ltd

1 Introduction

This book looks at those aspects of teaching and learning in schools that are important for effective teaching. Some people have voiced the opinion that anyone who knows their subject matter can teach. Nothing could be further from the truth. Effective teaching involves having a sound understanding of how and why certain activities lead to learning, and what factors influence their effectiveness. Teachers make use of a whole range of teaching skills to make sure learning occurs effectively. Only a combination of both subject matter knowledge and an understanding of the nature of effective teaching itself can provide a solid foundation for effectiveness.

Three of the key tasks of teacher education are:

- to help teachers build up their knowledge and understanding of effective teaching
- to help teachers to develop the key skills involved in classroom teaching
- to help teachers to critically reflect upon and evaluate their own teaching.

What has struck me about most books on effective teaching is that they largely fall into two camps. Some specifically concern themselves with common-sense observations about teaching, largely based on the professional experience of the writers, often termed 'craft knowledge'. Others concern themselves with theoretical discussion and research, stemming from mainly psychological and sociological perspectives. Such books do not satisfactorily meet the needs of teacher development for effectiveness. The former camp, whilst often giving good advice, does not provide the necessary framework of understanding that enables teachers to teach effectively. The danger of simply following advice is that it encourages an attempt to model one's practice upon some envisaged image of teaching, which does little to help you deal with the variety of classroom situations that occur. Books in the latter camp, however, often tend to gear their discussion towards the needs of other researchers, or those following academic courses, rather than the needs of those concerned to develop their own teaching effectiveness. These two camps are often discussed as the gap between theory and practice, i.e. between theoretical considerations drawing on academic concerns on the one hand, and a sound knowledge of the craft of good classroom practice on the other hand.

My own expertise lies within the psychology of education, but I have also taught in schools and observed many lessons given by both student teachers and experienced teachers. There is clearly much within the psychological perspective on teaching and learning in schools that can make an important contribution to effective teaching. However, the key to doing this is to make clear how sound craft knowledge is actually based on underlying psychological principles and processes. By doing this, it can be made clear what works well in the classroom and why.

The central aim of this book then, is to help develop and sharpen teachers' craft knowledge through a clarification of the key psychological considerations involved. This books aims to bridge the gap between theory and practice, by considering what is involved in establishing and maintaining the effectiveness of an educational experience, both at the surface level of what the teacher needs to be doing, and at the underlying level of what psychological processes underpin this.

The need to improve the quality of teaching in schools is a source of public debate in many countries throughout the world. In attempting to do this, some governments have introduced new forms of initial teacher training, the regular appraisal of established teachers, lists of teacher competencies, and statements about what should be taught and how. Indeed, it is not at all uncommon to witness one country making a major change towards something just as another country has decided to move in the opposite direction.

At the same time, there has been much debate among teacher educators concerning how teacher education can best foster effective teaching, taking account of the government's views on teacher training, the teacher educators' own professional views of how training is best conducted, and the findings of research studies looking at aspects of effective teaching and the impact of training.

Research into effective teaching is largely concerned with investigating three inter-related perspectives:

- *The teachers' perspective.* How do teachers view teaching and learning? What are their views about what works best and why? What factors influence their teaching practice? How much variation is there among teachers in their views and behaviour?

- *The pupils' perspective.* How do pupils view teaching and learning? What motivates them? What learning strategies do they use? What types of teachers and activities do they feel are effective and why? How much variation is there among pupils in their views and behaviour?

- *The activities perspective.* Are some activities more effective than others? What factors influence whether an activity will be effective? How well does the activity match the learning needs of the pupil? How can teachers and pupils get the most out of a particular activity? How frequently are different activities used? What factors influence the method of using different activities?

Within each chapter I have tried to encompass these three perspectives. In choosing the theme for each chapter, I have been very conscious of the extent to which each theme seems to relate to and touch upon considerations explored in other chapters. Such is inevitably the nature of effective teaching: a complex inter-relationship of a number of different concerns, each impinging on each other to greater or lesser extents. Nevertheless, I have attempted to focus on the themes that appear to me to be the most crucial ones in understanding effective teaching.

The book is broadly divided into three parts, which reflect the three key tasks of teacher education that I outlined earlier. The first part (chapters 2 and 3) focuses on providing an understanding of the key issues that underpin the nature of effective teaching and pupil learning. The second part (chapters 4 to 8) focuses on the delivery of effective classroom practice. Finally, the third part (chapter 9) deals with reflecting on teaching experience.

Chapter 2, 'Ways of thinking about effective teaching', considers three main approaches to looking at effective teaching. The first approach focuses on two central concepts:

'active learning time' and 'quality of instruction'. The former is concerned with the amount of time pupils spend during a lesson (or while at school) actively engaged in learning experiences related to the educational outcomes intended. The latter refers to the actual quality of the learning experiences themselves. These two concepts have dominated research on effective teaching aimed at explaining why some teachers are more effective than others. In essence, effective teachers are those who are able to maximise both the amount of active learning time and the quality of instruction. The second approach focuses on teaching as an essentially managerial activity, and has sought to identify key teaching skills that underlie the effective management of learning. The third approach focuses on the key psychological concepts, principles and processes that appear to be involved when effective teaching is taking place. This approach places emphasis on the pupil's psychological state and how it relates to the success or failure of an educational activity.

In chapter 3, 'How pupils learn', the nature of pupil learning itself is explored. Particular attention is paid to three psychological conditions that appear to be crucial for learning:

- The pupil must be *attending* to the learning experience.
- The pupil must be *receptive* to the learning experience.
- The learning experience must be *appropriate* for the desired learning to take place.

In chapter 4, 'Setting up the learning experience', the different ways in which teachers can set up learning activities are considered. One of the key features of effective teaching is the use of a diversity of approaches that enables the teacher to elicit and sustain pupils' interest and involvement in their learning. Much effective teaching involves allowing pupils to be more active and to have greater control over the direction and pace of the learning experience.

Chapter 5, 'Taking account of pupil differences', discusses the implications for effective teaching of a variety of important differences between pupils that can influence learning. There are many such differences, but the most important ones, which are explored here, are ability, motivation, social class, gender, race, and special educational needs. In attempting to consider the implications for teaching of these categories, what becomes very apparent is that the issues and strategies related to dealing with the needs of one group of pupils are also relevant to meeting the needs of *all* pupils. For example, in considering the needs of gifted pupils, a central problem is how to keep such pupils interested and challenged by the learning activities provided. In meeting their needs, it is evident that the same problem and possible response to it could be just as relevant to meeting the needs of all the pupils in the school.

The first half of chapter 6, 'Key classroom teaching qualities and tasks', attempts to identify the essential qualities of effective teaching. It is often claimed that it is easy to recognise good teaching when you see it, but few would claim that it is equally easy to break down such a global assessment into its constituent parts. This problem largely results from the fact that different observers actually mean different things by the notion of good teaching. Moreover, what a particular observer has in mind can often be achieved in different ways. Nevertheless, when one looks at the discussion of such qualities within the context of teacher education, there does appear to be a fair degree of consensus, although the exact headings and emphasis may vary from writer to writer.

In the second half of chapter 6, attention focuses on three key tasks underpinning effective teaching in the classroom: planning; presentation and monitoring; and reflection and evaluation. These three tasks need to be based on sound decision-making before, during and after the lesson. Planning deals with key questions regarding the basic format of the lesson and its content. Presentation and monitoring deals with how the teacher delivers a lesson and monitors its progress in order to establish and maintain its effectiveness. Reflection and evaluation deals with how the teacher evaluates the success of a lesson and reflects on implications for future teaching.

In chapter 7, 'Relationships with pupils', it is argued that a sound relationship between the teacher and pupils needs to be based on two qualities: the pupils' acceptance of the teacher's authority; and the establishment of mutual respect and rapport. The chapter looks at the way in which establishing a positive classroom climate forms an important aspect of effective teaching in promoting an expectation towards learning and in minimising pupil misbehaviour. Finally, the chapter also considers the way in which the teacher's pastoral care responsibilities also underpin teacher–pupil relationships.

Chapter 8, 'Dealing with pupil misbehaviour', looks at the major strategies and techniques that teachers can use to deal effectively with pupil misbehaviour. After considering the nature and causes of pupil misbehaviour and the strategies that can be used to pre-empt their occurrence, the chapter goes on to examine the use of reprimands and punishments, and the qualities that will increase their effectiveness.

In chapter 9, 'Appraising practice', three major professional concerns facing teachers are discussed: the curriculum; teacher appraisal; and teacher stress. The first concern explores the need for teachers to stand back from time to time and look afresh at the content and purpose of the school curriculum, both as a whole and in relation to particular areas. The second concern looks at how teacher appraisal can offer an opportunity for teachers to review their classroom practice and to consider their professional development needs. The third major concern is the issue of teacher stress. This reflects the fact that teaching is a demanding profession, and the ability to cope skilfully with the pressures and frustrations that can arise is an important part of maintaining one's enthusiasm for teaching and the capacity to perform well.

The final chapter, 'Conclusions', reflects on the various themes covered in this book and highlights the main priorities for fostering effective teaching in schools.

Useful websites

The following websites provide useful information about policy, practice and research on effective teaching.

Behaviour4Learning
www.behaviour4learning.ac.uk

British Education Index (BEI)
www.bei.ac.uk

British Educational Communications and Technology Agency (Becta)
www.becta.org.uk

British Educational Research Association (BERA)
www.bera.ac.uk

Centre for the Use of Research and Evidence in Education (CUREE)
www.curee-paccts.com

Department for Children, Schools and Families (DCSF)
www.dcsf.gov.uk

Educational Evidence Portal (EEP)
www.eep.ac.uk

Education Resources Information Center (ERIC)
www.eric.ed.gov

Evidence for Policy and Practice Information and Co-ordinating Centre
(EPPI-Centre)
www.eppi.ioe.ac.uk

Institute for Effective Education (IEE)
www.york.ac.uk/iee

Intute
www.intute.ac.uk

National Curriculum
http://curriculum.qca.org.uk

National Strategies
www.nationalstrategies.org.uk

Office for Standards in Education, Children's Services and Skills (Ofsted)
www.ofsted.gov.uk

Qualifications and Curriculum Authority (QCA)
www.qca.org.uk

Standards
www.standards.dcsf.gov.uk

TeacherNet
www.teachernet.gov.uk

Teacher Training Resource Bank (TTRB)
www.ttrb.ac.uk

Teachers TV
www.teachers.tv

Teaching and Learning Research Programme
www.tlrp.org

Training and Development Agency for Schools (TDA)
www.tda.gov.uk

What Works Well
http://whatworkswell.standards.dcsf.gov.uk

2 Ways of thinking about effective teaching

Objective

To consider the nature of effective teaching and the key concepts and processes involved.

Effective teaching can be defined as teaching that successfully achieves the learning by pupils intended by the teacher. In essence, there are two simple elements to effective teaching:

- The teacher must have a clear idea of what learning is to be fostered.
- A learning experience is set up and delivered that achieves this.

Over the years, thinking about effective teaching has been approached in a number of different ways. Until the 1960s, research on effective teaching was largely dominated by attempts to identify attributes of teachers, such as personality traits, sex, age, knowledge and training, which might have a bearing on their effectiveness. As long ago as 1931, for example, Cattell asked 254 people, including directors of education, teacher trainers, schoolteachers and pupils, to write down the most important qualities of the good teacher. Overall, the five most frequently reported were (in order of frequency):

- personality and will
- intelligence
- sympathy and tact
- open-mindedness
- a sense of humour.

Studies that attempted to relate such teacher attributes to educational outcomes have sometimes been referred to as 'black-box' research. The point being made is that such research on effective teaching completely ignored what actually went on in the classroom. Instead, it simply looked at input characteristics (attributes of the teacher and pupils), looked at the output (e.g. examination results), and tried to relate the two.

Since the 1960s, however, research on effective teaching has focused fairly and squarely on activities in the classroom, and in particular the interaction between the teacher and pupils. Moreover, since the 1990s, increasing attention has been paid, firstly, to establishing a research evidence base for effective classroom practices and using this to underpin the initial and continuing professional development of teachers, and, secondly, to gaining a deeper understanding of the teaching and learning that takes place in the classroom. As a result, there is now a good consensus regarding the basic framework for our thinking about effective teaching, within which we can make a useful distinction between three main classes of variables (Figure 2.1).

Context variables refer to all those characteristics of the context of the learning activity, usually a classroom-based lesson, which may have some bearing on the success of the learning activity.

Process variables refer to what actually goes on in the classroom, and deals with the perceptions, strategies and behaviour of the teacher and pupils, and characteristics of the learning tasks and activities themselves, and how these interact with each other. Such variables include:

- teacher's enthusiasm
- clarity of explanations
- use of questions
- use of praise and criticism
- management strategies
- disciplinary techniques
- classroom climate
- organisation of the lesson
- suitability of learning tasks
- type of feedback pupils receive
- pupil involvement in the lesson
- pupil-initiated interaction with the teacher
- pupils' strategies for learning.

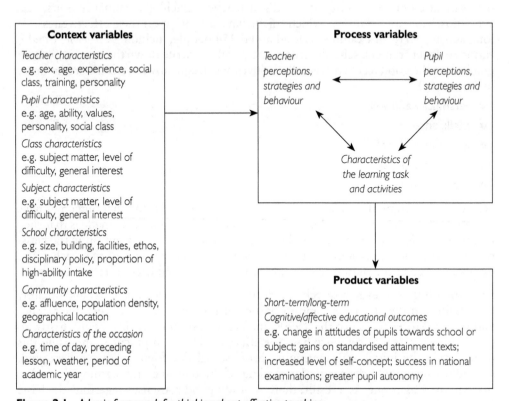

Figure 2.1   *A basic framework for thinking about effective teaching*

Product variables refer to all those educational outcomes that are desired by teachers and that have formed a basis of teachers' planning of lessons and the criteria they use or others use to judge effectiveness. The most important educational outcomes for pupils would appear to be:

- increased knowledge and skills
- increased interest in the subject or topic
- increased intellectual motivation
- increased academic self-confidence and self-esteem
- increased autonomy
- increased social development.

Many of these outcomes can be measured by tests, but others are often based on subjective forms of assessment, such as the teacher's opinion. Unfortunately, the methods used to measure these outcomes can often be very problematic, and may need to be treated with caution.

Conceptual and research problems

This overall framework of *Context–Process–Product* has provided the basis for almost all research on effective teaching reported over the last few decades (Borich, 2007; Muijs and Reynolds, 2005; Ornstein and Lasley, 2004). Such research has raised a number of important points concerning both our understanding of these three classes of variables and how research can provide evidence of the contribution made to effectiveness by different aspects of the teaching situation.

In considering context variables, it is clear that there are a vast number of aspects to the context of a teaching situation that may have a bearing on its success. The variety of ways in which these aspects can be combined to define a particular context in detail is enormous. The context for teaching in schools can range from a lesson based on adding small numbers for a mixed-ability class of five-year-old pupils in a small rural primary school to a lesson on electrolysis for a top-ability group of 16-year-old pupils doing science in a large urban secondary school. A major task facing a teacher is in deciding which aspects of the context need to be taken into account when considering the appropriate learning activity. Clearly, the variety of teaching contexts creates problems for research. Firstly, it means that each study undertaken can only take account of a few aspects of the context at any one time. Secondly, the influence of one variable on effectiveness may depend on which other variables are also present. Thus, for example, size of school may have a different effect in an affluent community than in a community containing much poverty.

In considering process variables, again it is clear that there are a large number of aspects of classroom activities that may well be related to effectiveness. In addition, a number of problems have been posed for researchers in considering how best to identify, monitor and record the various aspects of teacher and pupil behaviour and the learning activities. The use of questionnaires, interviews and classroom observation all have research problems associated with them that require great caution in the interpretation of the data collected. This can infuriate educational policy makers who often want simple and clear answers to the questions they pose about the effectiveness of teachers and teaching methods. Nevertheless, the wealth of studies of effective teaching conducted over the last few decades have now clarified the basic nature of the many process variables involved in teaching, ranging from very discrete observable behaviours (such as the frequency with which teachers use praise) to more global and more subjectively assessed qualities (such as classroom ethos).

Such research has emphasised the importance of looking at the meaning of classroom activities for pupils and teachers. Attention has been focused on looking at how teachers and pupils view each other's behaviour and the activities in hand, and the influence this has on determining whether effective teaching occurs.

In considering product variables, one faces a very difficult question: how can we judge whether effective teaching has occurred? At the outset of this chapter I stated that effective teaching is essentially concerned with how a teacher can successfully bring about the desired pupil learning by some educational activity. The problem that follows, however, is that there is very little consensus concerning the relative importance of the different educational outcomes that are taken to be the goals of effective teaching. The goals of effective teaching may emphasise *cognitive* (intellectual) aspects of learning or *affective* (social, emotional and attitudinal) aspects of learning; they may emphasise short-term goals (achievable by the end of a lesson) or long-term goals (achievable at the end of a course or even later). They may be amenable to objective monitoring and assessment or they may involve subjective monitoring and assessment – if assessment is possible at all.

In considering educational outcomes, there is a further difficulty. We must take account of the fact that teachers almost invariably appear to teach with a combination of outcomes in mind. Moreover, this combination of outcomes will vary from lesson to lesson, and indeed within a lesson itself it may vary with respect to each pupil in the class. For example, in dealing with one pupil's answer to a question, the teacher may take into account that pupil's lack of self-confidence, and thus may behave towards that pupil quite differently than towards another pupil giving a similar answer. An observer may find such apparent inconsistency in the teacher's behaviour hard to understand.

The difficulty of translating educational aims into product variables has led many research studies to focus on the most easily accessible, reliable and widely respected measures of educational attainment, namely standardised attainment tests and national examinations. Such a development has thus fostered and reinforced the assumption that the most important educational outcomes are those of intellectual attainment as displayed in such tests and examinations. Not only is such an assumption out of keeping with the professed educational objectives of many teachers, but it also offers greater academic credibility to such tests and examinations than they actually deserve.

Standardised subject attainment tests, for example, are actually suspect as indicators of effective teaching. They are designed to test progress in a particular subject area, but since pupils will not have covered the same material at the same time and in the same depth, there will be large differences between pupils that have little to do with the quality of the teaching. Another major shortcoming of such tests is that some teachers are adept at teaching for the test, by paying close attention to the type and nature of the questions and the mark schemes used and by giving regular practice with similar test material. This can inflate pupils' attainment marks above their real underlying level of understanding and competence in the subject.

National examinations are also suspect as a measure of effective teaching in that attainment in national examinations is influenced by school and teacher policies regarding which courses are offered, how pupils are selected for courses and examination entry, and problems over comparability between examinations set by different examination bodies. There can also be a mismatch between the teacher's own view of effectiveness and what the examinations measure. For example, a teacher may feel that one of the main educational outcomes of teaching science is that pupils should develop a good understanding of the nature of scientific experiment. As the same time, the examination adopted by the school may give little credit for such understanding, but instead emphasise more factual knowledge. As a result, all teachers are constrained to make a compromise between what they feel are the key educational outcomes they wish to foster and the outcomes expected by others who have a stake in the proceedings.

In considering the relationship between the notion of effective teaching and product variables, it is also important to note that researchers have used a variety of similar and overlapping terms to describe teachers, such as 'the good teacher', 'the successful teacher', 'the teacher I like best' and 'the teacher I learn most from'. Each of these terms means something slightly different, so one needs to be cautious in grouping the results of such studies together.

A number of studies have explored pupils' views of teachers and teaching (Cullingford, 2003; Haydn, 2007; Pollard et al., 2000). Overall, the picture that has emerged is that pupils view a good teacher as someone who:

- creates a well-ordered learning environment
- explains the work you have to do and helps you with it
- is friendly and supportive.

In addition, good teachers are often described by pupils as making use of a variety of teaching methods and learning activities, using a range of skills to maintain pupils' interest and to diffuse discipline problems quickly, and managing the lessons so pupils are kept engaged in what the teachers want them to do.

At this point, we need to make a clear distinction between 'effective teaching' and the other similar terms in common use. The essence of effective teaching lies very much in terms of whether the teaching is actually delivering the intended outcomes. Effective teaching implies identifying what actually works as indicated by outcomes. The notion of effective teaching derives from a psychological perspective on thinking about teaching, where the emphasis is placed on identifying observable behaviour in the classroom that can be linked to observable outcomes. In contrast, terms like 'good', 'liked' and 'preferred' teaching place emphasis on how an observer feels about the teaching and usually focuses on qualities and characteristics of teaching that the observer feels are desirable without necessarily any direct reference to outcomes.

Conducting research on effective teaching

As was noted earlier, almost all research on effective teaching reported over the last few decades has employed a basic framework of *Context–Process–Product* (Figure 2.1, p8). This section looks at the ways in which studies have attempted to explore effective teaching using this framework. In doing so, attention will be paid to the two main research strategies that have been adopted and which characterise the overwhelming bulk of research. The first strategy has attempted to relate process variables to product variables (called *process–product studies*); the second strategy has focused almost entirely on process variables alone (called *process studies*).

A number of types of studies have attempted to explore aspects of effective teaching. The main types are:

- studies based on teachers' opinions regarding effective teaching (usually employing questionnaires or interviews)
- studies based on pupils' opinions regarding effective teaching (usually employing questionnaires or interviews; some studies have sought pupils' opinions about their own teacher's teaching)
- studies based on classroom observation by an outside observer (using either recording schedules, video and audio tapes, rating scales or participant observation techniques)
- studies based on descriptions of the behaviour of teachers identified as effective by their headteacher, pupils or others
- studies based on teachers' descriptions of their own teaching
- studies by teachers of their own teaching (which may include keeping detailed notes about their lessons, and getting the reactions of others such as their pupils or colleagues)
- studies based on tests used to measure learning outcomes.

Process–product studies have dominated research on effective teaching for many years. This has led to the creation of a massive database from which many of the characteristics of effective teaching advocated in textbooks aimed at student teachers have been derived. Generally, such studies employ classroom observation to record the frequency of occurrence of various teacher behaviours and aspects of teacher–pupil interaction (the process variables), and then explore their association with the criteria for effectiveness being employed, such as gains in standardised subject attainment tests (the product variables). This association is most commonly explored by simply correlating the process variables with the product variables, with the assumption that the high correlations will pick out aspects of teaching that most strongly contribute to effectiveness. However, in recent years, a number of studies have made use of an experimental design to compare pupils being taught in one way with pupils being taught in another way.

Reviews of process–product studies (Good and Brophy, 2003; Petty, 2006; Stronge, 2007) have typically identified the following 10 characteristics of effective teaching:

- Clarity of the teacher's explanations and directions.
- Establishing a task-oriented classroom climate.
- Making use of a variety of learning activities.
- Establishing and maintaining momentum and pace for the lesson.
- Encouraging pupil participation and getting all pupils involved.
- Monitoring pupils' progress and attending quickly to pupils' needs.
- Delivering a well-structured and well-organised lesson.
- Providing pupils with positive and constructive feedback.
- Ensuring coverage of the educational objectives.
- Making good use of questioning techniques.

Two major problems, however, face such process–product studies. First, they employ a simplistic research design, attempting to focus on small, discrete, observable behaviours that are then associated relatively independently with the product variables. The idea, for example, that such discrete behaviours as 'use of praise' or 'repeating questions' can be explored independently of each other and everything else going on during the lesson, and that each will contribute in its own separate and identifiable way to effectiveness, is very suspect and has contributed to a mass of contradictory data. The second major problem is that such a research design cannot distinguish between those aspects of classroom processes that simply occur when effective teaching is in progress and those aspects which in themselves constitute effective teaching.

A number of process–product studies have attempted to meet the problem of focusing on too many discrete behaviours by grouping these together to form descriptions of particular *teaching styles*. Such studies have attempted to explore whether certain teaching styles are more effective (and if so, in what context and with respect to what type of outcomes). The problem with studies looking at teaching styles, however, has been the fact that teachers are very inconsistent in their use of teaching strategies, often moving from one style to another within a single lesson. In addition, some teachers may use a particular style well and others use the same style badly. This has made it very difficult indeed to reach any sensible conclusions about the effectiveness of different teaching styles, and the debate about this remains highly controversial.

A further problem with process–product studies is the diversity of the teaching context and intended outcomes. For example, what might be effective teaching of creative writing to 7-year-old pupils, as judged by project work, may be very different from effective teaching of mathematical formulae to 15-year-old pupils as judged by a recall test. As such, although we have some general ideas of what works well overall, this may not provide a sound guide as to what will work best in a specific teaching situation. In order to overcome this problem, a number of studies have focused on quite specific areas of learning, ranging from the teaching of reading in primary schools to the teaching of historical empathy in secondary schools. This more focused approach to the study of effective teaching often offers more powerful insights than those studies dealing with very broad levels of generalities.

Process studies have attempted to explore effective teaching by relating process variables to each other rather than linking process variables to product variables. Two main approaches have developed within this strategy. The first uses some aspects of pupil behaviour during the lesson as the criteria for effectiveness. The second relies primarily on the opinions and judgements of those involved, either the observer, the pupils or the teacher, as the mechanism for identifying effectiveness.

The first approach has much in common with process–product studies, but substitutes pupil behaviour during the lesson (e.g. pupils working hard and showing interest, or amount of time pupils are on task) in place of product variables. The strength of this approach is that it more easily identifies links between teaching and learning-related pupil behaviour. Its weakness is that one cannot be sure that what appears to be learning-related behaviour is actually producing the intended learning outcomes. Indeed, pupils are adept at giving the appearance of working hard and being on task when they are not.

The second approach, which makes use of teachers' and pupils' views, has also been fruitful. In particular, it has highlighted how crucial are teachers' and pupils' perceptions of each other and of the learning activities to understanding why a lesson was and was not effective. Indeed, numerous studies have employed a variety of classroom observation techniques to clarify classroom processes by observing lessons and then talking to the teacher and pupils afterwards to explore their views of the lesson. Such studies have enabled observers to offer a more powerful analysis of a lesson's effectiveness than would have been possible from a reliance on observation data alone. What is often particularly interesting in such studies is the richness with which the teachers talk about their choice of teaching methods and how they adjusted what they were doing to take account of the progress of the lesson.

Another important strand of research on effective teaching has been to look at the common difficulties faced by pupils in their learning of a particular subject matter. Such studies have looked at very specific topics (e.g. long division, radioactivity) with a view to identifying misunderstandings that often occur. Indeed, one aspect of the expertise of effective teachers is that they have built up an understanding of such problems, and can thereby help their pupils to avoid these difficulties when learning these specific topics.

Another issue of importance is the extent to which effective teaching may contribute to greater levels of educational outcomes than are achieved by less effective teaching. Some authors have argued that the main determinants of educational attainment are pupils' ability, motivation, social class, and previous level of attainment. They argue that the difference that results from being taught by a more effective rather than less effective teacher are small by comparison.

It has already been acknowledged that the tracing of cause and effect with regard to effective teaching is difficult. However, it is important to bear in mind the distinction between research on 'teacher effects' and research on 'effective teaching'. Research on teacher effects is primarily concerned with the extent to which having different teachers many contribute to explaining some of the *differences between pupils* in their educational attainment. In contrast, research on effective teaching is concerned with the *overall level of educational attainment* promoted by teaching and seeks to identify those aspects of teaching that are effective, even if they are used by the majority of teachers and thereby cannot account for differences between pupils in their final levels of attainment. Whilst research on teacher effects and effective teaching clearly overlaps, the fact that there are many influences on pupil attainment should not in any way underplay the crucial importance of effective teaching in promoting pupil learning.

A major development in research on effective teaching has been the attempt to evaluate the best available research evidence concerning which activities, programmes and practices have the most positive impact on learning outcomes for pupils. This approach has given rise to a number of 'systematic reviews' of the research literature commissioned by governments and other agencies to provide a base for the development of policies and practices that accord with research evidence. Such reviews are made widely available through the publication of these reports on websites aimed at schools and teachers. The What Works Clearinghouse (WWC) database in the US (**http://ies. ed.gov/ncee/wwc**) and the Evidence for Policy and Practice Information and Co-ordinating Centre (EPPI-Centre) database in the UK (**www.eppi.ioe.ac.uk**) provide examples of such syntheses of research evidence.

Whilst this approach has many advocates (Oakley, 2002; Slavin, 2008), it is important to note that the idea that particular classroom practices can be adopted by all teachers in a mechanistic way that will enhance pupils' learning outcomes is naive. Research evidence rarely has unequivocal implications for classroom practice. All such syntheses of research evidence need to be interpreted intelligently by teachers when they consider how their own classroom practices can be improved. The plethora of publications that claim to provide a basis for 'evidence-based teaching' thus need to be treated with some caution (Hattie, 2008; Petty, 2006; Stronge, 2007).

Models for thinking about effective teaching

As stated already, it is important when thinking about effective teaching to take account of the particular characteristics of the context of the learning activity (e.g. type of school, subject matter, and level of attainment) and the particular educational outcomes desired (e.g. increased pupil academic self-confidence, and examination success). Effective teaching is concerned with *what* aspects of the learning experience contribute to its effectiveness and *how* these aspects have the effect they do.

In considering the 'what' and the 'how' of effective teaching, three models of thinking about effective teaching have emerged (Figure 2.2). These three models are in fact complementary and consistent with each other. They represent three ways of looking at the same phenomena, but differ in the basic framework each model uses to elaborate on the key elements employed. Each framework has its own developmental history and its own distinctive contribution to make to the full understanding of effective teaching.

Model 1: A surface level of analysis

This model derives primarily from research studies and theorising about effective teaching. Such an approach has focused on two complementary constructs that appear to be crucial determinants of effectiveness. The first construct is *active learning time* (ALT), which is also often referred to as 'academic learning time' or 'time-on-task'. This refers to the amount of time spent by pupils actively engaged in the learning task

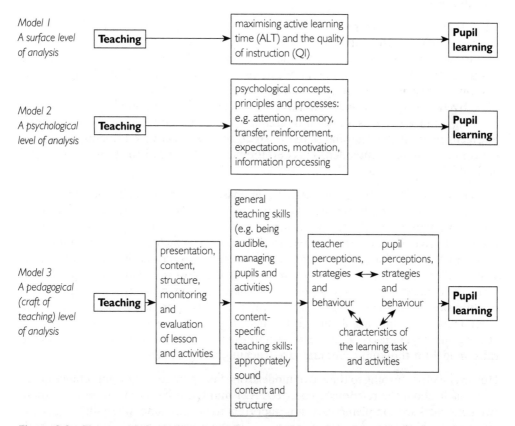

Figure 2.2 *Three models for thinking about effective teaching*

and activities designed to bring about the educational outcomes desired. The second construct is the *quality of instruction* (QI). This refers to the quality of the learning tasks and activities in terms of their presentation and suitability for bringing about the educational outcomes desired. In essence, model 1 equates effective teaching with maximising ALT and QI (Galton, 2007; Wilen *et al.*, 2008). This distinction forms a key part of the model of educational effectiveness developed by Creemers, in his analysis of effective teaching in terms of the 'management of time' and 'classroom learning environment' (Creemers and Kyriakides, 2008).

The construct of ALT has gradually been refined and made more sophisticated. Early research concentrated on the amount of time pupils spent on outcome-related tasks and indicated that greater time spent on task behaviour was associated with greater gains in educational attainment. This was generally true whether it resulted from the teachers allocating more curriculum time to task behaviour (for example, primary school teachers allocating more time during lessons for basic number work) or from individual teachers being more effective in keeping pupils on task during the lesson.

Such studies often highlighted the ways in which time was wasted during what was judged to be less effective teaching (for example, lessons where pupils had to queue for long periods to see a teacher, or where discipline problems were allowed to disrupt the work in hand). The notion of wasting time, however, must be treated with caution, given that some learning activities designed to foster certain educational outcomes (e.g. pupil autonomy, skills in using practical equipment) may appear to be costly in time if the researcher is using another educational outcome as the criterion of effectiveness.

Later research has attempted to move away from a simple 'amount of time' notion towards exploring the nature of being 'actively engaged'. It is argued that being on task in the sense of listening to a teacher or doing a task does not take account of the nature of that experience. Some pupils appear to be quite capable of doing the task without really being cognitively and affectively engaged in the fullest sense. The notion of 'actively engaged' represents a move away from a 'keeping pupils occupied' view of being on task towards a notion of creating and sustaining the appropriate mental engagement with the learning activities required to effectively bringing about the educational outcomes intended. This development makes the distinction between ALT and QI harder to sustain.

The construct of QI complements ALT by emphasising that the quality of teaching and learning is crucial for effectiveness. Clearly, a teacher who could sustain a high level of on-task behaviour, but who set up learning experiences that were of poor quality, would not be effective. QI, in essence, refers to the extent to which the instruction makes it easy for pupils to achieve the intended learning outcomes. Primarily, this involves considering if the learning experience is organised in the most sound and appropriate way when the context is taken into account. This may be done in two ways. First, by highlighting the psychological aspects of instruction. This approach is elaborated in the second model for thinking about effective teaching, outlined below. Second, by looking at the general qualities that appear to be important. This approach is elaborated in the third model for thinking about effective teaching, outlined below.

However, before turning to these two models, one final point of major importance needs to be made about the relationship between ALT and QI. It has been stressed that these two constructs are complementary. It is important to bear in mind, when thinking about effective teaching, that the vast majority of classroom process variables influence both

ALT and QI. This is because the aspects of teaching that maintain high levels of ALT often involve a high QI, and vice versa. Whilst it is useful to distinguish between these two constructs, they should not be perceived as operating in an independent fashion.

Model 2: A psychological level of analysis

The second model of thinking about effective teaching derives from attempts to identify the major psychological variables involved. As was noted above, it represents an elaboration of the surface level of analysis from a psychological perspective. Model 1 has been termed a 'surface level' of analysis because reference to the two central constructs of ALT and QI indicate the most crucial aspects of effective teaching in terms of the broadest constructs of value. In summary, process variables influence educational outcomes through their influence on ALT and QI. In a sense, this represents a 'surface level' explanation of effective teaching. The psychological level of analysis attempts to link the process variables with educational outcomes by explaining this influence in terms of the key psychological concepts, principles and processes involved, and as such offers a 'deeper level' explanation of effective teaching.

The psychological level of analysis attempts to make clear the psychological conditions necessary for learning to occur. If certain process variables influence educational outcomes, they must be doing so through influencing the pupil's psychological state and processes. Such an approach seeks to explain this. A vast number of psychological concepts, principles and processes have been identified as underlying effective teaching (Slavin, 2006; Woolfolk, 2007; Woolfolk *et al.*, 2008). These include: attention, memory, information processing, transfer of learning, reinforcement, feedback, motivation, ability, expectations and self-concept, to name but a few (these will be discussed in later chapters). Overall, it appears that there are three main aspects of pupil learning that are crucial to a consideration of effective teaching:

- The pupil must be *attending* to the learning experience.
- The pupil must be *receptive* to the learning experience (in the sense of being motivated and having a willingness to learn and respond to the experience).
- The learning experience must be *appropriate* for the intended learning outcomes (taking particular account of the pupil's initial knowledge and understanding).

These three aspects form the basis of the general conditions required for learning to take place. The analysis of effective teaching from a psychological perspective focuses on these three conditions and the factors that facilitate, or hinder, teachers in their efforts to achieve them. This analysis forms the subject of the next chapter, but also forms the central thrust of the whole of this book.

Model 3: A pedagogical (craft of teaching) level of analysis

The pedagogical level of analysis has emerged largely from the perspective of effective teaching used by teacher educators (Kerry and Wilding, 2004; Wragg, 2005). It concerns the attempt to describe the craft of teaching in a way that is of value to both student teachers during initial training and experienced teachers attending in-service courses. The emphasis within this perspective has been to describe effective teaching in ways that make sense to practitioners and relate to their professional needs and concerns. In this respect, model 3 is based as far as possible on the ways teachers themselves think and talk about their own teaching and the ways in which they offer advice to student teachers.

This approach largely sees teaching as a managerial activity, and seeks to identify the major tasks of teaching and the associated management activities required for effectiveness. This approach has had a major impact on researchers following the appearance of Kounin's (1970) seminal book on classroom management. Kounin drew attention to a number of managerial techniques used by effective teachers in contrast to less effective teachers, such as 'withitness', 'overlapping', 'smoothness' and 'momentum' (terms that will be dealt with in chapter 6). The particular importance of this study was that it focused attention on aspects of teaching that were subjectively much richer in meaning and significance than those types of process variables being studied at the time. Moreover, these aspects quickly established credibility within both the teacher education and the research communities.

Since the publication of Kounin's study, two major strands of development have been pursued. First, there has been an attempt to identify the management activities involved in effective teaching in terms of central 'teaching skills', with an implicit assumption that managerial activities can be broken down into such discrete component skills and that such skills can be developed and fostered within teacher education. Such studies also make a useful distinction between general teaching skills (such as being audible, and managing pupils and activities) and content-specific teaching skills (such the appropriateness of the content, method and structure of the learning activities for the desired educational outcomes). While these two sets of skills are complementary, the former focuses on general presentation and management skills, whilst the latter focuses on the 'intellectual packaging of the subject matter'.

The second major strand of development has been the exploration how teachers and pupils view and make sense of what happens in the classroom, and how they view each other and the learning activities that occur. This involves exploring the inter-relationship between three aspects of classroom processes:

- Teacher perceptions, strategies and behaviour.
- Pupil perceptions, strategies and behaviour.
- Characteristics of the learning task and activities.

Such research has highlighted how both teachers and pupils have expectations about learning activities, and both have strategies for attempting to deal with the demands each makes on the other. Studies of self-efficacy (beliefs people hold about their ability to bring about the ends they desire) indicate that pupil self-efficacy and teacher self-efficacy plays an important role in shaping how pupils and teachers behave in the classroom (Bandura, 1997; Woolfolk et al., 2008).

Pupils may thus respond to an activity in a way quite different to that assumed by the teacher. Such problems in part stem from assumptions made by teachers about pupils' level of motivation, understanding and competence, and in part because pupils may simply misunderstand what they have to do. To mitigate such problems, teachers need to be aware of the pupils' perspective regarding their experience of teaching and learning. This quality of 'social sensitivity' (the ability to see things from another's perspective) has received surprisingly little attention in thinking about effective teaching, although it can been seen to lie at the heart of many of the teaching skills frequently considered.

Summary

There were two major themes developed in this chapter. First, that in thinking about effective teaching there is a need to take into account the context and the nature of the educational outcomes desired. Second, that there appear to be three main models for thinking about effective teaching. These are complementary, but each of them makes a useful and important contribution to the understanding of effective teaching. Many of the issues and points developed in this chapter will be elaborated throughout the book. However, this chapter taken as a whole provides the overall framework for all that will follow.

Discussion questions

1 What do we mean by the term 'effective teaching'?

2 What do you see as being the most important goals of education?

3 What characteristics do you associate with an 'effective' teacher?

4 What factors will influence the quality of teaching and learning that takes place in the classroom?

5 How can a teacher best judge during a lesson that the lesson is progressing well?

6 In what ways might the teacher's awareness of pupils' views about a lesson help make the lesson more effective?

Further reading

Borich, G. D. (2007). *Effective Teaching Methods: Research Based Practice*, 6th edn. Englewood Cliffs: Prentice Hall. A detailed analysis of theories and research evidence on effective teaching.

Creemers, B. P. M. and Kyriakides, L. (2008). *The Dynamics of Educational Effectiveness*. London: Routledge. A thorough and insightful analysis of the interplay between factors at the pupil, teacher and school levels that underpin effective teaching.

Galton, M. (2007). *Learning and Teaching in the Primary Classroom*. London: Sage. An excellent overview of teaching in primary schools and the issues involved in effective classroom practice.

Haydn, T. (2007). *Managing Pupil Behaviour: Key Issues in Teaching and Learning*. London: Routledge. Draws on research on the views of teachers and pupils to consider the nature of effective teaching, largely focusing on secondary schools.

Woolfolk, A., Hughes, M. and Walkup, V. (2008). *Psychology in Education*. London: Pearson. This is an excellent overview of the nature of effective teaching considered in the context of psychological perspectives.

3
How pupils learn

Objective

To consider the nature of the learning process and the developmental, cognitive, and affective issues involved.

The essence of effective teaching lies in the ability of the teacher to set up a learning experience that brings about the desired educational outcomes. For this to take place, each pupil must be engaged in the activity of learning. The nature of the psychological state of being engaged in the activity of learning has been the focus of much debate and research. A number of important psychological concepts, principles and processes involved in both the activity of learning itself and in facilitating such activity have been identified (Bartlett and Burton, 2007; Slavin, 2006; Woolfolk *et al.*, 2008).

This chapter considers those aspects of how pupils learn that have the most practical relevance for effective teaching. Broadly, these fall into four sections. First, a consideration of the psychological nature of learning as it relates to effective teaching. What psychological state needs to be set up by the teacher for learning to take place? This will draw upon the work of those who have attempted to develop a psychological theory of instruction. Second, a consideration of the ways in which the study of human development has thrown important light on the nature of children's learning. Third, a consideration of issues regarding the mental processes involved in the activity of learning. Fourth, and finally, a consideration of the affective (emotional and motivational) issues involved in the activity of learning.

This chapter thus represents an elaboration of the psychological level of analysis as a model for thinking about effective teaching outlined in the previous chapter. The importance of this approach is that it provides a conceptual framework for teachers in thinking and decision-making about their own teaching and makes explicit why and how pupil learning may or may not be taking place effectively.

The nature of pupil learning

Many writers have considered the nature of pupil learning explicitly within the context of effective teaching (Fox, 2005; Jarvis, 2005; Schunk, 2008) and have explored four major questions concerning the nature of pupil learning:

- What mental processes are involved when a pupil is engaged in learning?
- What changes occur in the pupil's cognitive structure, which themselves constitute the pupil learning?

- Which psychological factors (concepts, principles and processes) facilitate pupil learning?
- What are the main types of pupil learning?

Although different theorists have elaborated their answers to these four questions in different ways, there are a number of points of convergence in their separate approaches. Thus it is possible to establish a degree of synthesis and consensus on which to build a basic framework for thinking about the nature of pupil learning, against which the different emphases of these and other authors can be considered.

The learning process

Pupil learning can be defined as changes in a pupil's behaviour that take place as a result of being engaged in an educational experience. Gagné *et al.* (2005) identified five main types of pupil learning:

- *Verbal information:* e.g. facts, names, principles and generalisations.
- *Intellectual skills:* 'knowing how and why' rather than 'knowing that'. These can be arranged in an increasing order of complexity, with more complex intellectual skills being built upon the simpler ones.
- *Cognitive strategies:* ways in which the pupil is able to control and manage the mental processes involved in learning, including strategies for attending, thinking, memorising and dealing with novel problems.
- *Attitudes:* an attitude may be defined as a pupil's feelings towards some particular object or idea. The fostering of certain attitudes, such as those towards ethnic minorities or towards school subjects, are important educational outcomes.
- *Motor skills:* e.g. playing a musical instrument or operating a word-processor.

The most detailed exposition of educational outcomes is Bloom's *Taxonomy of Educational Objectives* (Bloom *et al.*, 1956). This specifies three domains of learning: cognitive, affective and psychomotor. The cognitive domain, for example, is broken down into six categories of intellectual skills: knowledge, comprehension, application, analysis, synthesis and evaluation. This approach enabled the various categories of educational outcomes to be specified in great detail, and has formed the basis of specifying the objectives for teaching adopted by numerous curriculum developers.

Clearly, it is of prime importance for the teacher's planning and decision-making that the intended objectives of a course of study are as clear as possible. Curriculum developers have used such detailed specifications of objectives to help teachers ensure that they are able to match the content and teaching methods adopted to the objectives that they know are going to be assessed. At the same time, it is worth noting that taken to extremes, such an approach can become bureaucratic in its description of objectives and can lead to an emphasis on teaching towards the test in a way that makes the teaching excessively narrow in its educational value.

Ausubel's (2000) treatment of types of learning emphasises two important distinctions in pupil learning. The first is a distinction between reception and discovery learning. The second is a distinction between rote and meaningful learning.

In reception learning the entire content of what is to be learned is presented to the learner in its final form. The learner is required to internalise and incorporate the material presented. By contrast, in discovery learning the content of what is to be learned has first to be discovered by the pupil through some learning activity.

In meaningful learning, the essential characteristic of the learning is that it can be related in a meaningful, non-arbitrary way to what the learner already knows. In rote learning, however, what is learned is characterised by arbitrary associations with the learner's previous knowledge.

These two distinctions, reception versus discovery learning and meaningful versus rote learning, are seen by Ausubel to be independent of each other. Thus reception learning can be either meaningful or rote, and discovery learning can be either meaningful or rote. This is an important observation, since there is a tendency to assume that reception learning is also rote learning, and that discovery learning is also meaningful learning. Meaningful learning has important implications for the notion of teaching for understanding, since it places emphasis on the type of changes in the pupil's cognitive structure that takes place during learning, and on the consequent demonstration of learning that the learner can display.

The approaches adopted by such theorists as Ausubel and Gagné are based on the same essential model of information processing by the learner that must occur for learning to take place (Schunk, 2008). This model is illustrated in Figure 3.1. There are three main sections to this model. The first section is concerned with the initial reception of sensory information. This involves taking account of the learner's level of attention and the degree to which such attention is directed towards aspects of the whole range of sensory inputs available in the classroom. At the same time, initial reception is also subject to selective perception, which acts as a filter and alerts the learner to the most significant aspects of the sensory information available. The information processing that takes place here lasts for only a fraction of a second.

The second section is usually termed 'short-term memory' (STM). This is concerned with processing the information that is received through the initial reception. Such processing is in part experienced by the learner as conscious thinking, and involves the application of those cognitive processes outlined by Gagné and Bloom, for example, described earlier.

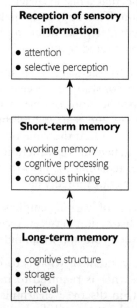

Figure 3.1   *The basic model of information processing which underlies the activity of learning*

Research on STM has focused on the distinction and interplay between verbal STM, visual-spatial STM and the central executive processes involved in coordinating different STM activities (Gathercole and Alloway, 2008; Goswami, 2008; Jordan et al., 2008). Such research has indicated how pupils with poor STM, particularly 'working memory' (the mental capacity used when manipulating ideas in order to carry out a task or series of tasks), can face problems in coping with the academic demands made upon them in the classroom and have highlighted strategies that teachers can use to support pupils with poor STM, such as restructuring a complex task into simpler components, repeating instructions and information, and encouraging the use of visual or diagrammatic memory aids.

The third section is usually termed 'long-term memory' (LTM). This is concerned with the changes that take place in the learner's cognitive structure as a result of the processing of information within STM. Such changes, in essence, constitute the learning that has taken place, as it is these changes that enable the changes in behaviour resulting from the learning to be demonstrated.

The raw stuff of the activity of learning is thus the interaction between the processing of information in STM and the cognitive structure in LTM. It is important to note that many of the cognitive processes involved in STM are also desired learning outcomes in themselves. Indeed, much education is designed to foster and develop those thinking skills, processes and strategies, which subsequently become part of the mental activity involved in STM processing. An interesting example of this approach to developing thinking skills is the work of de Bono (2004), who has designed a number of activities aimed to foster the perceptual and cognitive strategies involved in more effective thinking.

Ausubel (2000) has placed emphasis on the importance of meaningful learning for effective teaching. He argues that meaningful learning will involve changes in the cognitive structure of the learner, which will be based on 'meaningful associations' and hence contribute to more sophisticated behaviour. Ausubel has also advocated the use of 'advanced organisers'. These refer to the ways in which a teacher can usefully indicate at the start of a lesson how the content and learning activities of the lesson can be organised and related to pupils' previous knowledge and understanding, so that the learning that follows is made as meaningful as possible. Ausubel sees the principal function of advanced organisers as bridging the gap between what learners know and what they need to know before they can successfully learn from the task at hand.

At its crudest, the activity of pupil learning embodied in the model of information processes shown in Figure 3.1, can be outlined as:

attention ↔ thinking ↔ storage

A two-way direction of influence between each of these three sections is shown in the model. This is of crucial importance to understanding the processes involved in learning. This draws attention to the fact that at any given time, each of the three sections of the model is subject to influence by the other two sections.

Much has been written about the nature of LTM and the process by which the learner's cognitive structure changes. The work of Piaget, who was primarily a developmental psychologist and whose work will be considered in the next section, has been very influential. Piaget (e.g. Piaget and Inhelder, 1969) has argued that the cognitive structure of LTM essentially consists of *schemas*. Each schema is an organisation of information. These may range from schemas based on coordinating physical actions to ones that constitute conceptual understanding. Cognitive structure involves the acquisition of such schema and the gradual modification and organisation of existing schemas into more complex ones. This continuous process of the acquisition and modification of schemas is seen to result from the child's interaction with the environment. It involves two basic and complementary cognitive processes used in information processing: *assimilation* and *accommodation*.

Assimilation is the process involved when the learner's existing schemas are used to interpret the ongoing experience taking place. Accommodation is the process involved when the learner's existing schema are modified to take account of the new information, which stems from the ongoing experience taking place. During all information processing, there is a continuous involvement of both processes, but the relative degrees of assimilation and accommodation will depend on the activity. Piaget sees those experiences that involve a balance of assimilation and accommodation as being the ones that have the best educational significance for the learner. An important task for teachers is thus to get this 'cognitive matching' right for each pupil.

Bruner (2006) has explored the nature of the pupil's cognitive structure by considering how children appear to store information in and retrieve information from their cognitive structure. Given that the cognitive structure of the child is in some way an attempt to represent a model of the world, Bruner asks in what ways such a representation might be accomplished. He identifies three such models:

- *Enactive:* based on knowledge derived from actions concerning physical behaviour (such as learning to ride a bicycle).
- *Iconic:* based on knowledge derived from forming and organising images, either visually or by some other senses (such as imagining the shortest route between two well-known parts of one's locality).
- *Symbolic:* based on knowledge derived from the use of language, in terms of words or other symbols (such as discussing philosophically the 'meaning of meaning'!).

Bruner notes that human development appears to run the course of these three systems of representation until all three can be commanded for use.

Motivation and reinforcement

Having considered the basic information processing framework for the nature of pupil learning, two major concepts need to be related to the operation of this model: *motivation* and *reinforcement*.

What motivates pupil learning? In attempting to answer this question it is important to bear in mind a clear distinction between learning that must take place by an individual as a natural part of interacting with the environment, and the specific learning that is intended by the teacher. Within Piaget's approach, learning is the inevitable consequence of the individual's interaction with the environment. Such learning stems from the individual's biological drive towards adapting to the environment. In that sense, any educational experience that requires pupils to interact in some way with the learning task in hand will result in some learning. However, when we ask 'What motivates pupil learning?', we are really asking a question about the ways in which a pupil will make a positive mental effort towards the learning task. If pupils are asked when they felt most motivated towards school learning, their answers will fall into one of two main categories: 'When I was really interested in the work' or 'When I had to!' These two categories represent one of the most important distinctions made in considering pupil learning, that between 'intrinsic motivation' and 'extrinsic motivation'.

Simply speaking, *intrinsic motivation* stems from a biologically based drive of curiosity. Such motivation involves an interest in the learning task itself and also satisfaction being gained from the task. Human beings are born with a strong desire to explore their environment and to seek out stimulation. Almost any situation that is puzzling will gain a person's attention and interest. Indeed, a useful way of starting a lesson to present a topic in the form of a question or problem that needs to be addressed to elicit pupils' interest. Whilst most analysis of intrinsic motivation has focused on the intellectual curiosity aspect, there is another strand to the concept that often receives less attention, but which is also important. Intrinsic motivation also includes satisfaction from undertaking the task because one finds engaging in the task is satisfying in some way. For example, building up skills and competencies can often be pleasurable in themselves. Children can spend hours practising particular motor skills using hand-held computer games because the development of hand–eye coordination skills is intrinsically satisfying. In addition, a task can afford a way of working that is satisfying, such as learning as part of a group in a social context. The essence of intrinsic motivation is that the person finds the task pleasurable and satisfying in itself.

In contrast, *extrinsic motivation* refers to those learning situations where the impetus for the motivation stems from the fact that successful completion of the task is a means towards some other end. Here, the person's satisfaction is derived from the fact that completing the task leads to an end that they value and is not derived from the task itself. If the same end could be reached by engaging in some other task more easily, the person would happily switch tasks since it is the end that matters not the task itself. A simple example of extrinsic motivation would be doing a task for money. Here, the motivation stems from the desire for the money, not because one found the task interesting. Clearly, success in school learning can satisfy a whole range of needs that can form the basis for extrinsic motivation. One prime motive for school learning is the desire to earn status, esteem, approval and acceptance in the eyes of others (friends, peers, teachers and parents). These may be earned in the short term by means of obtaining good marks and teacher praise, and in the long term by entrance to degree courses and professional occupations. Another prime motive for school learning, at least of short-term value, is the avoidance of teacher reprimands and punishments. In both cases, such motivation is extrinsic because it is the end state that drives the motivation and not interest in particular learning tasks or activities.

Although intrinsic and extrinsic motivation are contrasted with each other, it is important to note that most tasks involve a mix of the two. Moreover, pupils may be high in their levels of both intrinsic and extrinsic motivation (i.e. they find the subject matter is interesting in its own right and success in the subject is important to the pupil in terms of achieving other ends). The notions of intrinsic and extrinsic motivation play a key part in the self-determination theory developed by Deci and Ryan (2002), which concerns how pupils' thoughts about motivation and learning regulate their behaviour. Within this approach, Deci and Ryan attempt to identify different components (or types) of intrinsic and extrinsic motivation in order to further refine how pupil motivation impacts on their academic behaviour.

The view of seeing motivation as deriving from an attempt to satisfy one's needs is very helpful in thinking about pupil learning. A particularly interesting development of this viewpoint is the work of Maslow (1987), who has argued that an individual's basic needs can be arranged in a hierarchy, with those lower in the hierarchy being 'pre-potent' (that is, needing to be satisfied as a matter of greater priority) in relation to needs higher in the hierarchy. Maslow's hierarchy, starting from the lowest level, is as follows:

- *Physiological needs:* e.g. need for food and oxygen.
- *Safety needs:* e.g. need for security, and freedom from anxiety.
- *Belongingness and love needs:* the need to feel one belongs, and the need to give and receive love.
- *Esteem needs:* the need for achievement, competence, mastery, and the need for status and prestige.
- *Need for self-actualisation:* the need to realise one's potentiality.

As well as basic needs, Maslow also identifies cognitive needs, based on the impulse to satisfy curiosity, to know, to explain and to understand. Maslow sees such cognitive needs as being inter-related with, rather than separate from, the basic needs. Indeed, the cognitive needs involve cognitive capacities (perceptual, intellectual and learning), which are used in part to satisfy the basic needs.

Maslow's hierarchy provides a useful framework for thinking about pupil motivation and needs. In particular, it draws attention to the importance of making sure that those needs lower in the hierarchy (particularly needs for comfort, safety, security and acceptance) are being met when educational experiences that draw upon the higher needs of esteem and self-actualisation are set up. Maslow has also discussed a related notion of 'peak experiences'. These refer to moments of intense delight and ecstasy involved in being 'at one' with an experience at the level of self-actualisation. Maslow has argued that a worthy and important goal for education is to generate such peak experiences as a result of ego-enhancing involvement and achievement in school learning.

The notion of 'need for achievement' (or 'achievement motivation') has also received a great deal of attention in relation to the motivation of pupils towards school learning. A number of studies have explored the nature and development of both the need for achievement in general and how it is expressed in the context of academic success (Alderman, 2008; Aronson, 2002). The need for achievement appears to involve both intrinsic motivation (particularly the need to develop competence), and extrinsic motivation (particularly the need for status and esteem). Research on pupils' level of need for achievement has highlighted how the expectations of others (teachers, parents, peers) can influence their aspirations and how they interpret success and failure to themselves (referred to as 'attribution theory').

The notion of 'reinforcement' has played a central role in the development of theories of learning by behavioural psychologists (Child, 2007; Schunk, 2008). The work of Skinner (1968) has been particularly influential. Skinner's approach attempts to account for learning (changes in behaviour) by focusing on the consequences for an individual of certain behaviour. He argues that where such behaviour is followed by reinforcement, it is more likely to occur in the same situation on a future occasion. In the absence of reinforcement, such behaviour is less likely to occur. This approach has been termed *operant conditioning*. It seeks to explain learning by identifying pieces of behaviour or actions (operants) and analysing the timing and nature of the subsequent reinforcement. Skinner has focused on two types of reinforcement that *increase* the likelihood of the behaviour occurring: positive reinforcement (rewards such as teacher praise) and negative reinforcement (the removal of an unpleasant consequence, such as having a detention cancelled). He defines three types of consequences that *decrease* the likelihood of the behaviour occurring: extinction (the absence of reinforcement), punishment (reprimands, detentions) and response costs (removal of expected rewards, such as loss of privileges).

Control over pupil learning by a teacher is seen to depend upon the teacher arranging the appropriate reinforcement to be contingent upon the desired pupil behaviour. Skinner's work on operant conditioning of animals relied heavily on the process of 'shaping'. This involved reinforcing those behaviours that gradually approximated the desired behaviour. Thus, if the desired behaviour was to jump up and touch an object, initial rewards would follow any jumping, then only jumping near the object, and finally only jumps that made contact with the object. The great advantage of working with human beings, is that one can indicate to pupils in the classroom what the desired behaviours are, and then reinforce their occurrence.

The behavioural approach to learning has a number of important educational implications. First, it draws attention to the relationship between pupils' behaviour (e.g. paying attention, disrupting other pupils) and how the consequences of the behaviour for the pupil influences its future occurrence. In particular, it advocates that teachers should make frequent use of praise to reinforce appropriate pupil behaviour. The systematic application of behaviourist principles to shape pupil behaviour, often termed 'behaviour modification', has been widely applied (e.g. Canter and Canter, 2001). Second, the research has identified a number of principles that can facilitate learning, for example, the use of quick corrective feedback. Such principles have been used to develop programmed learning packages, characterised by short learning steps and quick corrective feedback. These packages are designed to ensure a high probability of success on each step, which thus acts as reinforcement.

It is interesting to note at this point that reinforcement can be usefully linked to pupil motivation, since both success in learning tasks and the behaviours used by teachers to encourage pupil effort (e.g. praise, achievement awards, avoidance of sanctions) can constitute reinforcement. Moreover, the link between reinforcement and pupil motivation also draws attention to the danger of assuming that such teacher behaviours are in fact reinforcing when the opposite may be the case. For example, overt teacher praise for a pupil in the context of an anti-school ethos in the class may not be reinforcing at all, if that pupil's need for acceptance by peers as a member of an anti-school clique is undermined by such praise. Similarly, a reprimand for a pupil, as a form of punishment, delivered in a context where the pupil is attention-seeking may be experienced as a reward and act to reinforce the pupil's misbehaviour. To avoid this danger, the teacher needs to be sensitive to the pupil's social context and values in determining what actions will constitute reinforcement.

Pupil engagement in learning

Thus far, we have examined the basic model of information processing that underlies pupil learning, together with a consideration of the role of motivation and reinforcement. This model has a number of implications for effective teaching. Overall, there appear to be three central and crucial aspects to pupils' engagement in the activity of learning:

- *Attentiveness:* the pupil must be attending to the learning experience.
- *Receptiveness:* the pupil must be receptive to the learning experience, in the sense of being motivated and having a willingness to learn and respond to the experience.
- *Appropriateness:* the learning experience must be appropriate for the intended learning outcomes, taking particular account of the pupil's initial knowledge and understanding.

Effective teaching involves getting these three aspects of the learning activities right. *Attentiveness* relates to the ways in which teachers can elicit and maintain high levels of pupil attention and concentration (e.g. by varying the learning activities, getting pupils actively involved, and making use of pupils' interests). *Receptiveness* deals with the ways in which teachers can make use of the different sources of pupil motivation to facilitate and encourage motivation towards learning (e.g. by eliciting curiosity, offering the opportunity to be successful, and fostering a classroom ethos towards learning). *Appropriateness* refers to the ways in which teachers need to match the learning experience to each pupil's current state of knowledge and understanding, and at the same time ensure that the learning activities used actually foster the desired educational outcomes (e.g. by monitoring pupils' progress and giving quick corrective feedback, structuring and presenting activities that facilitate meaningful learning, and using questions and tests to check that pupils can demonstrate that the desired outcomes have been achieved).

The notion of 'engagement' refers to the extent to which pupils are seriously involved and engrossed in the academic work they are doing. It is interesting to note that many policy documents and research studies now address the need to engage pupils in their learning rather than the need to raise pupils' level of motivation as a key goal for effective teaching (Fredricks *et al.*, 2004; Glanville and Wildhagen, 2007). This, in part, reflects the idea that effective teaching can enable pupils who are otherwise poorly motivated to become engaged in learning. Whilst the terms 'motivation' and 'engagement' clearly overlap, pupil engagement appears to be viewed as more malleable than pupil motivation.

Developmental issues

The work of Piaget, in studying the cognitive development of children, has had a great impact on discussions of teaching and learning in schools. Although Piaget was earlier described as a developmental psychologist, strictly speaking his main concern was 'developmental epistemology', the study of how knowledge *per se* develops in children (Piaget, 1972). Piaget's research has focused on a number of important processes, including those of assimilation and accommodation, described earlier. Of these, it is his account of the quality of a child's thinking at different stages of development, and how such stages are characterised and linked, which has had the greatest impact on thinking about pupil learning. Although Piaget's writings are rather complex for the lay reader, synopses of the main elements of his approach are widespread, and can be found in most texts of educational psychology (e.g. Child, 2007; Woolfolk, 2007).

In essence, Piaget's theory of cognitive development deals with the gradual refinement of the child's cognitive structure through assimilation and accommodation. This refinement is governed by a combination of the child's interaction with the environment (with an emphasis on active exploration) and the processes of biological maturation of the child's nervous system. The nature of the child's knowledge and the cognitive processes the child displays follow a fixed, cumulative and hierarchical order of development through three main stages: the 'sensori-motor' period (lasting from birth to, on average, 18 months of age); the period of 'pre-operational and concrete operations' (lasting up to, on average, 11 years of age); and finally, the period of 'formal operations'. Each of these stages can be further broken down in tracing the development of particular knowledge and cognitive processes.

By identifying a child's knowledge and cognitive processes at a given time, one can place that child's point of development. For example, young children beginning primary school at around the age of five years old are characterised by being unable to 'decentre' (that is, they focus on one aspect of a situation and on their own perspective) or to 'mentally reverse' operations they have witnessed. Thus they cannot successfully acquire concepts such as the conservation of quantity, and appear to believe that changing an object's shape or appearance (by rolling out a ball of plasticine or stretching out a line of counters) will change its quantity. Piaget sees this as being the result of the child 'centring' on the increase in length and being unable to take into account that the original appearance could be restored. The development of 'decentring' and 'reversibility' plus the development of thinking involving the use of principles (such as the principle of 'invariance': that changes in shape do not change quantity unless something is added or subtracted) paves the way for the development of logical thinking. This normally occurs towards the end of the primary school years, although such logical thinking is at first limited to concrete examples, and only develops into abstract logical thinking, on average, during the secondary school years.

It is worth noting that a number of researchers have criticised aspects of Piaget's work. This includes the accusations that his notion of stages is too rigid; that children in the right context are able to develop certain understandings at a much earlier age than he suggests; and that Piaget underplays the role of social factors in pupils' cognitive development. Nevertheless, Piaget's framework continues to have a major influence in thinking about pupil learning and effective teaching.

One of the most important implications of Piaget's ideas for effective teaching is the notion of 'cognitive matching': the need to pitch the learning experience at the right level for each child. This has two aspects:

- The learning task needs to foster for the child an experience that can make useful links with what the child already knows, but that extends this knowledge and understanding further.
- The learning task must take account of the level of biological maturation of the child's nervous system and not over-reach the child's capacity for information processing.

A related notion is that of 'readiness'. This involves the teacher looking for signs that the child is both ready and able to cope with the intellectual demands involved in a particular curriculum topic or activity. There is a danger that exposing a pupil too early to particular curriculum demands far in excess of their level of cognitive maturity may well foster inappropriate learning strategies (such as a complete reliance on memorisation) or even painful experiences of failure and inadequacy that could lead to alienation from school learning.

A second important implication for effective teaching stems from the hierarchical and cumulative nature of cognitive development. This emphasises the need for teachers to structure curriculum activities in an order that makes intellectual sense in terms of the way knowledge is built up, and for teachers to make use of concrete examples in paving the way for pupils developing principles and relationships at an abstract level.

A third implication stems from Piaget's view of the child as an active learner who is trying to construct an understanding of the world. This has been termed a *constructivist* approach to learning, and has had a major impact on thinking about effective teaching. It emphasises that pupils do not passively accept and absorb what they are told or what they experience. Rather, they actively try to make sense of new experiences by relating it to what they already know and understand. As such, teachers need to be aware of pupils' previous understanding, so that possible misconceptions that pupils already have and that would otherwise be confirmed or extended by the new experience can be identified and corrected. It also implies that using activities that encourage pupils to be actively involved in the learning activity will better elicit and sustain their interest and their efforts to make sense of the new experiences, than activities requiring a relatively passive role for pupils.

Another influential approach concerning developmental issues that relate to pupil learning, perhaps second only to Piaget's, stems from the work of Vygotsky (1962). Vygotsky has developed the notion of the *zone of proximal development* to refer to the distance between the child's actual developmental level and the potential level of cognitive development that the child can achieve with help. If we apply this idea to a classroom situation where a pupil is working on a task, Vygotsky argues that an effective way to help a pupil who is having difficulties is to direct their attention to the key features of the task and prompt them in ways that will facilitate their understanding. Bruner has used the metaphor of *scaffolding* to refer to Vygotsky's view of this kind of teacher support (Smith *et al.*, 2003). The important feature of scaffolding is that it is still the pupil, rather than the teacher, who does the work, with the teacher simply helping to direct the pupil's cognitive processes. This notion of scaffolding focuses on how effective one-to-one teaching should be geared to helping the pupil relate a task to their previous understanding and directing their attention to the key features of the task necessary for success. A number of studies of classroom practice have shown that the teacher's ability to do this effectively, however, requires a high level of skill and a sensitive awareness of both the pupil's needs and of the subject matter in hand, and that it is very easy for a teacher to intervene too heavily by directing the pupil rather than by acting as a sensitive guide (Myhill and Warren, 2005).

So far this section has given greatest weight to considering general cognitive development. However, a number of other aspects of the child's development have important implications for effective teaching. First, there are particular aspects of cognitive development that require attention, most notably language development, particularly writing and learning to read. Both are crucial to the child's capacity to meet the demands of school learning. A major barrier to success for many pupils is that their competence in reading and writing is over-stretched by many academic demands, and teachers may sometimes infer a pupil is having difficulty with the intellectual subject matter of the lesson when the real problem stems from poor skills in reading and writing.

Second, as pupils progress through the school years, teachers increasingly make the assumption that pupils possess a variety of study skills that equip them with the strategies required for successful learning. The idea that pupils need to 'learn how to learn' has still not received sufficient attention. This is largely because most pupils seem to acquire such skills in an intuitive way, which makes many teachers feel that the need to explicitly teach study skills is unnecessary. Unfortunately, a lack of study skills lies at the heart of why many pupils fail to complete tasks adequately. Many schools, however, do devote curriculum time to fostering a range of study skills, such as information gathering, planning and writing an essay, revision and examination techniques, and self-organisation and time management (Guy, 2006). Some writers have gone further, and advocated that teachers should try to help pupils think about how they direct their cognitive efforts when engaged in a learning activity, termed 'metacognition' (Goswami, 2008; Woolfolk *et al.*, 2008). This idea that pupils ought to be encouraged to think about their own thinking, can help pupils develop more conscious control over the type and nature of their mental efforts, so that when faced with learning tasks they can think strategically about how to engage in them to best effect (Fisher, 2008).

As well as cognitive development, it is important not to overlook the implications of physical and personality development for effective teaching. Interestingly, both are linked at a most important phase during adolescence: the onset of puberty. This has a number of important influences on adolescents' attitudes towards school learning as part of their developing self-concept and on their negotiation of the crisis of adolescence involved in developing a sense of personal identity (Smith et al., 2003). Other aspects of such development, which may impinge on pupil learning, range from social problems that may stem from physical appearance or shortcomings (e.g. being very short or being clumsy) to difficulties over impulse control, which can undermine a pupil's ability to meet both academic and social demands and expectations.

Finally, the level of a child's need for achievement, and in particular the development of their motivation towards school learning, is influenced by many aspects of the child's home life. Some parents take a much more positive and active role than others in supporting their children's education, encouraging their children to value education, to develop high aspirations and self-belief in their own capabilities, and to make efforts to do well at school. Research studies indicate that such differences between pupils in their parents' child-rearing practices, the parent–child relationship, the child's general home circumstances and the parents' attitudes towards the importance of doing well at school, can have a marked influence in fostering and reinforcing the child's achievement-related efforts at school, or in undermining these (Smith et al., 2003).

Cognitive issues

Perhaps the most important cognitive issues arising from the nature of pupil learning outlined earlier, are those concerning the nature of STM and LTM (Child, 2007; Schunk, 2008). These issues concern three main aspects of learning:

- What is the nature of STM functioning?
- How is information relayed from STM and stored in LTM?
- How is previous learning brought to bear in meeting new demands (termed 'transfer of learning')?

The most interesting aspect of STM functioning concerns the conscious mental activity involved in learning. This includes the notion of 'mental effort', which can be conceived of, broadly, as a combination of attention and concentration, and the notion of 'metacognition', as described in the previous section, which concerns pupils' active and conscious direction of their mental activity towards learning. Both are clearly affected by pupils' general motivation and attitudes, and by pupils' previous experience of learning. When faced with a learning activity, the pupil is engaged in a complex web of decision-making, including such possible reactions as 'This is boring', 'I don't understand this', 'This is important so I must concentrate'. Such reactions will influence the effort and strategies that will characterise their STM functioning.

The question of how information is processed in STM and then relayed and stored in LTM is of immense complexity. What is processed in STM appears to be relayed to LTM and stored there. However, the main problem is that of retrieving the information from LTM. Retrieval failure is evident in the fact that a pupil may not be able to recall a piece of information but is readily able to recognise the correct answer if choices are offered. Forgetting appears to be largely a failure to retrieve stored information. Important learning, however, can be consolidated by practice and revision techniques, and by linking the learning to a number of different aspects of the pupil's understanding. Learning that is stored but that has very little association with other learning makes retrieval very difficult. This problem can be overcome, however, if the learning has been 'overlearned' by being well rehearsed and frequently used (e.g. a particular mathematical formula) or if a mnemonic device is used (e.g. use of a rhyme such as 'Thirty days has September', or through association by pairing with a strong visual image).

The advantage of meaningful learning for retrieval stems from the way LTM is organised in terms of a complex network of associations, within which meaningful links are of paramount importance. Overall, retrieval is dependent upon strength of initial storage (based on mental effort) and the existence of links (either meaningful or otherwise) that can be used to locate the required information. This is consolidated by subsequent practice and the establishment of further links.

'Transfer of learning' refers to the pupil's ability to make use of previous learning in dealing with new tasks and in new situations. To facilitate such transfer is perhaps one of the most important tasks of effective teaching. One of the major barriers to such transfer is that pupils tend to compartmentalise their learning, using retrieval plans that depend on matching specific characteristics of the learning task to the particular compartment of understanding. This is revealed by the frequent inability of pupils to transfer learning from one subject to another, or sometimes even from one topic to another within the same subject. This tendency partly arises because the majority of pupils see school learning as producing correct answers. Hence, doing school work successfully is primarily a matter of matching the appropriate behaviour to the task set by the teacher. As such, a pupil may fail to appreciate that behaviour that successfully dealt with one task could be relevant to another topic in the same subject area or to a topic in another subject area.

The term 'situated learning' is now widely used to refer to this powerful tendency to relate what is learnt to the situation in which it is learnt (Anderson *et al.*, 1996). It is thus clear that a major task of effective teaching is to make use of activities that highlight applications of what has been learnt in order to facilitate transfer of learning, particularly from school learning to 'real-life settings' (e.g. calculating mortgage interest rates, looking at rusting in cars, writing a letter to a newspaper, booking a hotel room in French).

As was noted earlier, LTM consists of an extremely complex network of associations. The development of such associations has been described in terms of Piaget's notions of assimilation and accommodation, and in terms of Skinner's notion of operant conditioning. However, it is worth noting that some associations are best explained in terms of another type of conditioning, termed 'classical conditioning', developed by Pavlov (1927). Classical conditioning is based on associations being built up between stimuli that are paired together, usually within a short time interval and in psychologically significant circumstances, so that the appearance of one signals the appearance of the other. Pavlov's most quoted example is that of a dog learning to salivate in response to the sound of a bell, the sound having previously been paired with the provision of food on a number of occasions.

In terms of effective teaching, classical conditioning theory has two major implications. First, it draws attention to the way in which associations can be built up through proximity in time. Second, that once a response comes to follow certain stimuli, the response can generalise to other similar stimuli. Thus pupils may build up associations between emotional responses, both pleasant and unpleasant, and particular stimuli. For example, a child may be very nervous of a teacher who resembles a feared father; or having had a panic attack in a reading test because of reading problems, the pupil may experience a subsequent attack in an arithmetic test even though they have no arithmetic problems.

Two other important cognitive issues concern *cueing* and *mental set*. Cueing refers to signals that can be used by teachers to alert pupils in appropriate ways to various demands. Such signals may be explicit, such as when a teacher says that a point will be difficult to grasp, or may be indicated by subtle nuances of a teacher's gestures or tone of voice, for example, when a teacher pauses for slightly longer than normal to signal that not everyone is paying attention. Mental set refers to the general expectations pupils have regarding a learning activity, ranging from its level of interest to which learning strategy is most likely to be effective. The teacher's use of cues throughout a lesson can help induce the appropriate mental set for the tasks in hand (being interested and attentive, expecting to succeed, and being ready to apply the appropriate learning strategy), which is crucial to establishing and maintaining successful pupil learning.

A further cognitive issue concerns the notion of feedback, as noted earlier. Quick corrective feedback is a great facilitator of learning, both because of its effects in correcting misunderstanding and because of its reinforcement and motivational value. However, pupils do appear to be quite sensitive regarding the type of feedback they prefer. In general, helpful and supportive feedback is seen to be an important characteristic of effective teaching, while hostile and deprecating feedback is not. Feedback is also important in giving pupils information about the general standard of attainment required, which may influence pupils' future expectations and aspirations about school learning.

Concept teaching is a particularly important skill involved in effective teaching. If a teacher fails to clarify key concepts that pupils are required to use in their school work, this can lead to all sorts of errors. For example, in calculating the length of a side in a right-angled triangle, it is important that the pupil realises that it is only the square of the side opposite the right angle that is equal to the sum of the squares of the other two sides. Many pupils fail to appreciate this, and simply treat any length they need to calculate as though it were the hypotenuse. Studies of pupil misconceptions (e.g. Hansen, 2005) indicate that in all subjects teachers need to spend time checking on pupils' understanding of key concepts by giving them exemplars and non-exemplars of the concepts so that they can see the difference.

Finally, a number of important cognitive issues concern individual differences among pupils in ability. These will be dealt with in chapter 5.

Affective issues

Many writers have pointed out that pupil learning is not simply a matter of cognitive processing. All learning occurs in a complex social context, and is influenced by a variety of important affective variables (Elliot *et al.*, 2005). In this context 'affective' issues refer to those emotional and social factors that impinge upon pupils' learning. They include, in particular, issues related to pupil motivation.

One of the most important affective issues related to pupil learning is the pupil's self-concept. The notion of self-concept has two main aspects: 'self-image', which refers to those general attributes that describe how an individual views himself or herself (fat, clever, an Asian, male), and 'self-esteem', which refers to the sense of worth that an individual ascribes to himself or herself. For some pupils, doing well at school can help develop a positive academic self-concept, which in turn helps sustain further effort and success (creating a virtuous circle). For other pupils, doing badly at school can lead to the development of a negative academic self-concept, which in turn may lead to a withdrawal of effort and general alienation from school learning (creating a vicious circle).

One of the major problems facing teachers is how to give positive feedback to high-attaining pupils without thereby making other pupils who are doing less well feel they are failures. The experience of failure is often painful. Pupils who consistently feel they are doing less well academically than their peers will often make less effort to succeed. After all, poor marks in academic work when you have not being trying is far less painful than failing after you have tried very hard. Some pupils who are doing less well academically try to compensate for this, by establishing a self-image and self-esteem amongst their peers in terms of other goals, such as success in sports, music, or even misbehaviour.

An important aspect of school life is the 'hidden curriculum'. The 'formal curriculum' refers to the subject knowledge that schools aim to foster. The *hidden curriculum* refers to all those messages conveyed to pupils by their experience of school regarding values, attitudes and expectations about themselves and their behaviour. Such messages may be intended or unintended by the teacher. Examples of the messages conveyed to pupils by the hidden curriculum typically involve the notion that 'you have to put up with boring lessons', 'the level of work done by high-attaining pupils is more valued by teachers' and 'teachers are in authority and have sole control over what you do in lessons'.

For some pupils, poor motivation towards school learning can reflect an attempt to preserve their own dignity and sense of worth by opting out of an involvement in academic tasks that have previously resulted in painful consequences, such as low marks, teacher criticism, or appearing to be 'dim' in front of peers. In our society, doing well or not doing well, whatever the activity, matters very much to people, and success and failure makes learning an emotionally charged activity. Recognition of this emotional aspect of learning has done much to explain why pupils often misbehave in apparently senseless ways to avoid learning. When seen from the pupil's perspective, such behaviour appears to be both a natural and rational response to their circumstances. Effective teaching thus requires teachers to nurture and support pupils' efforts, and to use forms of monitoring progress and giving feedback that reinforces pupil motivation and achievement across the whole ability range and across a wide range of school activities.

The influence of teachers' expectations on pupils' attitudes towards learning has been the focus of much attention. One of the most influential studies reported was that of Rosenthal and Jacobson (1968). In their study, a group of primary teachers were told by researchers that certain of their pupils had been identified on a test as likely to make marked gains in academic attainment in the forthcoming school year, when in reality, these pupils had been chosen by the researchers at random. Subsequently, these pupils did indeed make greater gains in IQ scores on average than their peers. Rosenthal and Jacobson interpreted this as evidence that the teachers' expectations must have influenced their behaviour towards these pupils in ways that promoted greater progress and produced a 'self-fulfilling prophecy' effect. Subsequent studies by other researchers using this type of research design have produced a mixed picture, but the findings of their original study and the notion of a teacher expectancy effect has had a great impact on thinking about pupil learning.

Whilst the relationship between teacher expectations and pupil learning may be more complex than a 'self-fulfilling prophecy' suggests, the importance of teachers needing to convey high expectations to their pupils is widely advocated. Indeed, in numerous reports by the Office for Standards in Education, Children's Services and Skills (Ofsted), the call for teachers to have high expectations is voiced as their most frequently expressed concern regarding effective teaching in schools (e.g. Ofsted, 2008a). Low expectations by teachers can easily come about because of the general inertia in the classroom, which acts to try and pull down the level of work expected for the class as a whole towards that produced by the lower-attaining pupils in the group. Indeed, hard-working, high-attaining pupils can often be ridiculed as 'swots' or 'creeps' by other class members because they provide ready evidence to the teacher of what can be achieved. It is important, however, to note that high expectations means expecta-tions that are challenging for pupils but that they can realistically be expected to achieve if they make sufficient effort. High expectations that are too demanding will not foster greater progress, and are simply likely to produce the sort of attack on pupils' self-concept mentioned earlier.

Another important affective issue concerning pupil learning is the psychological pro-cess of 'identification'. Identification is the tendency to identify with and subsequently model oneself upon and adopt the values of another person (usually a person who is loved, admired, or seen as having power and status). Young children normally identify with their parents, often with one more than the other, and not always with the same-sex parent. Such identification is a crucial process in the development of the child's values, attitudes and aspirations, including those towards school learning. During the school years, teachers can often be the object of identification, and where such iden-tification has taken place it can have a marked influence on the pupil's general behav-iour and motivation in that teacher's class. In addition, the process of identification can gradually become more generalised as pupils get older, so that instead of identify-ing with an individual, one can identify with a group, such as a group of friends who share common values, and where one can, as a result, experience strong peer-group pressure to conform to the group's norms and expectations regarding values and behaviour.

Studies of pupils in schools illustrate how pupils' attitudes and values regarding the nature of school and the importance of school learning is fostered and shaped by the expectations of their peers, parents and teachers (Cullingford, 2003; Pollard et al., 2000). Pupils need to strike a balance between the social side of school life (mixing in different friendship groups) and the importance of devoting time and effort to school learning. As they get older, pupils increasingly begin to appreciate the 'seriousness' of school learning through their encounters with teachers' reactions to their work and behaviour, the setting of homework, taking tests in examination-like conditions, being grouped into classes on the basis of attainment, the issuing of school reports on their progress, and the schools' operation of a system of incentives and rewards based on recognising effort and achievement.

Another affective issue worthy of attention concerns the effect of the pupil's level of anxiety on their cognitive processes. Anxiety is an important source of motivation. It arises whenever academic demands are made and success in meeting those demands is important to the individual. Anxiety is thus a common occurrence during tests and examinations, and during class activities where, for example, the failure to answer a teacher's question may cause embarrassment. Such anxiety can be elicited intentionally by the teacher in order to foster high levels of motivation. Two major dangers, however, are involved here. The frequent occurrence of anxiety in learning activities may well lead some pupils to reject such activities as being of no importance to them, thereby defending themselves from experiencing such anxiety. Furthermore, high levels of anxiety actually places constraints on the breadth and quality of one's cognitive processes, because the individual's own awareness of being anxious takes up some of the 'mental space' available for information processing. Indeed, if anxiety becomes too great, an individual literally becomes paralysed. In establishing an effective environment for teaching, the anxiety levels of pupils need to be carefully monitored by teachers to ensure they do not inhibit learning.

Finally, a number of writers have highlighted the importance of pupils' self-regulated learning (SRL) – the strategies pupils use to monitor, control and direct their learning (Hewitt, 2008; Schunk and Zimmerman, 2008). A useful distinction can be made between three types of SRL strategies:

- *Emotion control:* strategies to maintain a positive emotional frame of mind.
- *Motivation control:* strategies to maintain motivational effort.
- *Cognition control:* procedures to direct cognitive processes (metacognition).

There has been an increasing recognition of the need to help pupils develop effective SRL strategies to control and guide their own learning, and that doing this successfully involves a range of affective issues, which is why SRL is so easily influenced by the prevailing classroom climate and, in particular, by the attitudes displayed by important others (such as parents, peers and teachers).

Summary

This chapter has outlined the basic nature of pupil learning together with a consideration of the most important developmental, cognitive and affective issues involved. The main value of an understanding of pupil learning in the context of effective teaching is that it enables a teacher to reflect upon an explicit agenda of the major processes and issues involved in such learning. In the framework developed here, the notions of 'attentiveness', 'receptiveness' and 'appropriateness' acted as the focus for thinking about pupil learning. Teachers' thinking about their own teaching comprises much craft knowledge based on experience. The continued development of the quality of teaching stems from teachers thinking critically about their teaching. The processes and issues raised in this chapter lie at the heart of their consideration of pupil learning itself. In further chapters of this book, the major processes and issues identified here will form the basis of the discussion of the key tasks involved in effective teaching.

Discussion questions

1 What cognitive processes do teachers need to be aware of if they are to facilitate pupil learning?

2 What aspects of child development have important implications for effective classroom practice?

3 What part does pupil motivation play in effective teaching?

4 Which pupil needs must a teacher take account of in fostering learning?

5 How might a pupil's personal and social context influence their learning?

6 How might teachers' expectations influence pupils' effort to learn?

Further reading

Child, D. (2007). *Psychology and the Teacher*, 8th edn. London: Continuum. A comprehensive overview of the key psychological ideas involved in learning.

Fox, R. (2005). *Teaching and Learning: Lessons from Psychology*. Oxford: Blackwell. Provides a good overview of the psychological processes involved in learning, particularly strong on personal and social issues.

Jarvis, M. (2005). *The Psychology of Effective Learning and Teaching*. Cheltenham: Nelson Thornes. Deals with the ways in which cognitive, developmental and affective processes are involved in learning, and the implications these have for teaching.

Schunk, D. H. (2008). *Learning Theories: An Educational Perspective*, 5th edn. London: Pearson. A thorough overview of the key ideas, theories and issues involved in understanding how pupils learn.

Slavin, R. E. (2006). *Educational Psychology: Theory and Practice*, 8th edn. New York: Allyn and Bacon. Presents an excellent synopsis of the key principles and processes involved in pupil learning.

4   Setting up the learning experience

Objective

> To consider how the different types of learning activities used by teachers can promote effective learning.

This chapter is concerned with the types of learning tasks, activities and experiences that teachers can usefully set up to facilitate pupil learning. There is now an incredible diversity in the types of teaching methods used in schools (Muijs and Reynolds, 2005; Wilen *et al.*, 2008). There has been an increasing recognition by teachers of the importance of 'process' compared with 'product', and an appreciation that the way pupils learn is just as important as the content of what is taught. This move towards an increasing emphasis on process is part of a trend towards making use of learning activities that utilise more active pupil involvement (Watkins *et al.*, 2007). Such 'active learning' approaches (such as small group work and problem-solving investigations) have increased in use, not only because they can foster greater understanding, better skills and increased transfer of learning, but also because of their beneficial effects on motivation and attitudes towards learning.

As indicated in the previous chapter, the most important consideration involved in looking at pupil learning experiences is the degree to which they fulfil three major conditions for pupil learning: attentiveness, receptiveness and appropriateness. The basic task of effective teaching is to set up a learning experience in which pupils effectively engage in the mental activity that brings about those changes in the pupil's cognitive structure that constitute the desired learning. Teachers, therefore, need to be sensitive to the ways in which different teaching methods foster different types of mental activity, and the degree to which a particular mental activity brings about the desired learning.

Pupils' learning in school can be fostered in two main ways:

- *Teacher exposition:* listening to teacher exposition, which may include asking or being asked questions, watching a demonstration, and genuine teacher–pupil discussion.
- *Academic work:* being instructed to undertake or engage in academic tasks and activities, either on one's own or together with other pupils.

Teacher exposition tends to place emphasis on describing and explaining new information to pupils through direct teacher–pupil interaction, and is usually based on teaching the class as a whole. Academic work is much more diverse, and includes the whole range of tasks and activities in which pupils engage whilst the teacher takes on a more supportive role, and in some cases the teacher need not be present at all. The vast majority of lessons given in classrooms involve a mixture of exposition and academic work. However, as noted above, there has been an increasing move away from expo-sition-based teaching, towards more academic work, such as independent projects and small group investigations. In considering teacher exposition and academic work, two aspects of the learning experience taking place need to be constantly borne in mind:

- What type of mental activity is being generated by the teaching method used?
- What type of educational outcomes will this mental activity foster?

Taking account of the ways pupils learn is essentially concerned with the need to match as effectively as possible the mental activity being fostered by the learning activity with both the learner and the desired educational outcomes.

Teacher exposition

Teacher exposition is the most central stock-in-trade of teaching and serves a number of functions and purposes, often inter-related. The way pupils learn through teacher exposition is by listening, thinking and responding to what the teacher has to say. Overall, teacher exposition can best be related to pupil learning by looking at its three main uses:

- Making clear the structure and purpose of the learning experience.
- Informing, describing and explaining.
- Using questions and discussion to facilitate and explore pupil learning.

I Making clear the structure and purpose of the learning experience

One of the most important functions of exposition is to emphasise the essential ele-ments of the learning in hand. This is often characterised in terms of following the maxim: 'Tell them what you are going to tell them, tell them, and then tell them what you've told them.' In effect, the teacher needs to brief pupils about the learning tasks and activities that are going to be undertaken. Then, after they have been undertaken, the teacher needs to debrief the pupils about the nature of the learning that should have been accomplished. Unfortunately, there is a tendency for teachers to create well-established routines regarding the structure and organisation of their lessons and to assume that most learning is self-evident in its purpose and nature. This has resulted in a neglect of the briefing and debriefing function on occasions when it would have significantly improved the quality of the pupil learning that took place. This function has been strongly advocated by Ausubel (2000) in his call for greater use of 'advanced organisers' and 'end-of-lesson reviews', and forms an important feature of what many writers feel constitute effective classroom practice (Borich, 2007; Good and Brophy, 2003). As well as generally introducing the learning in hand, such exposition also serves to alert pupils to particular points of emphasis that are important if learning is to be successful. For example, when setting up a practical in science, the teacher may warn pupils in the initial exposition of some early difficulties that will be encountered and how they should be handled.

Another important function of teacher exposition is to induce the appropriate mental set towards the learning in hand, and in particular to elicit pupil motivation by either stimulating their interest and curiosity about the activity (intrinsic motivation) and/or by emphasising its importance and usefulness and the need for success in terms of future attainment (extrinsic motivation). A useful way of eliciting intrinsic motivation is to pose a question or a problem at the start of the lesson, and then indicate how the activity will help them address this.

The first main use of teacher exposition is thus concerned with the effective setting up of the learning tasks and activities and with the effective drawing of conclusions following these. This use can be extended to explicitly indicating how a particular lesson may relate to previous and future lessons or to activities in other subjects, in order to create a greater sense of coherence for the course as a whole and to foster greater transfer of learning.

2   Informing, describing and explaining

A degree of informing, describing and explaining is clearly involved in the first usage of teacher exposition outlined above. The second usage can be distinguished from the first usage by being concerned specifically with the transmission of the intellectual content of the subject matter itself. That is, it is concerned with the role of the teacher either as instructing or in supporting academic tasks.

At its extreme, teacher exposition can constitute the only activity, as in a lecture. While the use of the lecture mode in schools is less frequent than it once was, it is by no means rare to find such teaching occurring. In addition, the lecture mode is sometimes used in short bursts to ensure that an accurate and correct piece of writing concerning some topic is recorded. There are two major dangers in the use of such extended exposition. First, pupils are psychologically incapable of attending to such activities for long periods. Second, the experience does not in itself constitute meaningful learning, and must be explicitly linked to other learning tasks and activities if it is to be of value.

Another extreme use of teacher exposition is the teacher demonstration of some technique or activity, which pupils are asked to observe, note and copy. The most common example of this occurs in the teaching of mathematics, but it also appears to a marked extent in many other subjects. The essential characteristic of such a form of teacher exposition is that no pupil need say a word throughout the entire lesson.

The most common form of teaching, in fact, consists of a mixture of teacher exposition and academic tasks, where the teacher exposition takes the form of a mixture of informing, describing, explaining and questioning interspersed with or alongside the academic tasks. Such a mixed approach enables a dialogue between teacher and pupils to develop, which is more meaningful for pupils and better sustains their attention and interest.

An emphasis on teacher exposition in a lesson tends to go hand in hand with a general approach towards teaching called 'expository teaching' or 'didactic teaching'. This is often contrasted with 'discovery learning'. In expository teaching, the teacher uses academic tasks to exemplify what pupils have already been told about the subject matter. In discovery learning, pupils are given an opportunity to approach a problem and identify its significance before the teacher offers an explanation. Ofsted surveys of classroom practice in both primary and secondary schools indicate that discovery learning has been increasing over the years, but that overall, expository teaching is much more widely used than discovery learning and there is still a need for teachers to make more frequent use of investigations and discovery learning in their teaching (e.g. Ofsted, 2008a).

Teachers spend a large proportion of their time teaching the class as a whole, with the teacher exposition being directed at the whole class, and with interaction with individual pupils being directed at a selection of pupils to check on general class understanding (Good and Brophy, 2003; Myhill *et al.*, 2006). Such whole-class teaching poses two major tasks for teachers. First, the exposition must gain and sustain the attention of pupils. Second, the exposition must be appropriate for all the pupils in the class. These two tasks are not easily achieved, and require a high level of expertise. Gaining and sustaining attention depends on a mixture of classroom management skills, non-verbal cues (e.g. use of eye contact, facial expression) as well as clarity in the content of the exposition itself. Keeping the exposition appropriate for the whole class depends on the teacher's ability to take account of the pupils' previous level of knowledge and understanding and the level of the cognitive demands the exposition is making upon them.

All classes contain a range of pupil interests, abilities and motivation. In general the exposition tends to be pitched so that the least able or least receptive pupil can be carried along with the rest. However, where the range of differences among pupils is particularly large, teachers tend to pitch the level just above that of the least able, and then use subsequent elaboration or help with academic tasks to meet the needs of those having problems. Two dangers arise when such whole-class exposition has not been fully successful. First, the teacher may need to give individual help to a large number of pupils (indeed, some pupils may come to expect this and thereby develop a habit of paying little attention to the teacher's initial exposition). Second, some pupils may not recognise their lack of understanding or are reluctant to ask for help, and hence approach the academic tasks using faulty techniques yielding little success.

Research on teacher exposition has indicated that an overwhelmingly high proportion of teacher exposition in both primary and secondary schools comprises simple information and data giving, with a contrastingly small proportion dealing with challenging ideas involving a consideration of concepts, reasons, explanations and generalisations (Ornstein and Lasley, 2004). However, effective explaining is still widely regarded as the most important of all the skills involved in effective teaching (Wragg and Brown, 2001a,b).

At the heart of the teacher's ability to explain effectively, is being able to take account of the pupils' current knowledge and understanding, and then being able to structure the content, level and steps in the explanation so that it is meaningful. Overall, the key aspects that underpin effective explaining are:

- *clarity:* it is clear and pitched at the appropriate level
- *structure:* the major ideas are broken down into meaningful segments and linked together in a logical order
- *length:* it is fairly brief and may be interspersed with questions and other activities
- *attention:* the delivery makes good use of voice and body language to sustain attention and interest
- *language:* it avoids use of over-complex language and explains new terms
- *exemplars:* it uses examples, particularly ones relating to pupils' experiences and interests
- *understanding:* the teacher monitors and checks pupils' understanding.

3 Using questions, dialogue and discussion to facilitate and explore pupil learning

During a professional career, the number of questions asked by a teacher runs into tens of thousands. Indeed, there can be no other profession where one asks so many questions that one already knows the answer to! Over the years a great deal of attention has been paid to the effective use of questions as a key teaching skill (Hayes, 2006; Walsh and Settes, 2005). What makes questioning such a useful but complex skill is that it can be used in a number of different ways, ranging from a simple and quick check that a particular pupil has been paying attention, to an integral part of developing a dialogue and genuine discussion with a pupil about the topic in hand.

With regard to the types of questions teachers use, one first needs to consider the type of thinking that the question is designed to promote. For example, in terms of Bloom's categories of cognitive processes, it might be knowledge, comprehension, application, analysis, synthesis or evaluation (Bloom *et al.*, 1956). One important distinction in categorising question types is between those that require the recall and reporting of facts or information (lower order questions) and those that require some manipulation of information, such as reasoning about, evaluating or applying information (higher order questions). Whereas lower order questions tend to have answers that are clearly right or wrong, higher order questions tend to be judged in terms of general qualities related to the thinking involved. A second and related distinction is that between 'closed' questions, which only have one right answer, and 'open' questions, where a number of correct answers are possible.

Studies of teachers' use of questions indicate a much greater use of lower order and closed questions, rather than higher order and open questions. Given that the latter are seen to be more intellectually challenging than the former, it is important for teachers to use a good mix of both. However, given that the teacher's use of questions to promote thinking among pupils is inter-related with its use for other purposes, particularly of a social and managerial nature, it is perhaps not surprising that lower order and closed questions are used more frequently.

The reasons given by teachers for asking questions are various (Kerry, 2002; Wragg and Brown, 2001c,d), and include:

- To encourage thought, understanding of ideas, phenomena, procedures and values.
- To check understanding, knowledge and skills.
- To gain attention to task, enable the teacher to move towards teaching points, as a warm-up activity for pupils.
- To review, revise, recall, reinforce a recently learnt point, remind of earlier procedures.
- For management, settling down, to stop calling out by pupils, to direct attention to teacher or text, to warn of precautions.
- Specifically to teach the whole class through pupil answers.
- To give everyone a chance to answer.
- To prompt bright pupils to encourage others.
- To draw in shyer pupils.
- To probe children's knowledge after critical answers, redirect questions to pupil who asked or to other pupils.
- To allow expressions of feelings, views and empathy.

In looking at the skills underlying effective questioning, five key aspects stand out: quality, targeting, interacting, feedback and extending pupils' thinking. The *quality* of the question itself, in terms of clarity and appropriateness for meeting its intended function, is clearly of importance. In part, this depends on the teacher's ability to take account of the pupil's perspective when asking the question.

The *targeting* of questions refers to the way in which teachers select pupils to answer. Of major importance here is the need to distribute questions to as many pupils as possible, and certainly not to focus on volunteers. At the same time, targeting also involves matching the question to the target pupil.

Interacting refers to the techniques used by teachers to deliver questions and to respond to pupils. They involve making use of eye contact, the manner and tone of voice used, the use of pauses to give pupils thinking time, the use of prompting to help pupils in difficulties, and using follow-up questions or points to enable and encourage pupils to elaborate or improve the quality of their initial answer. Teachers' use of questions often involves stringing together several questions to develop a particular theme or explore the issue in hand. This technique of sequencing can be a very effective form of dialogue, particularly when the teacher is sensitive to and takes account of pupils' responses. The greatest danger in sequencing is that of sticking too rigidly to a pre-planned sequence, so that pupils' responses are largely ignored or regarded as incorrect simply because they do not fit the teacher's intended sequence.

The role of *feedback* concerns the effect on pupils of the teacher's use of questions. Answering questions is often a high-risk and emotionally charged activity, in part because it is usually public and in part because it usually involves explicit teacher judgement. The teacher's use of questions can thus have a profound influence on the whole tone of a lesson and on the rapport that develops between the teacher and pupils. In order to protect a pupil's self-esteem and develop pupil self-confidence the teacher needs to ensure that questioning takes place in an encouraging and supportive atmosphere. In particular, this requires praise and encouragement to develop pupils' answers and to convey the message that all attempts to answer will be respected and valued. A teacher should certainly avoid scorning an answer or allowing other pupils to do so. Pupils are very sensitive and alert to such aspects of interaction in forming their views of the teacher's expectations of their efforts. Teachers also need to be aware of the many unintended consequences that may follow from their reactions to pupils' answers. For example, if a teacher frequently corrects the language used by pupils in answering, these pupils may feel reluctant to contribute answers in future because of their perception that 'correct language' is as important to the teacher as the meaning of what is said.

Extending pupils' thinking refers to teachers using questions as a means of developing higher quality dialogue in the lesson that extends pupils' thinking. It is very important for the teacher to go beyond the traditional initiation-response-feedback (IRF) style of discourse interaction with a pupil, in which the teacher asks a question (initiation), the pupil responds (response), and the teacher then gives an evaluative comment (feedback). In order to make use of asking questions to establish high-quality dialogue with pupils, the teacher needs to ask follow-up questions, such as asking the pupil to explain their answer, or using the pupil's answer as a stimulus for asking another pupil to comment. Going beyond IRF can help engage pupils in higher quality thinking and also give the pupils a sense of co-constructing knowledge and understanding with the teacher, rather than a sense of being a passive recipient to a teacher's use of a transmission style of teaching. Alexander (2008a) refers to a type of use by teachers of teacher–pupil dialogue to promote pupils' learning as 'dialogic teaching', which is characterised by:

- structuring questions to provoke thoughtful answers
- using pupils' answers to establish dialogue
- developing a strand of thinking through the use of dialogue.

For Alexander, dialogic teaching offers a particular kind of interactive experience, which is characterised by five principles:

- *Collective:* teachers and pupils address learning tasks together.
- *Reciprocal:* teachers and pupils listen to each other and share ideas.
- *Supportive:* pupils express ideas freely within a supportive climate.
- *Cumulative:* teachers and pupils build on their own and each other's ideas.
- *Purposeful:* teachers plan and steer talk towards specific educational goals.

Fisher (2008) has illustrated how the use of dialogic teaching, interspersing teacher–pupil dialogue with pupil–pupil dialogue that is characterised by intellectual challenge, creates a powerful learning environment for pupils, by actively engaging pupils in questioning and explaining.

Effective questioning overlaps with the use of discussion to explore the topic in hand. In this section the focus is on teacher-directed discussion rather than the discussion between pupils that occurs in small group work, as the former can be regarded as an extension of teacher exposition. Numerous Ofsted reports have pointed to the need for teachers to make greater use of discussion to explore and develop pupil learning (e.g. Ofsted, 2008a). The skills involved in the effective use of teacher-directed discussion have received much attention (Walsh and Settes, 2005).

Overall, there appear to be two main skills involved. First, the ability to get as many pupils as possible to make a contribution. This means the teacher may need to be relatively less critical and less censoring of pupils' contributions in order to encourage their participation. Second, the teacher needs to probe and encourage pupils to develop their contributions. Such teacher-directed discussion most often occurs when teachers are exploring general aspects of a topic that are later to be shaped and refined. For example, in looking at a topic such as the advantages and disadvantages of family life, the teacher may begin with generating pupils' ideas on this before focusing on key themes in the subsequent work. Full discussion takes place when pupils are given more control over the course of their contributions and indeed when pupils begin to comment on each other's contributions. The teacher's skill in relaxing control over the direction of contributions, while at the same time retaining appropriate control over the nature and procedure of the discussion is important. Mercer (1995) refers to the teacher's role in such interactions as a 'discourse guide' and has illustrated how teachers can adopt this role. Mercer also advocates the use of 'exploratory talk' in which partners engage critically but constructively with each other's ideas. Mercer and Littleton (2007) have pointed out that one of the key reasons why engaging pupils in 'exploratory talk' in the classroom is so beneficial is because of its collaborative quality in which partners can co-construct knowledge and understanding in a purposeful manner. However, for this to be successful, the teacher needs to adopt a more equal stance with pupils in respecting what they have to say, and being prepared to go with the pupil wherever the dialogue takes you.

The introduction of the National Literacy Strategy in 1998 and the National Numeracy Strategy in 1999 directed teachers to make use of 'interactive whole-class teaching' in order to promote high-quality teacher–pupil dialogue in lessons designed to encourage and support pupils' thinking and intellectual engagement. Research studies of classroom practice indicate that teachers' use of 'whole-class teaching' markedly increased as a result, but unfortunately the type of 'interactive' quality advocated in these strategies has not featured prominently. Indeed, whole-class teaching remained rather didactic, based on repeated waves of low level teacher–pupil IRF discourse patterns (Smith *et al.*, 2004; Webb and Vulliamy, 2007). This didactic style of teaching also seems to be evident when interactive whiteboards are being used, which in part were intended to introduce more opportunity for a more genuinely interactive style of teaching to occur.

Before leaving teacher exposition, a special note is required in relation to the teaching of a foreign language, where teachers spend a great deal of time demonstrating and repeating particular words and phrases with pupils, acting as a model for good delivery. This type of teaching behaviour, called 'modelling', involves a mix of skills. Of particular importance for foreign language teachers is the need to be aware of pupils' sensitivities to the demands of such oral work, and hence the need to establish a very supportive and encouraging classroom atmosphere, where pupils are happy to participate and can make errors and mistakes without feeling unduly upset by the experience.

Academic work

Academic work refers to the academic tasks, activities and experiences used by teachers, usually in conjunction with teacher exposition. In essence, this is based on pupils learning by doing, and the learning derives from the thinking involved in undertaking the academic work. Of particular interest here are the findings of a number of studies that have focused on the way in which pupils approach academic tasks (Hayes, 2006). Such studies have indicated that the type of thinking used by pupils to meet the academic demands set, and the strategies they employ, may often be very different from that intended by teachers. Research has pointed to the ways in which pupils are continually attempting to make sense of what is required of them by the teacher: 'What do I have to do and how do I do it?' From the pupils' perspective, attention is primarily focused on how to perform successfully (or at least give the teacher that impression), often referred to as 'performativity', and not on thinking and learning in a genuine intellectual sense.

As such, when pupils give incorrect answers it is important that teachers explore the method the pupils used to obtain their answer, rather than merely repeat the correct method. In addition, if a teacher wishes to foster understanding rather than performativity, this must be reflected in the nature of the academic demands made. For example, being able to add fractions competently will not of itself foster an understanding of the addition of fractions. Pupils gear their learning towards the type of assessment they expect the teacher will be employing. This, in part, explains why pupils may be reluctant to pay attention to learning that they know will not be tested.

There is a large variety of academic work teachers can set. In looking at the range of such tasks, two important aspects seem to be central to the pupils' perception of their appeal. First, the degree of teacher control and direction over the nature of the task. This aspect is often characterised as the difference between 'direct instruction' (or 'direct teaching') and 'indirect instruction'. In direct instruction, the activities and tasks are highly structured and organised by the teacher, and usually involve written work that enables pupils to acquire, demonstrate and practise the knowledge, skills and understanding covered during an initial phase of teacher exposition. A common example of direct instruction would be in a mathematics lesson, where pupils undertook an exercise that consisted of examples of a type of question that was explained at the start of the lesson. In contrast, indirect instruction involves tasks where pupils are given a significant degree of initiative and responsibility in deciding how the tasks are organised and undertaken and in deciding on the nature of the learning that takes place. An example of indirect instruction would be a foreign languages lesson in which the pupils are asked to script the dialogue for a short sequence of interaction (e.g. arriving at a hotel and booking a room), which they are then asked to perform in front of the class.

The second aspect of a task's appeal concerns the degree of risk and cost involved for the pupil engaging in the task. This aspect relates to pupils' perception of how likely it is that they will succeed at the task in hand (which relates to its intellectual difficulty), the nature of the work itself (e.g. copying out), the nature of the mental effort involved (e.g. memorising, applying rules, applying understanding), and its apparent value in terms of interest and relevance.

It is important to note that pupils differ markedly in the extent to which certain characteristics of the task set by teachers increase or decrease its appeal. It is thus important that teachers employ both direct and indirect instruction, and both high- and low-risk/cost tasks, in order to foster a broad range of educational outcomes. The skill involved in using a mix of teaching methods effectively lies in thinking creatively about how different methods can be used to foster the different desired outcomes.

There are six main categories of academic work employed by teachers to complement teacher exposition. These will now be considered in turn:

- Structured reading and writing tasks.
- Investigational work.
- Individualised programmes of work.
- Small group work.
- Experiential learning.
- Using ICT.

1 Structured reading and writing tasks

Structured reading and writing tasks refer to those activities where what is read and written is tightly prescribed and directed by the teacher. Such a task often takes the form of an elaboration or consolidation of what has been presented during teacher exposition. The most classic example of such tasks is the use of exercises or lists of questions in a textbook where the pupil's ability to answer correctly is derived from the preceding teacher exposition or material presented in the textbook itself. Other examples of such structured tasks are copying maps, diagrams or notes out of a book or off the whiteboard, or simply being asked to read some text. The essential feature of such structured tasks is that they are passive, in the sense that they provide the pupil with little initiative or control over the work. This is not to decry their importance, particularly in enabling pupils to practise and apply a whole variety of skills. Over the years, there has been a gradual shift away from the use of structured reading and writing tasks towards other types of academic work. However, it has been noted by Ofsted in a number of their reports that such tasks appear to occupy too great a proportion of the academic work undertaken by some pupils. Where such tasks are less structured and offer more initiative, they begin to take the form of genuine investigational work, which will be considered in the next section.

One example of such tasks is worthy of particular note. This is the development of paired reading schemes, which involve pupils being asked to read books at home in the presence of a parent. Such schemes have had marked benefits for pupils, because of the extra time pupils thereby devote to reading and the help parents give through prompting, and also because it conveys a message to pupils that their parents value this activity.

In the context of structured reading and writing tasks, specific mention needs to be made of the use of tests. Regular tests and examinations act as a stimulus for both teachers and pupils. In addition, they serve to provide both teacher and pupils with feedback concerning the quality of learning that has taken place, and the general standard of attainment that has been achieved. Tests and examinations can, however, have a corrupting influence on education, particularly where both teacher and pupils gear the teaching and learning towards success in the tests and examinations. Indeed, many teachers and educationists have noted that the importance placed on test and examination results as the prime index of educational success is the single most influential barrier against the development by teachers of more desirable forms of educational experience. Furthermore, the fact that some pupils must inevitably do less well in their test and examination results than others, communicates to many pupils an unequivocal message of failure. One of the greatest challenges facing effective teaching is to devise methods of monitoring progress and attainment that do not alienate those pupils who do relatively less well. One interesting development in this respect is the use of objective criteria of performance whereby pupils progress through various levels of attainment at their own pace. Such criteria take the form of knowledge or skills required for a given level of competence to be displayed. Attainment tests thereby emphasise what pupils can do and succeed at by setting an appropriate level to be aimed at for each pupil. Success is dependent on achieving set criteria and is not explicitly measured by performance relative to other pupils. Examples of this approach include grade tests in musical instruments and grade tests in modern languages.

2 Investigational work

Investigational work refers to those activities where pupils are given a degree of initiative, autonomy and responsibility towards planning and conducting their own learning in order to investigate some topic or task set by the teacher. The essential ingredient of genuine investigational work is that it involves a degree of problem solving and/or discovery learning, which is in part or totally independent of teacher support. Its prime value lies in the qualities and skills it fosters in pupils, although in addition it has been widely advocated as an effective way of promoting deeper understanding. Indeed, teaching and learning in schools places much greater emphasis than in the past, on pupils developing investigational skills rather than simply acquiring knowledge. The most notable examples of this are in the teaching of science and history, which, as subjects, have moved very much away from being the accumulation of facts towards being seen as investigational and interpretive activities.

Effective use of discovery-learning and problem-solving activities in schools requires teachers to:

- clearly formulate the problem that is to be undertaken
- explicitly foster the types of information-gathering skills that are required
- systematically debrief pupils on the learning that should have occurred.

The ability of pupils to undertake investigational work also has to be cultivated carefully, otherwise such activities may result in little learning actually occurring. Indeed, pupils are adept at appearing to be active and looking busy, when they are making little productive progress in the ways the teacher intended.

Another important aspect of investigational work is that of developing the pupil's ability to go beyond the recording and description of what they have done towards making interpretations and explanations. Some problems may appear to involve investigational work, but in fact merely foster simple information gathering. For example, asking pupils to give three reasons why the Romans invaded Britain after reading a page of a textbook that clearly lists three reasons is not investigational, although it might be a precursor of such work. Now, asking pupils to analyse some information about both Britain and Rome at the time from which to identify possible reasons for the invasion would involve a genuine investigation based on analysis and interpretation.

Investigational work does not only foster intrinsic motivation but also those qualities and skills that pupils need to be able to apply to meet many demands in adult life. Attempts to facilitate such transfer of skills from school to the real world have involved setting tasks that have real-life relevance. For example, a mathematics task might ask pupils to plan all the arrangements for a class trip by using maps, train timetables and a budget for meals and other expenses.

Another benefit of investigational work is that it can foster creative thinking. One of the key skills of effective teaching in this context is indeed to encourage pupils to explore their own ideas. Quite naturally, teachers often have in mind the type of responses and comments they are seeking from pupils. Unfortunately, this can sometimes foster an atmosphere where pupils are encouraged to guess what the teacher has in mind (often assisted by the teacher through giving clues and prompts). Pupils will be inhibited from making creative responses if they feel there is a danger that their comments and ideas will be publicly judged by the teacher to be unwanted or incorrect. Indeed, it takes a fair degree of skill by the teacher to encourage genuinely creative exploration of a topic by pupils that is not unnecessarily constrained by the teacher's expectations. As such, it is imperative for the teacher to be very supportive of all pupil efforts, particularly as the giving of such efforts is exactly what investigational work is attempting to foster.

A particularly interesting development in a number of schools is the use of resource centres to support investigational work. Such centres have tended to develop from their original function as school libraries to include a whole range of materials and equipment (such as ICT packages, internet sources, video and audio tapes, slides and photographs, objects, and self-access learning packs). These resources are then linked to particular pieces of investigational work that a pupil or small group of pupils can undertake. The investigation set by the teacher will specify the type of information that needs to be gathered or the problem that needs to be addressed, along with the sources and activities housed in the resources centre that need to be used. Such centres have been developed widely in both primary and secondary schools, and appear to be very successful.

3   Individualised programmes of work

Individualised programmes of work refer to a substantial piece or course of academic work extending over a number of hours or days, which the pupil is able to undertake on an individual basis. The major advantage of such an individualised programme of work is that it enables pupils to work at their own pace and at their own level. Given the importance of matching pace and level to the pupil in order to maximise the quality of the pupil's learning experience, it is not surprising that such programmes of work have been widely used.

The three main types of individualised programmes commonly used in schools are project work, computer-based learning programmes and schemes based on structured word cards and booklets. There are however two major dangers facing the effective use of such schemes. First, the teacher can spend a great deal of time dealing with a range of trivial resource and organisational matters, rather than actually teaching and giving the pupil on-task support when needed. An over-reliance by a teacher on the content of the materials used for the development of pupils' understanding can easily lead to problems. Indeed, the main rationale for such schemes is not that they replace the teacher, but rather that the teacher is given more time to teach on a one-to-one basis. Second, it is commonly assumed that the most crucial task for teachers is indeed to help pupils when they get into difficulties. In fact, the major task is to brief pupils properly before they begin about what they are expected to do and achieve as result of the activities.

Project work has been widely used as a means of developing independent study skills, and has been widely incorporated into national examination assessments. Project work can act as a very important source of motivation (particularly of intrinsic motivation) through the degree of choice and control it offers to pupils in undertaking the work. However, it is very important for teachers to make clear to pupils what qualities will be looked for when project work is assessed and, if possible, for them to see examples of project work produced by other pupils. It is very easy for pupils to feel that as long as the work displays evidence of much time and effort being devoted to it, that of itself will largely contribute to a good mark. This can lead pupils to spend insufficient time on polishing up its intellectual and academic content because too much time has been spent in accumulating bulk.

The use of individualised programmes of work has also become widespread. The tasks and activities may direct pupils to support resources. The crucial aspect of using such schemes effectively is to maintain a careful record of the progress made by each pupil. While some degree of pupil self-assessment is often involved, teacher assessments are essential if a whole range of qualities (such as spelling, handwriting, presentation and explanation) are to be monitored. One danger with such schemes is that pupils may waste much time waiting for a teacher to help, mark and give direction, before they can proceed further. As such, an effective system of organisation that minimises such problems is very important. Indeed, there is little doubt that a teacher supervising a class of pupils who will be working on different topics, at different speeds, and who demand different types of help, requires a high level of sound planning and organisation, as well as a high degree of mental energy.

4   Small group work

One particularly healthy development in schools over the years has been the greater use of small group work. Small group work refers to academic tasks and activities undertaken by a group of pupils, which involves some degree of discussion, reflection and collaboration. The optimum size for small group work for most types of tasks is probably about five, although small group work can be undertaken by groups as small as two (termed 'paired work'). Advocates of the value of small group work have stressed the importance of the skills developed by the processes involved in small group work (e.g. social and communication skills) as being educationally as important, if not more important than, the intellectual quality of the work produced (i.e. the aims may often be process rather than product oriented in emphasis). The importance of the collaboration involved in such work has received particular attention, and this is often referred to as 'collaborative learning'. The point is frequently made is that effective small group work must involve genuine collaboration, not simply pupils working alongside each other relatively independently and occasionally sharing answers. The value of small group work includes:

- creating a climate in which pupils can work with a sense of security and self-confidence
- offering the optimum opportunity for pupils to talk reflectively with each other
- promoting a spirit of cooperation and mutual respect.

Studies of small group work (Gillies, 2004; Kutnick, 2006) have indicated that its effectiveness is enhanced when the teacher:

- helps pupils to understand and develop the skills involved in doing group work
- makes clear to pupils what they are expected to do and gives a positive lead before the group work begins
- follows up the group work by pooling the discussion and giving feedback on the work produced.

Many might regard science practicals, usually involving two or three pupils working together, as a common example of small group work. However, many science practicals simply involve pupils carefully following instructions and directions given by the teacher. They thus offer little room for discussion and collaboration other than the cooperation required for the conduct of the practical. In fact small group work involving genuine collaborative learning occurs most often in English, history and social studies in secondary school, and in topic and project work in primary school. The greater use of small group work in science and mathematics will depend on these subject teachers recognising the value of the skills being fostered as an important part of their own subject area and not regarding them as the more proper concern of others.

There are two main types of small group work. The first is where the pupils are given a specific task to achieve (e.g. 'Prepare a leaflet about the working conditions a sailor could expect to find on a seventeenth-century ship from the materials given'). The second is where pupils are asked to explore an issue through information gathering and discussion (e.g. whether fox hunting should be banned). The former is thus focused on the production of a tangible end product as the stimulus, whereas the latter is open-ended. Other types of small group work range from activities based on pairs of pupils interacting (a common feature of modern languages teaching) to 'buzz sessions' (where pupils are asked to identify ideas connected with some problem).

The use of group work in primary school has, however, been the subject of some controversy, in part because it has been discussed in the context of the debate over the relative effectiveness of 'formal' versus 'informal' teaching styles. Group work has been seen as a key feature of progressive teaching, characterised as involving the use of more open-ended investigational tasks, pupils being seated together in small groups around a table, a more relaxed classroom ethos, and greater pupil involvement in the pace and direction of activities. In contrast, traditional teaching is characterised as involving more whole-class teaching, pupils being seated at individual desks in rows, the use of expository teaching, and greater teacher control and direction over classroom activities. One danger with the use of small group work, is that teachers may assume that pupils already possess the skills and maturity to produce a high of quality work within this context when in fact they do not. As such, it is important for teachers to help pupils develop these skills and to behave appropriately in order to use such approaches to best effect. Unfortunately, some teachers avoid using group work simply because pupils do not appear to already possess the necessary skills, when in fact it is part of the teacher's task to help such skills develop. It must be remembered that the development of group-work skills by pupils takes practice and confidence, and that a substantial period of teacher support and guidance is needed before pupils can show what they are capable of.

A particularly interesting development in schools has been the use of peer-group tutoring, which involves one pupil helping or teaching another on a one-to-one basis. The most common application of peer-group tutoring has involved older pupils helping younger pupils, for example, in learning to read or in arithmetical computations. Interestingly, the older pupils themselves often benefit from the exercise, as having to teach leads them to improve their own competence and understanding. This form of tutoring has been widely used to help less confident younger pupils. Earlier in this chapter, mention was made of paired reading programmes, which involve pupils reading to their parents at home. Studies of such programmes indicate that it is often an older brother or sister, rather than a parent, who acts as a tutor, particularly among minority ethnic communities, which is in fact a form of peer-group tutoring. For some reason, the use of confident pupils helping less confident pupils in the same class appears to have been less successful than the use of older pupils, in part perhaps because a classmate as tutor may serve to highlight one's sense of failure and relatively lower status.

5 Experiential learning

It is important to note that there are two common uses of the term 'experiential learning'. The first denotes the process of coming to understand and make sense of oneself and one's own experiences, particularly aspects of oneself or experiences one has sought to suppress. In education, this definition is applied to the need to develop 'the whole person' and is an aspect of the humanistic psychology that essentially sees the teacher's role as involving a degree of emotional help and support in fostering such learning (Rogers and Freiberg, 1994). The second use of the term 'experiential learning' refers to the use of activities such as role playing, or direct experiences such as spending time working in a local firm, which are used by teachers to help pupils better understand, both intellectually and emotionally, the issue being explored. It is this second use of the term that will be considered here.

Experiential learning, as defined above, involves providing pupils with an experience that will totally and powerfully immerse them in 'experiencing' the issue that is being explored, and will as a result influence both their cognitive understanding and also their affective appreciation (involving their feelings, values and attitudes).

The most common examples of experiential learning are:
- role play (utilising drama, simulation activities and games)
- watching plays performed in the school by professional acting groups
- viewing films or videos that focus on a particular person's perspective
- direct experiences (based on tasks or visits).

An example of the use of role play would be acting out an industrial dispute at a factory, with pupils allocated various roles, such as managers, union officials and workers. Plays and films can provide powerful experiences, for example, exploring prejudice through the experience and perspectives of the victims. Direct experiences can utilise visits in various ways. For example, pupils can discover far more about the nature of working on a production line in a factory from a visit to one than is possible by more 'indirect' means. An interesting opportunity for a visit, which also includes role play, is offered in some historic houses where pupils can take on roles (often in period dress) in the household at an appropriate historical period. Direct experiences can also utilise a whole variety of tasks in the authentic situation (e.g. work experience in a local firm) or in some contrived way (such as being required to wear a purple armband for three days in school without divulging the reason to anyone, in order to parallel aspects of racial discrimination).

Where the use of experiential learning has been employed in personal and social education programmes, as a means of fostering the pupil's personal development, it links up with the first usage of the term 'experiential learning' outlined above.

As with group work, careful planning, briefing and debriefing by the teacher are of fundamental importance for the success of experiential learning. In addition, this approach calls for a very different form of teacher–pupil relationship and classroom climate than that which commonly exists during expository teaching, as discussed earlier in this chapter. In experiential learning, the role of the teacher is to set up a learning experience that encourages pupils to reflect upon their own feelings, ideas and values. The climate of the classroom during debriefing work needs to be supportive and enabling rather than intellectually prescriptive.

In thinking about experiential learning, it is interesting to note that the pupil's whole experience of schooling is in itself an example of experiential learning. After all, the myriad of experiences that pupils encounter throughout their schooling shapes their feelings, ideas, values and attitudes about themselves. If one thinks of schooling in terms of experiential learning, one can focus upon a number of experiences schooling typically offers to pupils, collectively referred to as the 'hidden curriculum', which was outlined in the previous chapter.

Teachers and pupils often find experiential learning uncomfortable at first. Teachers tend to feel drawn towards exposition and interpretation, and find it difficult to not keep intervening with comments. Pupils often feel unsure of what is expected from them. As with group work, both teachers and pupils need to develop the skills to make such learning successful. Teachers and pupils should not be disheartened or put off by their first experiences with such forms of teaching. Indeed, it is worth noting that schooling also involves experiential learning for teachers about themselves. By trying various teaching methods, they learn about their own capabilities as teachers, their strengths and weaknesses. Like pupils, teachers also prefer to stay on safe ground and use tried and tested learning activities, which in part explains why some teachers are reluctant to make more use of such approaches.

6 Using ICT

Perhaps the single most significant development over the years regarding academic work has been the growing use of learning activities based on the use of information and communications technology (ICT). ICT-based learning activities include:

- *blended learning:* combining the use of ICT activities with face-to-face non-ICT activities
- *e-learning:* the use of online technologies such as blogs, email, discussion boards
- *computer-assisted learning:* the use of computer-based software packages designed to aid learning
- *learning platforms:* a collection of web-based ICT resources and interactive discussion forums
- the *virtual learning environment (VLE):* pupil and teacher access to software systems that support learning, which are brought together in a way that enables teachers to monitor and track pupils' engagement.

This growth has led to many exciting developments (Leask and Pachler, 2005; Wheeler, 2005). ICT-based teaching is expected to be used across the whole curriculum. Schools are expected to foster a wide range of pupils' skills in the use of ICT and to use ICT to enhance the quality of pupils' learning within subjects.

ICT-based activities present schools with three challenges:

- Financial, organisational and logistical.
- The need for teachers to develop sufficient expertise in using ICT.
- Using ICT to enhance the quality of pupils' learning experiences.

Research on aspects of this third challenge regarding the quality of pupils' learning experience has highlighted that there are two levels of ICT use in the classroom. The first level deals with the stimulating aspects of using ICT. Pupils often report that they enjoy using ICT, they become more engaged in the work, and their motivation for learning increases. The second level deals with the genuine increase in the quality of pupils' learning by enabling their knowledge and understanding of the topic in hand to be enhanced through the use of ICT.

Whilst the 'first-level use' of ICT is important and beneficial, particularly in terms of the motivational value that using ICT can provide to pupils who might otherwise be disaffected or disinterested in the work, it is only when 'second-level use' takes place that we can say that the effectiveness of the teaching and learning has been enhanced by the use of ICT to promote higher quality pupil learning. For example, numerous evaluation reports and guides for schools illustrate how developments in the use of ICT have provided a host of new ways in which teachers can scaffold pupils' learning and promote new forums within which high quality pupil–pupil dialogue can occur (e.g. Becta, 2007, 2008). In many lessons, however, pupils and teachers have only developed sufficient expertise in the use of ICT for the work to remain at the first level. It can take quite some time for pupils and teachers to develop the necessary skills and understanding in the use of ICT for second-level use to take place, but when this is achieved, the progress and insights that it offers can be substantial, and sometimes unique (in the sense that it is hard to see how the particular type of deeper understanding by pupils of the topic gained by using ICT could have occurred using any other type of teaching method).

Summary

In this chapter the diversity of the learning tasks, activities and experiences that a teacher can set up to facilitate learning have been considered. While a number of distinct categories have been used to make this diversity clear, in practice effective teaching involves a complex combination of such tasks, activities and experiences. Effective teaching involves a number of skills concerned with the planning and organisation of such tasks and their presentation, and with matching the tasks to the educational outcomes the teacher wishes to foster. Much of the discussion of effective teaching in the past has relied heavily on an image of teaching that is traditional both in terms of the teaching style it implied (expository teaching) and in the educational outcomes it focused upon (performance on attainment tests). If there is one thing that characterises schools nowadays, it is the greater diversity of teaching activities that are adopted, ranging from computer-assisted learning to role play. Our thinking about effective teaching needs to keep pace with such changes in the character and nature of learning.

Discussion questions

1 What are the relative strengths and weaknesses of expository teaching versus small group work activities?

2 What qualities are involved in the effective use of questioning by teachers?

3 In what circumstances is experiential learning particularly useful?

4 How can ICT-based learning activities be used to best effect?

5 How might the teacher's choice of learning activities be influenced by the intended learning outcomes?

6 What role does teacher feedback play in the use of different types of learning activities?

Further reading

Hayes, D. (2006). *Inspiring Primary Teaching: Insights into Excellent Primary Practice.* Exeter: Learning Matters. An excellent analysis of the key features involved in setting up effective learning activities the primary school classroom.

Muijs, D. and Reynolds, D. (2005). *Effective Teaching: Evidence and Practice*, 2nd edn. London: Sage. An overview of the key factors and issues involved in promoting learning.

Myhill, D., Jones, S. and Hopper, R. (2006). *Talking, Listening and Learning: Effective Talk in the Primary Classroom.* Maidenhead: Open University Press. An excellent analysis of the way language is used to promote learning, with a focus on the primary school classroom.

Watkins, C., Carnell, E. and Lodge, C. (2007). *Effective Learning in Classrooms.* London: Paul Chapman. Looks at ways of promoting effective learning by focusing on classroom activities that provide for greater pupil involvement and engagement.

Wilen, W., Hutchinson, J. and Ishler, M. (2008). *Dynamics of Effective Secondary Teaching*, 6th edn. New York: Pearson. Presents a detailed overview of the key instructional techniques and the factors that influence their effective use.

5 Taking account of pupil differences

Objective

To consider the key ways in which pupils differ and their implications for effective teaching and learning.

There are a large number of differences between pupils and between groups of pupils that may influence teaching and learning (Arthur *et al.*, 2006; Ellis, 2007; Jacques and Hyland, 2007). Many of these sustain books in their own right. This chapter, however, will focus on the six major pupil differences that warrant particular attention: ability, motivation, social class, gender, race and special educational needs.

Taking account of pupil differences is a key factor in thinking about effective teaching. It enables the teacher to be more sensitive to the context of the educational experience to be set up and the issues involved in ensuring that this experience will facilitate the desired learning by a particular group of pupils. Essentially, the same message occurs from each pupil difference considered: that teachers need to carefully monitor the match between the teaching and the pupils being taught. The skills involved in getting this match right, and the implications for the teaching methods and processes adopted, will almost certainly benefit *all* pupils, not just the specific individual or group being considered. For example, in considering how best to sustain the interest of gifted children, it becomes evident that the strategies and considerations involved are relevant to sustaining the interests of all children. Each of the six major pupil differences that will be considered in this chapter in effect thus serves to raise a number of agenda items about teaching and learning that carry with them similar implications, although the details of the prescriptions that emerge will be different. This similarity of implications is perhaps not surprising, given that the categories of pupil differences commonly identified as important are not mutually exclusive. Indeed, such categories overlap to a considerable extent, as for example in the case of 'ability' and 'social class', which will be discussed later. In looking at pupil differences, the central message invariably says something about *all* pupils and about *each* pupil. This point needs to be borne in mind throughout the chapter.

Ability

The 1944 Education Act stated as a legal requirement that all children should receive an education related to their 'age, ability and aptitude'. While the need to take account of age is currently reflected in the widespread grouping of pupils into single-year-span classes (although not exclusively so), ability and aptitude are currently the subject of diverse provision. Ability is closely linked to the notion of 'intelligence'. Intelligence refers to a child's ability to learn and to meet cognitive and intellectual demands through the application of current knowledge, understanding and intellectual skills. Indeed, the notion of intelligence arose from research findings that indicated that children appeared to differ in performance in a consistent way across a wide variety of cognitive and intellectual tasks (Jordan *et al.*, 2008). This indicated the existence of some 'general ability' that contributed to relative success in each such task. Aptitude refers to particular talents, such as mathematical, musical or in foreign languages.

Two important points need to be made concerning this view of general ability (or intelligence). First, it is clear that at any given moment a pupil's general ability is in part a reflection of their previous learning experiences. Second, a pupil's level of educational attainment is not simply a function of general ability, but is influenced by a number of other considerations, such as the pupil's motivation and aspirations, parental encouragement and help, and the nature of the content and processes involved in the school curriculum. Thus, distinguishing between 'less able' pupils and 'low attainers' is important in its implications for effective teaching. After all, low attainers may well include some able pupils.

Much discussion has taken place over the years concerning the teaching of 'very able' and 'gifted' children (e.g. Gross, 2004; Tunnicliffe, 2008). The major concern in this respect is that such pupils are not sufficiently stretched by the teaching they would normally experience in schools, and that this may well result in gross underachievement. Given that gifted children may well be able to make a very significant contribution to society in their future working careers, additional support for the education of such children can be justified not only in terms of the pupils' needs, but also in terms of the possible future benefit to society as a whole.

However, providing additional provision for gifted children is no easy matter. One problem lies in the implicit elitism involved and the feeling that extra resources may be directed at pupils who are quite capable of doing well from the education system anyway. Another problem is the difficulty involved in identifying such children. For many years the label 'gifted' has been restricted by most educationists to those with very high IQ test scores (the cut-off point differs from writer to writer, but the top 0.5 to 2 per cent of the age population is common).

Recently, however, there has been a tendency to refer to the needs of 'very able' pupils and to encompass a much broader range of pupils under the label of 'gifted' or 'very able' and to use these two terms synonymously. The DfES's (2001) 'gifted and talented programme' for pupils in inner city schools is a good example of this stretching of the term gifted. However 'very able' more properly denotes a broader range of IQ test scores, covering the top 20 per cent. Using the concept of gifted to cover such a broader range of ability simply undermines its meaning and usefulness.

In addition, there has been much concern expressed about the use of IQ scores as a rigid method of identifying gifted pupils, and increasing attention is now paid to looking at more general indicators of giftedness, such as the quality and style of the work produced by a pupil, which can take account of motivational factors and more specific aptitudes. However, those gifted pupils who attempt to mask their ability (for example, so as not to appear to be too different from their peers) may well be overlooked, whatever approach to identification is used.

Three main types of additional provision are available for gifted pupils. The first approach involves acceleration through existing provision, such as when a pupil is promoted to a class of older pupils or follows the normal coursework but does so at a faster pace so that they may be using texts normally undertaken in later years. The second approach involves specialist provision for groups of gifted pupils, such as at specialist schools for particular talents (most notably in music) or at specialist centres where gifted pupils in the region can meet together perhaps once a week to engage in advanced work of various types. The third approach involves school-based enrichment materials and activities, used with the normal class teacher.

The DCSF (2007a) has also outlined how the notion of 'excellent teaching' can be applied to meeting the needs of gifted and talented pupils through effective classroom practice. In particular, the DCSF guidance highlights how the learning environment needs to provide opportunities for gifted and talented pupils to engage in meaningful and high-quality dialogue and discussion.

At present, in the vast majority of schools, teachers are rarely given either additional time or additional resources to meet the needs of gifted pupils, despite extortions to do so. With a few notable exceptions, school practices have given gifted pupils a low priority when the allocation of resources is decided. As such, what provision is made in schools to meet the needs of a gifted pupil have rested almost entirely on the efforts made by particular teachers to do this. In addition, however, some parents with the ability to provide enrichment activities at home, or through activities organised with other parents, have been able to make their own provision outside school.

The most central need of gifted pupils is to be stretched. This does not mean working faster, or doing more of the same. Rather, it means engaging in a higher quality and more stimulating course of work. Fortunately, a more general awareness of the need to stretch *all* pupils across the ability range has led to changes in teaching methods and activities, such as the use of project work, individualised programmes of work, and supplementary materials, so that there is now much more scope for teachers to match work to the needs of the very able pupils.

At the other end of the range of ability and attainment are pupils variously described as 'the less able' or 'slow learners'. Following the 1981 Education Act, we now speak of such pupils whose attainment falls well below the average expected for their age group because of their low general ability, as having *mild learning difficulties* (see the section later in this chapter on special educational needs). This category also includes pupils whose learning difficulties are the result of environmental, motivational, social, behavioural or health problems. The current expectation is for pupils with mild learning difficulties to remain with their normal classroom teacher, in 'mainstream' schooling. Their educational needs may be met by their normal classroom teacher alone, or with support from colleagues, or through periods of withdrawal for remedial attention. Where the pupils' needs relate to physical disabilities, additional provision may include special materials and equipment (Lewis and Norwich, 2005).

Pupils with a very low general ability, whose educational needs are not able to be met in an ordinary school in the normal way, may be described as having *moderate learning difficulties*, and may, if assessed as appropriate, attend a special school. Pupils with more extreme problems are referred to as having *severe learning difficulties*, and in the most serious cases, such pupils will almost certainly have their needs met by residential (rather than day attendance) special schools or hospitals.

The picture is complicated by the fact that many pupils with a very low general ability remain in ordinary schools, whilst some pupils with a higher general ability may attend a special school. The cut-off point in terms of general ability together with the surrounding circumstances that together determine whether a pupil will attend an ordinary or a special school are subject to a variety of other considerations. In addition, a further term is frequently employed, that of children with a *specific learning difficulty*, which refers to apparently 'normal' pupils who have a marked difficulty in one area of their basic educational progress, such as in reading, writing, spelling or number work. A particularly widely discussed example is that of dyslexia, which refers to pupils whose general level of educational ability seems sound, but who have a particular problem with written language. Pupils with a specific learning difficulty may be found in both ordinary and special schools. Overall, the relationship between pupils' general ability, learning difficulties and attendance at an ordinary or special school, is not a simple one.

Much has been written about the effective teaching of less able pupils. Research by Dweck (2000) has highlighted how pupils' self-perception of their own level of ability has a major impact on their feeling of self-worth. Overall, the most important point to emphasise is that such pupils need to regularly experience success and encouragement. In providing the opportunity for regular success, however, there is a real danger of viewing less able pupils as simply needing more practice in, and consolidation of, lower level work. This can easily lead to much repetition in their work. In fact, such pupils need to be excited, challenged and stimulated by their learning just as much as their more able peers. Their teachers thus need to give much thought to how to create variety in their coursework whilst continuing to address those basic skills and areas of understanding that need to be fostered.

The most sensitive problem concerning less able pupils is that they have often experienced failure in the school. Hence they may well have built up an emotional resistance regarding future effort to succeed, largely because it exposes them to further risk of failure. In such cases, remedial teaching can often involve counselling and activities based on building up the pupil's self-confidence and self-esteem. A particularly interesting development in schools is the use of a support centre to provide additional teaching both for pupils needing remedial attention and also for pupils undertaking individualised programmes of work in the normal way. This dual purpose, in catering for the whole-ability range whilst concentrating on the remedial aspect, to some extent reduces the overt labelling that occurs in many schools if a centre is only used by pupils requiring remedial attention. Many pupils may experience problems in handling academic work set by the teacher primarily because of underlying basic problems in their reading and writing skills or in number work, rather than in any lack of understanding of the topic being covered as such. It is thus important for the classroom teacher to be alert to pupils' learning difficulties that may arise from such underlying problems and that will require appropriate remedial attention. This is no easy task, since many pupils are quite adept in masking the real nature of their difficulties, particularly by indicating that their poor work reflects a lack of interest or understanding, when in fact the real problem lies in the poor level of their basic skills in language or number work.

The fact that the teaching of very able and less able pupils has received particular attention in writings on teaching methods does not, of course, mean that teaching average ability pupils is in any sense less of a problem. Clearly, because a majority of pupils are of average ability, the classroom tasks and activities, together with resources and materials, tend to be more specifically geared to them. However, the need to match the work to meet the needs of average ability pupils is just as much a challenge for teachers, as meeting the needs of the extremes in the ability range.

In addition, all classes of pupils, even those where some selection has occurred in terms of attainment, will involve a range of ability. As such, effective teaching of a class will always have to involve differentiation. The term 'differentiation' refers to the extent to which the teaching caters for the needs of the different levels of pupil ability within the same class (Bills and Brooks, 2007; Coffey, 2007; Johnston, 2007). More recently the term 'inclusive teaching' has been used to denote the use of teaching methods and practices that can cater for pupils across a range of ability and learning needs (including those with learning problems stemming from disability, disaffection, or socio-economic disadvantage). Inclusive teaching practices thus obviate the need to attach the label 'special provision' when teaching 'pupils with special educational needs' (Avramidis, 2006; Ofsted, 2004).

Seven types of differentiation have been highlighted:

- Differentiation by *task*, where pupils cover the same content but at different levels.
- Differentiation by *outcome*, where the same general task is set, but they are flexible enough for pupils to work at their own level.
- Differentiation by *learning activity*, where pupils are required to address the same task at the same level, but in a different way.
- Differentiation by *pace*, where pupils can cover the same content at the same level but a different rate.
- Differentiation by *dialogue*, where the teacher discusses the work with individual pupils in order to tailor the work to their needs.
- Differentiation by *support*, where the degree of support is tailored to the needs of individual pupils, with less support offering more challenge and opportunity for initiative.
- Differentiation by *resource*, where the type of resource used (worksheets, internet, graphical calculator) is tailored to the pupil's ability and skills.

One key aspect of the organisation of teaching in schools, is whether to make use of setting of pupils in terms of ability, or whether to allocate pupils to a class so that each class comprises a wide spread of ability. One of the main arguments in favour of having a spread of ability in each class, is that it avoids less able pupils being grouped together and thereby being labelled as low attainers. Classes comprised of less able pupils often generate a vicious circle of low expectations, and the class can gradually develop a strong anti-school ethos and become hard to teach. As such, to avoid this problem, many schools make use of mixed-ability teaching groups, but in order for mixed-ability groups to work successfully, the teacher needs to be very skilful in their use of differentiation. This is no mean feat, since it is far easier to organise teaching materials and methods for a more homogeneous group. The main danger with teaching mixed-ability groups is that to some extent, at least one of the three ability levels in the class (the more able, the average and the less able) tend to lose out depending on how the teacher prioritises their preparation and teaching time. In addition, there are some subject areas, notably mathematics and modern languages, where knowledge, understanding and competence is overtly hierarchical and cumulative, and where, as a result, it becomes very difficult and less sensible to sustain mixed-ability grouping beyond the early years of secondary school.

Before leaving the topic of ability, it is worth noting that the concept of ability as a single all-encompassing 'general ability' has been challenged by others who prefer to look at ability as a set of different abilities. The most well-known framework developed along these lines is Howard Gardner's (2006) notion of 'multiple intelligences'. This comprises eight types or dimensions of intelligence:

- *Kinaesthetic:* ability to perform and think through physical activity.
- *Logical-mathematical:* ability to sequence items, identify patterns and understand symbols including number.
- *Interpersonal:* ability to relate well to other people.
- *Intrapersonal:* ability to understand one's own feelings and emotions.
- *Musical:* ability to appreciate and respond to sound and music.
- *Naturalistic:* ability to make sense of natural objects and processes.
- *Verbal-linguistic:* ability to understand, absorb, manipulate and use words.
- *Visual-spatial:* ability to perceive, create and recognise images and pictures and make sense of visual data.

Motivation

Motivation towards learning is undoubtedly one of the key aspects of pupil learning, and it is also a source of important differences between pupils (Alderman, 2008; Slavin, 2006). Yet, whereas differences in ability between pupils are almost taken for granted, differences in motivation are subject to extensive debate and discussion. Indeed, in my own research, many teachers reported that teaching poorly motivated pupils was a major source of stress for them in their work as teachers (Kyriacou, 2000). The notion that the vast majority of pupils 'could do better' is probably the most widely used cliché found in teaching.

Differences between pupils in their academic motivation are a reflection of a number of influences, ranging from experiences in their upbringing to their experiences of success and failure at academic tasks and activities in school. The role of the home and parental encouragement is widely acknowledged to be of major importance in influencing the level of pupils' academic motivation, although the relationship is a complex one, as many parents of 'unmotivated' pupils can testify. Studies of child rearing practices have highlighted how such pupil motivation to do well at school can be fostered by parents through developing the child's self-confidence regarding their own capabilities as individuals, and praising them whenever they have undertaken tasks successfully (Smith *et al.*, 2003). This also reinforces the child's belief that doing things well is valued. Many parents also help their children prepare for school in the pre-school years by engaging them in school-related tasks, and also by helping them with school work once they have started school. All this means that some pupils find the demands of school in the early years less of a culture shock, and are also better able to concentrate on the academic tasks demanded in school and to complete these successfully. In contrast, some pupils from homes where there was less opportunity to develop pro-school attitudes and values and to engage in school-type work, may well find school an alien place at first, and fail to adapt and thrive as quickly as other pupils. For these pupils, a vicious circle can develop if early failures are allowed to engender lower motivation, as this can soon result in gross underachievement in school. Such differences in upbringing vary from home to home, but those characteristics linked with higher levels of pupil motivation do seem to be more prevalent in middle-class homes than in working-class homes (the influence of social class is explored in the next section). Differences between pupils in their self-confidence and perseverance, and in their attitudes regarding the importance of school attainment, are evident from the early years of schooling, and as a result teachers do try to take care to make the early years of school as pupil-friendly as possible. This helps to limit the possibility of such a vicious circle of underachievement developing in this first phase of schooling for those children less well prepared to cope with the demands of school life.

Another aspect of the influence of the home stems from the tendency for pupils to identify with and take on the aspirations of their parents. To the extent that becoming like their parents (or living up to their parents' aspirations) in lifestyle and occupation may require educational success, such pupils may be prepared to make great efforts at school to succeed. This is most noticeable in the learning strategies pupils are prepared to adopt to be successful. For example, countless pupils have used rote learning to memorise information or techniques, without understanding what the learning addresses. This strategy of reproducing what the teacher or examiner wants, even if they do not understand the material, is often use by highly motivated pupils who are keen to gain high-attainment grades. In contrast, poorly motivated pupils are likely to complain or simply not do the work if they do not understand or see the importance and relevance of the learning tasks in hand.

Teachers' concern about poor motivation in pupils, however, is not just restricted to a small, relatively low-attaining group of pupils. Rather, it is a concern about the vast majority of pupils. Teachers themselves are aware that the compliance towards learning of many pupils (across the whole range of ability) lacks that quality of intellectual involvement and excitement about academic work that is the hallmark of the highest quality of educational progress. Teachers often contrast the attitude of most pupils with the enthusiasm that adult learners bring to a subject during evening classes. For teachers, improving pupil motivation reflects a concern to develop and foster a more positive and enthusiastic approach to their studies, involving a degree of autonomy, independence and self-generated activity. The task of increasing pupil motivation does not only relate to pupils alienated from school work altogether.

Increasing pupils' motivation depends on giving pupils more control over their learning, fostering greater self-confidence and increasing the perceived relevance and interest of the academic work undertaken. It is quite crucial, however, that the teacher is skilled in identifying the source of a particular pupil's low motivation. Underlying a pupil's low motivation may be a lack of understanding, poor self-confidence, reluctance to apply the required mental effort, or fear of failure. The teacher thus needs to diagnose the problem carefully before deciding on how best to give remedial attention to deal with this effectively.

A particularly important influence on pupil's motivation is the teacher's expectation, as noted in chapter 3. The interplay between pupils' and teachers' expectations of each other and how this influences pupil motivation is a complex one. Teachers clearly need to have expectations, since expectations are crucial to their ability to match the learning experience to pupils. What is problematic is that such expectations inevitably reflect pupils' previous attainment, rather than what they may be capable of producing if fully motivated. For pupils with low motivation and low levels of attainment, it is easy for teachers to increasingly expect less and less from them. As such, teachers need to retain a stance of being positive and encouraging in their expectations in order to combat such slippage. The problem also applies to teaching very able pupils, where it is easy to accept consistently good work when a very able child is capable of even better, and for whom 'good' work may reflect marked underachievement. Again, it requires determination from the teacher to sustain a demand for higher level work from very able pupils, when both they and the teacher know the work produced is well above that being produced by other pupils.

It is also of prime importance in fostering pupil motivation that the teacher maintains a stance of conveying the view, through their actions and expectations, that academic work is interesting, worthwhile and of value, and that the progress of each pupil really does matter. If a teacher's actions convey this is not the case, this can rapidly undermine pupils' efforts.

Pupils differ not only in their overall level of motivation, but also in the underlying make up of that motivation. In particular, pupils differ in the extent to which they are intrinsically and extrinsically motivated. Whilst all pupils will respond to some extent to both intrinsic motives (e.g. making the learning interesting and eliciting curiosity) and extrinsic motives (e.g. merit awards for good work and praise from parents), some pupils appear to be more responsive to some aspects of the learning experience than to others. For example, some pupils seem to thrive in a more task-oriented classroom climate, whereas for others a warm and friendly relationship with the teacher acts as the main basis for enhancing their motivation. In addition, pupils differ in their personality in terms of a number of characteristics. One personality dimension that has been well researched is that of 'introversion–extraversion' (being inward-looking and reserved versus being outgoing and sociable). Another important dimension is that of 'locus of control' (a generalised belief that things in life are to a large extent within one's own control versus a view that they are largely outside it). Although the relationship between a pupil's personality and what will best foster their motivation and educational progress is a complex one, these do seem to play an important part in explaining why some pupils seem to thrive more in one class or with one teacher than do other pupils. In part this may reflect the extent to which the pupil feels able to establish a comfortable rapport with the teacher, and in part it may reflect how they respond to the teacher's working style and expectations.

Research by Dweck (2002) has also indicated how pupils make a distinction between learning goals (based on wanting to learn about the material being studied) and performance goals (based on wanting to perform well in tests and examinations). Dweck (2002) has noted that teaching strategies that are effective in motivating pupils who are learning-oriented may be different from those strategies that are effective in motivating pupils who are performance-oriented. Moreover, Dweck argues that the picture is also complicated by whether pupils hold a belief that, in a given academic situation, success will largely depend on their level of ability or whether it will largely depend on their level of effort. Research by Bandura (1997) and Covington (1998) has highlighted how pupils' self-attributions and self-efficacy beliefs concerning the reasons for their success or failure in a given academic task can also influence how much motivation they are prepared to exert in the future. In addition, a pupil's academic self-concept is also influenced by their social context and social frame of reference. This is well illustrated by the work of Marsh (2007) on the 'big-fish-little-pond effect' whereby a pupil's academic self-concept tends to be higher if they are doing better than other pupils in their class/school, than it is when they are doing less well than their peers but placed in a social context comprising higher ability pupils.

Social class

The relationship between social class (or socio-economic status) and educational attainment has been the subject of much discussion and research (Wyness, 2008; Power *et al*., 2003). The term 'social class' has not been used in a single and consistent way, but it is generally taken to include two main elements. First, the relative power, wealth and status that derive from one's occupation; second, the set of cultural values, attitudes and aspirations that typify the different occupational groups. The main distinction made is between 'middle class' and 'working class' but different authors have placed differing emphasis on how individuals are assigned to these two categories.

The most widely used categorisation classifies middle-class occupations, or those with relatively high socio-economic status (SES), as those involving managerial and professional occupations, and working-class occupations, or those with relatively low SES, as those involving semi-skilled or unskilled manual work.

Pupils with middle-class parents achieve higher educational attainment markedly more often than their working-class counterparts. Indeed, an analysis of data regarding pupils' GCSE performance by Connolly (2006) indicates that social class exerts a more powerful influence on pupils' attainment than either ethnicity or gender.

A number of influences have been advanced to account for this. First, middle-class homes are more likely to provide the child rearing experiences that foster greater intellectual development, motivation towards success in school and greater academic self-confidence. Second, middle-class parents provide a stronger model for identification that requires and expects higher educational attainment if pupils are to enjoy the same lifestyle as their parents or relatives, which shapes their aspirations towards gaining middle-class occupations. Third, working-class homes are more likely to contain the extremes of poverty, overcrowding and poor housing, and the associated social tension and distress, which may undermine a child's capacity to deal positively with the demands of schooling. Fourth, the middle-class home is more likely than the working-class to provide the cultural milieu of experiences, interests, use of language and assumptions about worthwhile activities that is in tune with the cultural milieu of schools. Fifth, middle-class pupils are more likely to have attended pre-school playgroups or nursery classes, which acts as a useful preparation for starting school.

It is extremely important to bear in mind, however, that such 'pro-school' characteristics may be present or absent in both middle-class and working-class homes. Indeed, many working-class homes display the whole range of such characteristics: parental encouragement, high aspirations, high income, good housing, and value for education. In addition, in those working-class homes where most or all of these characteristics are absent, many pupils are still educationally successful. Nevertheless, it remains the case that the social class of pupils' parents is a strong predictor of their educational attainment, ranging from success in learning to read in the early years of school, right through to examination success at the end of secondary schooling, and beyond, including university entrance.

It is clear that a number of factors influence educational attainment, including ability and motivation. To the extent that differences in social class are bound up with differences in the ability and motivation of pupils, then it is not social class *per se* that influences attainment, but rather the underlying psychological experiences associated with middle-class and working-class homes respectively. A crucial question is thus whether the notion of social class draws attention to the way social class may influence educational attainment over and above its influence through general aspects of ability and motivation.

There appear to be two ways such an additional influence may operate. The first is the school's response to pupils from working-class homes. Indeed, many authors have criticised the way in which research on the relationship between social class and educational attainment has focused much more on the home rather than the school, and has sought to explain the association by highlighting 'deficits' in working-class homes. In fact, the way in which the school responds to pupils can have a powerful influence on the pupils' educational progress. Particular attention has been paid to the way in which teachers' use language in the classroom, and the way in which the curriculum content and activities assume certain shared interests and experiences. This is not to say that teachers should use working-class vernacular or that they should provide specialised activities based on working-class areas of interest, so that working-class pupils can feel more at home. However, it does mean that teachers need to be careful not to unnecessarily correct pupils' use of language and discourage them from making contributions. In addition, teachers can usefully undertake activities based on a broad range of cultural and community-based interests, so that an excessively middle-class bias is avoided.

The second main way in which social class may have an additional distinctive influence on educational attainment is through the influence of class consciousness. This refers to the extent to which working-class and middle-class families adopt a general view of the world (a set of general attitudes, expectations, values and ways of behaving) that derives from their type of occupation and associated status and method of working. In general, this view is reflected in the middle-class emphasis on the virtue of individual enterprise and personal advancement, in contrast to the working-class emphasis on a collectivist outlook. In the context of schooling, this can in part explain the way in which working-class pupils may develop a type of group solidarity in the classroom towards rejecting a teacher's attempts to encourage them to work harder, and the way in which this group may taunt an individual pupil who appears to be betraying the group by working hard. Conversely, middle-class pupils see competition between pupils as a challenge, which helps them strive for success.

Two important caveats need to be borne in mind, however, concerning the notion of social class. First, that each social class in practice covers a great diversity of experiences. Second, that social changes in lifestyles and occupations over the years have influenced the nature of class consciousness and identification. Having said this, the extent to which social class still operates as an area of pupil differences that impacts on their educational attainment is surprising. Part of this continuing influence would appear to derive from the strong tendency for middle-class and working-class families, and in particular pupils, to associate primarily with others from their own class, and thus reinforce and consolidate their class-associated values and attitudes.

In the context of discussion about social class, the term 'educational disadvantage' has been widely used to refer to pupils whose opportunity for educational attainment has been markedly constrained by either 'social disadvantages' (e.g. poor housing, poverty) or 'cultural disadvantages' (e.g. impoverished mother–child interactions, absence of cultural experiences in the home) or any other set of factors (e.g. poorly resourced local school). While some writers have discussed the aspects of disadvantage stemming from being working class, the term has more usually been applied to a smaller group of pupils, normally within the working class, who experience the extremes of such disadvantage or deprivation, typically accounting for about 5 per cent of the pupil population. These problems are often compounded because such pupils are frequently concentrated in communities based in deprived urban areas and are also much more likely than other pupils to be identified as having learning difficulties, stemming from low ability and social and emotional problems.

Ofsted have frequently reported evidence of the ways in which the educational provision and attainment for pupils attending schools in such disadvantaged urban areas fall short of the standards expected: the proportion of lessons judged to be good or better, the standard of pupils' work, and the rate of school attendance, all tend to be lower in schools serving disadvantaged communities compared with schools sited in more affluent areas (Ofsted, 2008a).

A number of 'compensatory education' programmes have been launched to meet the needs of educationally disadvantaged pupils (Smith et al., 2003). Most of these have focused on the pre-school years in preparing disadvantaged children for school or in providing additional support in language and number work during their early years of schooling. Relatively few schemes have focused support during the secondary-school years. The key philosophy underpinning such schemes has been to ensure that disadvantaged pupils get off to a sound start in their schooling so that they can avoid getting caught in the vicious circle of low motivation and underachievement.

Three main problems have handicapped the success of such programmes. First, the whole nature of what compensatory education meant was unclear and controversial. Was it to address all working-class pupils or merely the extremely disadvantaged minority? Was it correct to refer to aspects of working-class culture, and in particular their use of language, as deprived or impoverished, or is this simply a reflection of a bias towards middle-class norms? Second, educational provision would appear to have little impact on the effects of gross deprivation. A successful intervention programme needs to deal with the underlying deprivation, which involves both the family's social interaction and their material circumstances. Third, the enduring influence of the child's circumstances, such as the effects of poverty or living in a community with low expectations of educational success, has a tendency to reassert itself once the period of the intervention has come to a close, and the educational gains made typically regress back towards the norm for the deprived group (this phenomenon has been termed 'washout').

Before leaving the discussion of social class, particular attention needs to be given to the use of language by middle-class and working-class pupils (Smith et al., 2003). A very influential theory has been developed by Bernstein (1971). In the early exposition of this theory, he argued that a distinction could be made between two kinds of language used by speakers: 'elaborated code' and 'restricted code'. The former is characterised by a richer use of language to make the meaning of what is said explicit to the listener. The latter is characterised by a grammatically simpler utterance, shorter in length, and depending on shared understanding. An example would be 'Would you like a cup of tea?' versus 'How about one?' Bernstein argued that middle-class pupils were able to use both codes while working-class pupils were limited to using the restricted code. He further argued that as a result, working-class pupils were severely disadvantaged in their intellectual growth, and were less able to meet the demands of schools. This crude version of the theory is extremely dubious, and is no longer subscribed to by Bernstein. Nevertheless, it has influenced much of the discussion about compensatory education, and to a large extent has entered the educational folklore about working-class pupils.

Subsequently Bernstein developed a more sophisticated notion of these codes and argued that middle-class homes, through their child-rearing practices and socialisation patterns, foster a use of language that emphasises a more generalised and explicit use of speech, and it is this that may advantage middle-class pupils in schools. At this stage in our understanding, it is not at all clear if and how social class differences in speech patterns (be it in terms of dialect or grammatical qualities) may impact on pupils' educational attainment. The notion that the use of non-standard English *per se* may limit educability certainly is very suspect. However, teachers' expectations of pupils' ability may well be influenced by the pupils' speech characteristics, just as some pupils' may find the teachers' use of language alien compared with that used at home. As such, teachers need to be sensitive to the possible influence of such factors on pupils' motivation and progress.

Gender

In looking at differences in educational attainment between male and female pupils, reference is made to both 'sex' and 'gender'. The term 'sex', strictly speaking, refers to biological differences. In discussing the influence of sex differences on attainment, the focus is on the ways in which underlying biological differences between males and females may influence attainment. In contrast, the term 'gender' refers to the ways in which boys and girls who grow up in a particular society develop certain attitudes, values, expectations and ways of behaving that are regarded by members of that society as typical and appropriate for males and females. In other words, a person's gender is a social construction. In discussing the influence of gender on attainment, the focus on the ways in which male and female pupils see themselves, or are seen by others, as behaving in male-appropriate or female-appropriate ways, may influence attainment.

For many years, most studies attempting to account for differences in attainment between male and female pupils looked at biological differences. However, it became increasingly clear that it was social influences rather than biological factors that were having the main effects on attainment. As such, many researchers began to refer to 'gender' rather than 'sex' to highlight this distinction. Clearly, sex and gender overlap, and the choice of term made by a particular author to some extent indicates the emphasis they wish to place in their consideration of the sources of differences in attainment between male and female pupils.

The complex inter-relationship between pupils' biological makeup and development on the one hand, and their perceptions, attitudes and values concerning their sex (i.e. gender) on the other hand, makes the examination of their individual and distinctive influence on educational attainment difficult to conduct. For example, the onset of puberty for female pupils during early adolescence seems to be coupled with a heightened awareness of themselves as 'female' and an increasing concern with their sex-role and sex-appropriate behaviour. While some aspects of differences between male and female pupils in education may have a biological basis, the vast literature in this area indicates that the main differences reported during the school years (ranging from learning to read in the early years to the choice of option subjects in the later years) appear to result mainly from gender-linked experiences, both at home and at school. Indeed, even such developments in infancy, such as the tendency for girls to develop their use of language earlier, or for boys to develop greater spatial ability, seems to be more a reflection of the type and pattern of parent–child interactions rather than biological development *per se*.

The challenge for effective teaching is to try to ensure that both male and female pupils are able to receive a broad-based education, with the opportunities to follow up specific interests and activities, without pupils' progress and choices being unjustifiably constrained by gender. Many studies have highlighted the ways in which pupils' and the schools' response to gender can contribute to these constraints (Jackson, 2006; Martin, 2008). A major area of concern regarding gender is that more girls than boys achieve five or more GCSE passes at grade C or better (the so called 'gender gap' in attainment) and a number studies have highlighted how this appears to be related to more boys than girls viewing working hard at school as 'uncool'.

Gender differences also exist in relation to how pupils view different school subjects. Numerous studies have highlighted a number of factors that seem to influence the development of such gender-related perceptions (e.g. Colley and Comber, 2003). These include:

- whether the subject is usually taught by a male or female teacher
- whether the subject is related to sex-stereotyped career aspirations
- whether the sexes differ in their perceptions of the subject's interest and their general ability in the subject
- whether the activities and materials used in the subject display sex bias, making it more appealing or more related to the experience of boys or girls
- whether the pupils' and teacher's behaviour in the classroom reinforces sex-stereotyped perceptions
- whether school documentation or organisation relating to the curriculum includes in-built assumptions about sex-stereotyped behaviour.

The greater emphasis now evident in schools to promote equal opportunities means that much more effort has been taken to improve school practices in this respect, and programmes of personal and social education typically deal with gender issues and how problems these pose may be overcome. Examples include having visits from women engineers to talk to female pupils about the possibility of careers in engineering, and encouraging boys to take part in singing, dancing and reading books. Interventions such as these do seem to have had an effect in moving the attitudes of both boys and girls towards holding more positive attitudes concerning activities regarded as more typical of the opposite sex. What has proved harder to achieve is converting a change of attitude (e.g. there is nothing wrong in boys going to dance classes) to actual changes in behaviour. This in part reflects the fact that one can hold more liberal attitudes concerning what constitutes sex-appropriate behaviour, but that need not impinge on real choices based on what are felt to be real preferences. For example, boys who actually do find playing football in the lunch hour more enjoyable than going to a choir practice are unlikely to change their behaviour, but for those boys who prefer to go to the choir, they may now feel less inhibited from doing so.

A particularly interesting intervention has been the use of single-sex lessons in some subjects in coeducational schools as a means of allowing girls to avoid being in classes where boys tend to dominate the teacher's attention and teacher–pupil interactions, and to enable boys to feel less inhibited in some subjects that are perceived to be more feminine. In addition, there is a tendency to regard doing well at school as a reflection of conformity and conscientiousness, which sits less easily with the development of boys' self-image, in part exaggerated by the presence of girls, and which may help explain why there is a tendency for boys' overall educational attainment during the school years to be slightly lower than that of girls. After years of advocating the social benefits of coeducation, the realisation that coeducation can inhibit attainment (in different ways for both boys and girls) poses a problem for schools in considering how this can be overcome.

Anti-sexist initiatives in schools can also sometimes unwittingly promote or confirm sexist assumptions. For example, by making efforts to encourage more girls to study physics, one is implicitly conveying the message that this is unusual for girls, and may make a girl who was intending to do physics think twice about doing so as a result. As such, greater care needs to be taken concerning how one promotes equal opportunities in this way.

In addition, one also needs to recognise that the efforts being made in schools to promote equal opportunities, are limited by factors outside the school that have a powerful impact on pupils' attitudes and aspirations. These include the influence of the family and the attitudes generally held in the local community and by society at large. In addition, there are realistic choices that need to be made by individuals based on how they feel things typically operate at the moment rather than how they might operate in an ideal world or at some point in the distant future. For example, whereas some girls may well have the ability to develop a professional career of some sort, their perception might be that becoming a wife and mother is a much more attractive and compelling lifestyle, and at the moment they feel it is not possible or that it is at least very difficult to do both. Overcoming strongly held views such as this may help such pupils feel they have more of a choice in life, but this depends on convincing them that it can apply realistically to their circumstances. One danger with efforts to promote equal opportunities is that they can raise aspirations and extended perceived choice, only for individuals to find these are difficult to achieve. In addition, there is also an important question concerning which aspirations the school can or should legitimately encourage. For example, is following a professional career necessarily to be advocated as more worthwhile than full-time motherhood? Equal opportunities is in part to do with helping pupils to develop options and choices, but leaving it up to them in the final analysis to choose which ones to pursue. What is undesirable is for individuals to only have choices within an unnecessarily narrow range. Education is nothing if it is not about widening horizons and choice.

Race

The concern with race stems from the apparent lower-than-average educational attainment of pupils from particular ethnic groups (Stanley, 2008; Tomlinson, 2008). To some extent, the greater underachievement among pupils from some particular minority ethnic families can be attributed to the effects of poorer housing, relatively lower income, different cultural values and attitudes regarding the role of schooling, use of language and patterns of family life. All this parallels the earlier discussion of educational disadvantage and the working class. However, the fact that black and Asian pupils are readily identifiable has added to the problem. Successive immigrants to Britain have often faced initial problems in achieving parity of educational attainment with the indigenous community. By and large, this has not been a continuing problem for those born in Britain, be they Jews, Italians or Cypriots. However, it has become apparent that black West Indian pupils born in Britain, in particular, have not attained the expected levels of attainment despite many decades of 'assimilation'. A number of reasons for this have been suggested. The most significant factor would appear to stem from a mixture of racial prejudice and West Indian cultural values, which has meant that black West Indian families have not become more prevalent in middle-class occupations. As a result, this group's spectrum of social class amongst UK-born pupils is still not in line with that of the indigenous population. In this respect, the achievement of many black pupils is still constrained by their socio-economic circumstances. In contrast, Asian families have been much more successful in establishing themselves in a range of middle-class occupations ranging from shopkeepers to doctors, and their children have thereby benefited from sharing this range of educational and career aspirations. It has been well recorded that nearly all the children in schools for pupils with moderate learning difficulties are drawn from the poorest sections of society, and are proportionately over-represented by children from African-Caribbean backgrounds. Moreover, a relatively greater proportion of Afrian-Caribbean pupils are excluded from schools for emotional and behavioural problems. If black West Indian families continue to remain proportionately more economically and socially disadvantaged than other minority ethnic groups and the indigenous community, this will continue to act as a barrier against their achieving educational parity.

The Swann Report (1985) provides an excellent overview of the issues and problems concerning the education of minority ethnic groups. In addition, it stresses the importance of taking a wide view of these issues and problems by considering the role of education for all pupils within a multi-racial society. In considering the role of racism in schools, the report made a very important distinction between direct racism, which refers to prejudiced attitudes concerning ethnic groups (both hostile or well-intentioned) and indirect or institutionalised racism, which refers to the ways in which systems, practices and procedures in education unwittingly discriminate against minority ethnic groups. Such institutionalised racism can be entirely unintentional. For example, organising a school trip or a parents evening that coincides with a religious festival for a particular minority ethnic group, may make it very difficult for those pupils or parents to attend. Both direct and indirect racism can contribute to underachievement by excluding such pupils from the mainstream of society and school life.

The need for schools to respond effectively to meeting the twin needs of educating pupils from minority ethnic groups and preparing all pupils for life in a multi-racial society have received much prominence. Two main themes have been developed for this. The first is 'multicultural education', which is based on teaching and learning about the different ethnic cultures. Advocates of this approach argue that it fosters a better understanding of and respect for the different minority ethnic cultures and thereby undermines prejudice, and also boosts the self-respect of minority ethnic pupils by showing that their culture is deemed of value to the school community. The second main theme is 'anti-racist education', which is concerned specifically with addressing questions of race and prejudice as they operate in society, with a view to undermining prejudice among pupils. Anti-racist education has utilised a range of teaching activities to do this, such as group work based on cooperation between pupils of different ethnic origins, role play and simulations. Clearly these two themes overlap in many respects. They both place emphasis on fostering a critical and sensitive appreciation of the different minority ethnic cultures that make up our society, and developing a pluralist and non-prejudiced perspective. To do this successfully, however, requires the whole school to consider and deal with both direct and institutionalised racism within the school. This involves establishing a non-racist bias in the curriculum and dealing with racist attitudes and behaviour such as racist graffiti and harassment. Schools also need to be sensitive to racist attitudes amongst teachers, which can often be disguised or simply be naive and patronising, such as asking a black pupil whether they visit their homeland often, which implies that their homeland is not Britain. It is important to note however that this whole area is emotionally charged, and can involve intense clashes of value judgements among and between teachers and pupils, both inside and outside the classroom. In addition, certain activities may also invoke criticism from parents. The development of a school policy regarding race needs to be carefully thought out and implemented with sensitivity. One school's multicultural policy is shown in Table 5.1.

As well as developments concerned with racist attitudes and behaviour, the school also needs to address how best to help pupils from minority ethnic groups to achieve higher levels of educational attainment. A number of initiatives have been concerned with this. Particular attention has been paid to the importance of language skills. For all pupils, the acquisition of competence in Standard English is crucial for their progress. Pupils from minority ethnic groups include those who speak virtually no English at all when they first arrive at school. Some will have a first language based on a non-Western

---

We aim to develop an understanding of different cultures and lifestyles, in order to prepare pupils for life in our multicultural society. This policy affects every aspect of school life and all staff are committed to opposing any form of racist behaviour.

I The multicultural curriculum

The school aims to encourage respect between individuals by increasing their understanding of cultural diversity. It is important that pupils recognise the equality, worth and dignity of people from all cultures. Pupils will have opportunities to learn about their own and other cultures throughout the school curriculum. We aim to foster a sensitive, informed attitude amongst its pupils, creating a caring atmosphere in which diversity can flourish.

2 Equality of opportunity

The school will endeavour to meet the needs of all pupils and staff regardless of racial origin, colour, religion or sex. Every member of the school is held to be of equal value. Every pupil has rights to the best possible education, and equality of opportunity must be afforded to all.

3 Racial prejudice

Racist behaviour is unacceptable at the school. Actions by pupils which are clearly hurtful to others include:

(a) Racist jokes, graffiti, name-calling, insults and threats.
(b) Language deliberately offensive to others' beliefs.
(c) Behaviour such as wearing racist badges or bringing racist literature into school.
(d) Racist comment in the course of discussion in lessons.
(e) Physical assault against a person or group because of colour or cultural background.

The school will act to deal with racial prejudice in an appropriate manner and support the sufferers.

4 Multicultural harmony

It is the responsibility of all governors and staff at our school (teaching, support, library, administrative, catering and cleaning staff) to implement this policy.

Table 5.1   *One school's multicultural policy*

alphabet script. Some will speak English with a strong foreign accent, or even a dialect of English. Such pupils will need much language-support work to establish a sound basis for their progress across the school curriculum. An important implication of this for effective teaching is that pupils' lack of confidence or expertise in English may result in their appearing inarticulate or reticent to take part in more public activities, such as whole-class discussion, and they may need more time for their written work. Until their English has developed to a reasonable level, their classroom performance will poorly reflect their real level of subject knowledge and understanding.

Providing equal opportunities for pupils from minority ethnic groups also involves many of the issues mentioned in the earlier discussion of social class and gender. These include providing role models, intervention programmes to prevent circles of under-achievement developing, and attention to developing pupils' academic self-esteem and self-confidence. One interesting development has been the operation of Saturday schools organised by black parents. Another interesting development has been the attempt to improve access to higher education by identifying and removing forms of institutionalised racism governing the admission procedures.

One final point concerning teaching in a multi-racial school involves the way in which race is an important construct for pupils from minority ethnic groups in perceiving their educational experiences. For example, a study by Richards (2008) included the perceptions regarding schooling held by male African-Caribbean pupils in order to explore why these pupils are more likely to underachieve and be excluded from schools. The complexity here is well illustrated by the fact that, in contrast to the male pupils, the female African-Caribbean pupils generally perform better than average. Her study highlights the important role played by their self-identity as a black African-Caribbean male. Richards argues that it is how they perceive and experience schooling and, in particular, how they choose to react to the academic demands made upon them, which marginalises them from the 'academic game' they need to play in order to achieve academic success.

Special educational needs

For many years the term 'special education' primarily referred to the educational provision made in special schools, or in special classes and units attached to ordinary schools, or in the most severe cases, in residential homes and hospitals. Such special provision was made for pupils categorised as having one or more of a number of handicaps (mental, emotional, social and/or physical), which resulted in ordinary schools not being able to cater adequately for their education. The main categories of handicap referred to include the following: blind or partially sighted, deaf or partially hearing, educationally subnormal, epileptic, physically handicapped, speech defect, delicate, and maladjusted. Approximately 2 per cent of the school-age population received such special and segregated provision.

In 1978 the Warnock Report introduced a much broader notion, that of children having 'special educational needs' (SEN). The report recommended that this broader term be used as it focused attention on pupils' *educational needs* rather than their handicaps. The report also advocated that this term should be used to cover both those pupils whose needs were typically being met up to then by special and segregated provision (the '2 per cent' referred to above) and to a much larger proportion of pupils who experience learning difficulties (in the short term or long term) and whose educational needs could be met by special provision being made in the ordinary school. The report estimated that about one child in five would require such special educational provision at some time during their school careers. It is important to emphasise that this broad notion of SEN sought to cater for the needs of many pupils who encountered particular problems for a variety of reasons at some point in their school careers, for which special provision was needed. It was not in any way intended that such pupils were to be considered as having a disability in the way normally applied to the much smaller group (the '2 per cent') of pupils, although in some cases these pupils might indeed have a short-term disability. The report placed emphasis on the child having a 'learning difficulty' as the essential criterion for identifying the child's SEN.

The recommendations of the Warnock Report was embodied in the 1981 Education Act, which defined the key terms as follows:

- A child has *SEN* if s/he has a learning difficulty that calls for special educational provision to be made.
- A child has a *learning difficulty* if s/he has a significantly greater difficulty in learning than the majority of children of his age or if he has a disability that prevents or hinders him from making use of educational facilities of a kind generally provided in schools for children of his age.
- *Special educational provision* means educational provision that is additional to, or otherwise different from, the educational provision made generally for children of his/her age.

The Act included pre-school-age children for such provision. The degree of learning difficulty is described as 'mild', 'moderate' or 'severe'. In very broad terms, the report saw SEN as likely to take the form of the need for one or more of the following:

- The provision of special means of access to the curriculum through special equipment, facilities or resources, modification of the physical environment or specialist teaching techniques.
- The provision of a special or modified curriculum.
- Particular attention to the social structure and emotional climate in which education takes place.

While the report advocated that children's SEN should be met by the ordinary school wherever possible, this decision needed to take account of appropriate economic considerations. In addition, it envisaged that special schools (and other segregated special provision) would be required for most pupils with moderate learning difficulties and almost all pupils with severe learning difficulties. The Warnock Report also envisaged four main types of special provision located in the ordinary school, which would help encourage integration where possible:

- Full-time education in an ordinary class with any necessary help and support.
- Education in an ordinary class with periods of withdrawal to a special class or other supporting base.
- Education in a special class or unit with periods of attendance at an ordinary class and full involvement in the general community life and extra-curricular activities of the ordinary school.
- Full-time education in a special class or unit with social contact with the main school.

The notion of SEN has had a major impact on school practices, not only in terms of how best to cater for those pupils deemed to have such needs, but also in terms of its impact on thinking about catering for the educational needs of all pupils in the school. For example, once it is felt in a school that a particular individualised learning package could help meet the special needs of one particular pupil, this may quickly lead to the realisation that perhaps this same package might be educationally more effective for all pupils following the course.

This shift in focus has now occurred away from how best meet the needs of those pupils with moderate and severe learning difficulties who are 'integrated' into ordinary schools towards using the notion of inclusion: how can ordinary schools meet the needs of all pupils in such as way that schools can thereby cater for those pupils who have SEN (Ellis, 2007; Jacques and Hyland, 2007; Ofsted, 2004). In other words, successful inclusive teaching practices means that the notion of 'integration' becomes redundant (Avramidis, 2006; Kellett, 2008).

The essential feature of a whole-school approach regarding inclusion is that the educational provision for all pupils in the school needs to be flexible enough (particularly in terms of organisation, teaching methods and access to materials) to accommodate most pupils with SEN without too much difficulty (Evans, 2007).

With regard to effective teaching, teachers need to undertake two very important tasks. First, the teacher needs to be alert to the possibility that a particular pupil having learning problems may have an underlying SEN that will need to be identified. Such pupils will need to be monitored carefully and, if there is a cause for concern, a proper assessment will need to be conducted, often involving an educational psychologist. Second, the teacher will be involved in the school's programme for meeting the SEN of particular pupils in the school. This may require the teacher to develop new skills, particularly if special equipment or materials are involved or if the teacher needs to liaise with other teachers or work with a support teacher provided for the pupil.

In an analysis of research on whether inclusion (or 'mainstreaming') has been effective in meeting the needs of pupils with SEN in ordinary schools, Lindsay (2007) concluded that the picture was equivocal, and that the quality of provision and practices adopted in mainstream schools for pupils with SEN was variable. However, Lindsay was able to identify a number of teacher practices that were likely to benefit pupils with SEN. These included scaffolding, creating a positive classroom ambience, the use of feedback, collaboration between teachers, and implementing individualised plans of support.

Whilst the system of meeting pupils' SEN has been successfully in many ways, there have also been many enduring problems (Ofsted, 2008a). These include major problems involved in identifying the nature and extent of pupils with learning difficulties. Despite the operation of LA- and school-based screening programmes and the alertness of both teachers and parents, there are still many pupils whose underlying problems are not picked up until well into their school careers, if at all. In addition, once a cause for concern has been identified and a formal assessment involving an educational psychologist is put in motion, in many cases the process of establishing a formal statement of the pupil's needs has taken well over a year. At the same time, problems can arise over how best to meet the pupils' needs, particularly when LAs and schools have to pay regard to the cost implications, the availability and appropriateness of certain types of provision and the wishes of the parents. In order to improve the procedures used to identify and support pupils with SEN, the Special Needs and Disability Act (SENDA) 2001 introduced a revised 'Code of Practice', which recommended that schools should operate a 'graduated response' to pupils with SEN, starting with making changes in curriculum and teaching, before embarking (if necessary) on making a formal assessment ('statementing') of the pupil's needs. The code of practice also identified four main areas of SEN:

- Behaviour, emotional and social development.
- Cognition and learning.
- Communication and interaction.
- Sensory and/or physical.

One major benefit of introducing this code of practice is that it has helped to maintain the profile of SEN pupils and the importance of ensuring that proper provision is made to meet their needs.

Given the range and types of learning difficulties pupils may have and the types of provision that may usefully be made, the task of identifying and matching a pupil's SEN with the provision to be made is not an easy one (Lewis and Norwich, 2005). In addition, in many cases, it is extremely difficult to decide what the exact nature of the pupil's SEN is. Poor reading attainment in a primary school, for example, may involve one or more of a mixture of underlying causes: mental, emotional, social or physical in nature. An identification of educational need and provision requires a sound diagnosis of the learning difficulty. In reaching a diagnosis, reference may be made to underlying causes that are themselves the subject of much controversy. Two such causes have received particular attention. The first is 'dyslexia', which is described as a constitutional brain dysfunction that impairs reading development specifically, while not affecting general intelligence. The second such cause is 'emotional and behavioural disorder' characterised by disturbing behaviour, either emotional and/or anti-social, that impairs educational progress. The factors that influence whether and how a pupil is assessed seems to depend not just on the child's behaviour but also on a number of other circumstances. For example, the accusation is often made that the children of middle-class parents having problems learning to read and write are more likely to be diagnosed as dyslexic than comparable children with working-class parents. Similarly, misbehaviour by pupils from certain minority ethnic groups seem to be more likely to be diagnosed as resulting from emotional disorder than comparable behaviour by other pupils. Whilst such differences in assessment patterns are indeed reflected in various statistics, making such an unequivocal interpretation of the reasons for such differences is very problematic. It does however highlight the way in which the assessment of SEN and the delivery of appropriate provision is not a simple matter.

Summary

In this chapter a number of important differences between pupils have been explored: ability, motivation, social class, gender, race and SEN. This theme of pupil differences highlights some very important concerns and observations. First, the importance of knowing the pupil as an individual with his or her own particular educational history and perspective towards schools, teaching and learning. Second, that a consideration of such pupil differences highlights how and why certain pupils are more successful than others in terms of their educational attainment. Third, that in highlighting such differences, and the ways in which schools attempt to meet the needs of *some* pupils more effectively, schools are forced to consider changes in their practices that are also relevant to meeting the educational needs of *all* pupils in the school more effectively.

Discussion questions

1 How should a teacher take account of the differing levels of ability amongst a class of pupils?

2 How can teachers best meet the needs of disadvantaged pupils?

3 What particular challenges are posed for teachers when teaching pupils from a mix of ethnic backgrounds?

4 How can a teacher best promote equal opportunities among pupils by taking account of differences between pupils in terms of race, gender and social class?

5 How can teachers meet the needs of gifted pupils?

6 How can having a whole-school policy help meet the needs of a particular group of pupils?

Further reading

Alderman, M. K. (2008). *Motivation for Achievement: Possibilities for Teaching and Learning,* 3rd edn. London: Routledge. Looks at the role of motivation in learning and how this is influenced by pupils' attributional beliefs.

Ellis, V. (ed.) (2007). *Learning and Teaching in Secondary Schools,* 3rd edn. Exeter: Learning Matters. This book presents a succinct overview of the personal character- istics and social factors influencing teaching and learning in secondary schools.

Evans, L. (2007). *Inclusion.* London: Routledge. An excellent book that looks at 'inclu- sion' in its widest sense – how schools can meet the needs of all pupils, but particularly those pupils who, for whatever reason, are at risk of becoming marginalised.

Jacques, K. and Hyland, R. (eds) (2007). *Professional Studies: Primary and Early Years,* 3rd edn. Exeter: Learning Matters. This book presents a succinct overview of the personal characteristics and social factors influencing teaching and learning in primary schools.

Matheson, D. (ed.) (2008). *An Introduction to the Study of Education,* 3rd edn. Lon- don: David Fulton. This book contains chapters dealing with key aspects of pupil differences.

6 Key classroom teaching qualities and tasks

Objective

To consider the key qualities that underpin effective teaching and how they provide a basis for effective classroom practice.

At this point it is worth reminding ourselves of the theme that has been developed so far. It has been argued that in thinking about effective teaching, it is important to take account of the *context* of the lesson (e.g. the subject matter, the age and ability range of the pupils and the school ethos) and the desired educational *outcomes* the teacher wishes to foster (e.g. increased interest in the subject matter, the development of some particular intellectual skill). What may constitute effective teaching in one context and with one set of desired outcomes in mind, may not be as effective in a different context and with a different set of desired outcomes in mind.

The earlier chapters of this book paid attention to how pupils learn, the ways in which pupils learn and the types of pupil differences that have a major bearing on the effectiveness of teaching and learning. I argued that pupil learning required the pupil to be *attentive* to the learning experience and *receptive* (i.e. the pupil must be motivated and have a willingness to learn and respond to the experience). In addition, the learning experience must be *appropriate* for the desired learning to take place. In thinking about the qualities and tasks of effective teaching, the question is one of how to effectively marshal aspects of one's teaching and set up a learning experience such that it:

- elicits and sustains pupils' attention
- elicits and sustains pupils' motivation and mental effort
- fosters the type of learning desired.

In looking at effective teaching, a useful distinction can be drawn between the general *qualities* of effective teaching and the component *tasks* involved. The qualities focus on broad aspects of teaching that appear to be important in determining its effectiveness, such as good rapport with pupils or pitching the work at the appropriate level of difficulty. The tasks refer to the activities and practices involved in teaching, such as planning a lesson or assessing pupils' progress. Clearly, qualities and tasks are closely interrelated. However, the discussion of the former tends to be in answer to a question such as 'what qualities would you expect to find in an effective lesson?' A consideration of the latter tends to be in answer to a question such as 'what tasks are involved in effective teaching?' In effect, the search for qualities is explicitly judgemental in character and may cut across a number of different tasks involved in teaching. The first part of this chapter will explore the key qualities involved in effective classroom teaching. The second part will explore the key tasks involved.

Key classroom teaching qualities

Over the years, many studies have sought to identify those characteristics of teaching that contribute to effectiveness (see chapter 2). Such studies have varied immensely in the type of focus they have used to describe teaching qualities. At one extreme are studies that have sought to focus on a small number of key dimensions. For example, an analysis of teaching qualities by the Organisation for Economic Co-operation and Development (OECD, 1994) focused on five key dimensions:

- *Knowledge* of substantive curriculum content.
- *Pedagogic skills* involved in the ability to use a repertoire of teaching strategies.
- *Reflection* on one's own teaching and the ability to be self-critical.
- *Empathy* in acknowledging the dignity of others.
- *Managerial competence* within and outside the classroom.

The OECD framework is based on the view that teaching qualities should be regarded as a holistic concept made up of competencies displayed across these five key dimensions.

It is also interesting to note that the OECD analysis lists the teacher's knowledge of subject content as a key quality, as subject knowledge is often overlooked in studies in effective teaching. This may be because its importance is so obvious that is taken for granted. However, a number of international comparisons of effective teaching have emphasised the importance of the teacher's subject knowledge and indicated how poor teaching can sometimes stem from the teacher's lack of understanding of the topic in hand (Akiba et al., 2007; OECD, 2007). It is also noteworthy that when governments attempt to produce a list of the qualities needed by teachers, subject knowledge is often the first quality listed (TDA, 2008).

At the other extreme are those studies that attempt to itemise in detail the numerous attributes that may characterise a lesson, and then to explore the extent to which each of these attributes is associated with some measure of effectiveness (the criteria used may range from teachers' perceptions of their importance, to pupil performance on a standardised test of educational attainment). For example, a study by Haydn (2007) looked at secondary school pupils' views of the 'pedagogical qualities' of teachers that the pupils feel has a positive influence on their attitude to learning. The four most highly rated qualities were:

- Knows their subject really well.
- Explains things well.
- Makes it interesting.
- Is good at stopping other pupils from spoiling the lesson.

When the pupils were asked about the 'personal characteristics' of teachers that they feel have a positive influence on their attitude to learning, the four most highly rated qualities were:

- Talks to you 'normally'.
- Is friendly.
- Is enthusiastic about their subject.
- Has a sense of humour.

Surveys of research on the qualities identified as underpinning effective teaching cover similar qualities (Petty, 2006; Stronge, 2007). However, a major problem with studies that attempt to itemise the qualities involved in effective teaching, is that they tend to produce fairly long checklists of these characteristics. Thus there is a danger of losing sight of the holistic quality of teaching referred to in, for example, the OECD analysis. In making judgements about teaching, we react to the sense of the whole lesson as a single unit. While this unit can be usefully broken down into a handful of key teaching qualities, once such a list becomes too lengthy, the interplay between the qualities is lost. Yet, it is this interplay that, in many respects, is the most important aspect of the analysis of teaching.

Another very valuable source of information concerning teaching qualities comes from attempts by teacher educators to develop rating schedules that can be used to assess the classroom teaching of student teachers as part of their initial teacher training courses. In addition, similar schedules have also been developed for use with experienced teachers as part of teacher appraisal (or performance management) systems. By way of example, one of the most widely used rating schedules has been the *Stanford Teacher Competence Appraisal Guide* (Stones and Morris, 1972). This lists a total of 17 qualities, grouped together under five headings: 'aims', 'planning', 'performance', 'evaluation' and 'community and professional'. Each of these qualities is then rated by an observer of a lesson on a seven-point rating scale, labelled from 'weak' to 'truly exceptional'. For example, the six qualities grouped together under the heading of 'performance' are:

- *Beginning the lesson:* pupils come quickly to attention; they direct themselves to the tasks to be accomplished.

- *Clarity of presentation:* the content of the lesson is presented so that it is understandable to the pupils; different points of view and specific illustrations are used when appropriate.

- *Pacing of the lesson:* the movement from one part of the lesson to the next is governed by the pupils' achievement; the teacher 'stays with the class' and adjusts the tempo accordingly.

- *Pupil participation and attention:* the class is attentive; when appropriate, the pupils actively participate in the lesson.

- *Ending the lesson:* the lesson is ended when the pupils have achieved the aims of instruction; there is a deliberate attempt to tie together the planned and chance events of the lesson and relate them to the immediate and long-range aims of instruction.

- *Teacher–pupil rapport:* the personal relationships between pupils and the teacher are harmonious.

Research studies of effective teaching have made extensive use of such rating scales. In large measure, this approach to exploring effective teaching in terms of key teaching qualities owes much to the work of Kounin (1970). Kounin's seminal study attempted to identify the effective techniques used by teachers in dealing with pupil misbehaviour by contrasting the videotaped classroom behaviour of teachers known to be successful with that of teachers who had continuing discipline problems. Surprisingly, the two groups differed little in how they dealt with actual misbehaviour. Rather, what seemed to differentiate the two groups was that the successful teachers were much more effective in their teaching, particularly in terms of their instructional management and in keeping pupils actively engaged in the lesson, thereby minimising the time in which pupils were bored or restless. The qualities identified by Kounin included:

- *withitness:* the teacher communicating to pupils through his behaviour that he knows what the pupils are doing at all times (has 'eyes in the back of his head')
- *overlapping:* being able to deal with two matters at the same time, particularly that of dealing with a pupil's misbehaviour while keeping other pupils engaged in the work
- *smoothness:* maintaining the flow of academic activities (avoiding 'jerkiness' such as making a sudden interjection while pupils are busy, or leaving an activity too early and then having to return to it later)
- *momentum:* maintaining an appropriate rate of flow (avoiding 'over-dwellings' and 'slowdowns'), such as by not staying too long to deal with a point, or by not breaking down an activity into parts that could be better performed as a single unit.

While the use of a set of key classroom teaching qualities identified by various authors cannot be regarded as providing an unequivocal analysis of effective teaching, such lists of qualities do provide a very useful set of agenda items, which serves to focus attention on different aspects of classroom teaching.

In thinking about such qualities, we need to make an important distinction between qualities, tasks and skills. Firstly, we can think of classroom teaching as involving a number of key *tasks* (e.g. planning a lesson, classroom organisation, dealing with mis-behaviour). Secondly, in order to carry out these tasks effectively, the teacher needs to display a variety of teaching *skills* (e.g. vigilance, giving clear instructions). Thirdly, it is a reflection of how well these skills are applied to the key teaching tasks, which conveys the particular *qualities* of the teaching displayed during the lesson. A consideration of how teaching qualities are related to tasks and skills serves as an elaboration of the first part of the model presented in Figure 2.2 (p15) dealing with the pedagogical (craft of teaching) level of analysis. In essence, the notion of skill focuses on how well a teacher is able to carry out the tasks of teaching (Johnston *et al.*, 2007; Kyriacou, 2007).

This approach of judging qualities by relating these to how well the teacher displays certain skills in addressing the key tasks of teaching, is the main approach adopted by Ofsted in a number of its reports and associated documentation (Ofsted, 1995, 2002, 2003, 2008a). Looking at its reports over the last two decades dealing with aspects of effective classroom teaching, there appear to be 10 qualities that have been consistently referred to by Ofsted over the years. These are:

- the teacher has good subject knowledge
- the teacher has high expectations for pupils' work
- the work is challenging for pupils
- the teacher has established good relations with pupils
- the teacher manages the class well
- the lesson is well planned
- the teacher adopts a variety of teaching methods, including ICT
- the needs of the different ability groups within the class are catered for
- the teacher makes good use of a variety of questioning techniques
- classroom dialogue is used to extend pupils' thinking.

The annual report by Ofsted summarising the findings of its school inspections pro-vides a useful indication of the quality of teaching evident in schools and the areas of concern. These reports typically indicate a gap between aspects of government policy regarding the qualities of effective classroom practice and the extent to which these qualities are evident during school inspections. For example, whilst the National Strategies have advocated forms of classroom discourse that are 'interactive' and that promote high-quality classroom dialogue, Ofsted has typically reported that classroom practice is still over-shadowed by a teacher-dominated and transmissive form of interaction and use of dialogue (Ofsted, 2008a).

The key qualities and skills underpinning effective teaching have been incorporated by the Training and Development Agency for Schools (TDA, 2008) into a list of 'professional standards' that student teachers in England need to display during their teacher training course in order to obtain Qualified Teacher Status (QTS). The QTS standards are followed by a further list of standards associated with the performance required by Newly Qualified Teachers (NQTs) at the end of their first (induction) year in post as a full-time teacher (the core standards), and three further sets of standards covering their continuing professional development (the post-threshold standards; the excellent skills teacher standards; and the excellent teacher standards). The descriptions of these standards are largely skills-based in tone (Kyriacou, 2007).

An exploratory study

Any attempt to break down the holistic quality of teaching into a number of key qualities of effective teaching presents a major challenge for those involved in teacher education to 'lay their cards on the table' and make explicit their own view of such qualities. This challenge led me to formulate my own set of qualities, drawing from research on effective teaching. My initial 'melting pot' of attributes included the whole variety of specific behaviours at one extreme (frequently maintains eye-contact with pupils, follows up pupils' ideas, etc.) to general qualities at the other extreme ('withitness', enthusiasm, warmth, etc.). It became clear that any attempt to define an unequivocal set of qualities that would describe effective teaching was doomed to failure. There are a number of different ways in which teachers may be effective and these different ways appear to rely on different characteristics. However, what did seem to be justifiable was an attempt to formulate a set of qualities that have been widely identified in writings and studies on effective teaching. Such a set of qualities could then be used as a basis for exploring the extent to which lessons given by different teachers might be usefully described and discussed in terms of variations in these qualities. If a set of qualities proved useful in this way, it could then be further explored in terms of its relationship to effectiveness. If it failed to describe differences between lessons, that in itself might be important for our thinking about effective teaching. I felt the most useful approach in developing such a set of key classroom teaching skills, would be to outline each quality in terms of teacher and pupil behaviour and lesson characteristics that would typify the two extremes of a dimension of appraisal based on that quality. Following a development study based on classroom observation and discussion with teachers, a set of eight such qualities was identified. The corresponding dimensions and the descriptions are shown in Figure 6.1.

The basic theme of each of these dimensions was as follows:

I Preparedness

The notion of preparedness was intended to be seen from the viewpoint of the pupils in the class in terms of the appearance that the lesson gave of being well organised, having a coherent structure and creating the impression of purposefulness from the

1 Preparedness

Teacher is well organised and prepared both for teaching during the lesson and for setting work; lesson well structured; teacher knows where they are going and how to get there.

vs   Teacher is not sure how they want lesson to start or develop; frequently not sure what they want to do next; materials required not to hand; some problems caused by lack of foresight.

2 Pace and flow

Teacher keeps up an appropriate pace for maintaining interest and attention; lesson flows smoothly; teacher is able to attend to more than one thing at a time and thereby does not break flow of lesson in order to give individual help or discipline individuals.

vs   Teacher dwells on minor points; talks longer than necessary for pupils' understanding of points and tasks; holds up lesson whilst disciplining, or whilst dealing with minor matters (e.g. getting a pupil a pencil); distracted by questions or actions of individuals; lesson progresses slowly and is disjointed.

3 Transitions

Teacher is able to establish attention quickly at the start of a lesson and re-establish it when required, such as at transition between activities; lesson begins smoothly and moves smoothly between activities; teacher is sensitive to how lesson is progressing in deciding when to initiate transitions.

vs   Beginning of lessons and transitions are jerky, long and awkward; teacher is unable to establish and maintain attention when required; jerkiness caused by having to repeat instructions or by referring back to previously omitted points or instructions; new instructions are disruptive because they contradict earlier ones or because they are not relevant or appropriate for the whole class.

4 Cognitive matching

Lesson is well suited to pupils' ability and interest; teacher is able to accommodate individual differences by varying the difficulty and pace through individual attention where appropriate; work is challenging as well as instructive.

vs   Lesson is boring and ill suited to pupils' ability and interests; no attempt is made to meet the requirements of individuals.

5 Clarity

Teacher's instructions and explanations (both verbal and written) are clear and at pupils' level.

vs   Teacher instructions and explanations are vague, ambiguous, or take no account of pupils' level of comprehension.

6 Business-like

Lesson is essentially conducted in a business-like manner; authority is firm; teacher reacts calmly when dealing with misbehaviour; exudes confidence and positive expectations for quality of work and behaviour.

vs   Lesson conducted hesitantly; authority is uncertain, and reactions are over-emotional; teacher lacks confidence and conveys expectation of underachievement and misbehaviour.

7 Withitness

Teacher is aware of and continually monitors what is going on in all parts of the classroom; frequently maintains eye contact with pupils, and scans whole class; pre-empts misbehaviour or acts with speed when it appears.

vs   Teacher gets wrapped up in what they are doing and is unaware of parts of the classroom; is slow to recognise and react to misbehaviour, and when they do so, fail to identify the culprits correctly.

8 Encouragingness

Interaction with pupils is essentially encouraging and positive, such as to build up pupils' self-confidence and self-esteem; teacher uses plenty of praise and instructive criticism (explaining where pupil went wrong or how they could do better rather than criticising pupils themselves; conveys enthusiasm and some good humour.

vs   Interaction with pupils is hostile and deprecating; teacher frequently uses personal criticisms; remains aloof; teaches with little enthusiasm and shows no sense of humour.

Figure 6.1   *The teaching assessment rating scales*

teacher. Attached to this notion was also the idea that the unexpected could be catered for in the lesson without disrupting its structure or intent.

2 Pace and flow

This dimension dealt with two complementary notions. Pace concerned the idea of keeping up the rate of events in the lesson so that all pupils are kept involved and attentive. The idea of flow was to do with maintaining a continuous sequence of learning throughout the lesson. An important aspect of this is Kounin's notion of overlapping: the teacher being able to deal with more than one thing at a time so that the thread of the lesson was not lost while an individual pupil's problem concerning work or discipline was dealt with.

3 Transitions

Transitions focus on three key elements in the lesson. First, the establishment of attention at the start of the lesson. Second, sensitivity in deciding when to move from one activity to the next. Third, maintaining pupils' attention when moving between activities.

4 Cognitive matching

This dimension contains three elements. First, whether the lesson is suited to pupils' abilities and interests. Second, whether the work is challenging and instructive. Third, whether individual differences between pupils are accommodated.

5 Clarity

The notion of clarity refers to the extent to which the teacher's instructions and explanations are clear and are pitched at the appropriate level for pupil comprehension.

6 Business-like

This dimension is concerned with the manner in which the lesson is conducted. It focuses on matters of authority, reaction to misbehaviour and teacher expectations, which together create an impression that the teacher is in control. This impression is conveyed by the tone of confidence and firmness regarding teaching and control, together with positive expectations regarding the quality of work and behaviour occurring in the lesson.

7 Withitness

This notion, developed by Kounin, deals with the teacher's monitoring of the lesson. It refers to the teacher being alert to learning problems and misbehaviour, so that he or she can largely pre-empt their occurrence or take swift action when they do occur.

8 Encouragingness

This dimension explicitly examines the nature of teacher–pupil interaction in terms of the extent to which the teacher uses a mixture of praise, instructive criticism, enthusiasm and good humour to develop a positive and encouraging tone in the lesson, which will foster and support pupils' self-confidence and self-esteem.

While these eight qualities overlap in some respects, they appear to represent the key classroom teaching qualities that warrant attention. In a study based on using these scales, 40 lessons (each given by a different teacher) were observed in two secondary schools (Kyriacou and McKelvey, 1985). Each lesson was rated on each of these eight dimensions using a scale of 1 to 5, where 1 denoted the right-hand (less desirable) description and 5 the left-hand (more desirable) description. The findings of the study indicated, surprisingly, that for all but one dimension, more than half of the 40 lessons received a rating of 5. This is a much higher proportion of positive qualities being displayed than was expected. The exact number of lessons (out of 40) receiving a rating of 5 on each dimension was as follows:

Preparedness	31
Pace and flow	24
Transitions	24
Cognitive matching	24
Clarity	33
Business-like	26
Withitness	22
Encouragingness	14

The fact that only 14 of the 40 lessons received a rating of 5 on encouragingness reflected the somewhat tired or bored or bored tone of some teachers, and instances of teachers using sarcasm or being deprecating in their interaction with pupils.

Four of the 40 lessons rated all 5s. These were all characterised by:

- a coherence of presentation
- a pace that seemed to suit the pupils' needs and maintain their interest
- an ability to deal with matters of discipline without interrupting the lesson (although few incidents of misbehaviour were evident)
- ease in moving between activities without spending time repeating or controlling the class
- a general awareness of what was going on
- a positive and enthusiastic relationship with pupils.

Nevertheless, there were also notable differences between these four lessons. One lesson was very formal and highly structured, requiring a great deal of individual work from pupils and little discussion. In contrast, in another lesson, the teacher read to the class, talked to pupils, and pupils talked among themselves and reported back to the teacher. Although these two lessons received identical ratings (all 5s), they had very different learning atmospheres.

Of the 40 lessons, a further 14 received a profile of ratings that contained only 5s and 4s. This bias in the lessons observed towards ratings of 5s and 4s (the desirable descriptors) was no doubt in part a reflection of the fact that the 40 teachers observed were all experienced teachers, and had all agreed to allow the researcher to observe a lesson (some teachers who were approached did not agree to take part in the study). In this respect, the descriptions used for the eight qualities did not sufficiently discriminate between such lessons.

Using such rating scales in the context of initial teacher training has been very useful indeed. It raises an agenda of qualities against which student teachers can discuss and compare their views of effective teaching and their assessment and evaluation of videotaped lessons. The views of student teachers, together with the lack of discrimination between the lessons of experienced teachers shown above, points to three important observations concerning the search for the key qualities of classroom teaching. These apply not only to the qualities discussed here, but to all such sets, including those used by Ofsted and in the *Stanford Teacher Competence Appraisal Guide* already discussed. The first observation is that a list of rating scales fails to do justice to the intellectual quality of the lesson (how the content and learning activities are marshalled to set up the educational experience appropriate to achieving the teacher's intended outcomes). In part, this requires one to consider the development of the lesson as a whole unit. This becomes very evident when one looks at a description of a whole lesson and sees how the different parts and activities were related. Rating scales fail to adequately convey this.

The second observation is that such ratings also fail to do justice to the nature of the rapport between teacher and pupils, and to measure how such rapport is developed. Such rapport extends beyond its purely affective tone to include the hidden curriculum, in terms of the types of activities used and the 'language climate' of the classroom. The language climate, which refers to the teacher's choice of words and phrases to describe and comment on pupils' behaviour, and how they exert control over when and how pupils may speak, is particularly important. In addition, the rapport between teacher and pupils can change many times during the course of a lesson, as the teacher puts on 'different hats' (e.g. encouraging, explaining, counselling and reprimanding).

The third observation concerns the importance of teachers being able to see the progress of a lesson from the pupils' perspective and to make appropriate decisions and modifications to the lesson while it is in progress. Many regard this quality of social sensitivity (seeing things from another's perspective) as an important contributor to all qualities of effective teaching, since it relates to a teacher's awareness of how their own actions will be experienced by pupils.

Together these three observations have a common thread. This is that the dynamic nature of a lesson, in terms of how the scenario unfolds and how the qualities and phases of a lesson are interrelated, is fundamental to one's overall judgement and appreciation of a lesson taken as a whole. As such, the value of using ratings scales is that they provide a valuable set of agenda items for discussion and reflection. However, it is how one discusses these qualities that is important, since no one set of qualities alone can adequately capture the full richness of a lesson. In effect, rating scales are best regarded as a very useful heuristic device that enables one to probe the nature of effective teaching in terms of its underlying characteristics.

The study reported here also highlights how such rating scales seem to provide a useful basis for considering the general qualities underlying effective teaching, but cannot adequately discriminate between 'good teaching' and 'outstanding teaching'. In other words, both 'good teaching' and 'outstanding teaching' will share these same general qualities, but what makes outstanding teaching different from good teaching owes something to the notion of 'master classes' or 'virtuoso performance'. This involves a variety of additional factors, such as exceptional teaching skills, charisma, first-class commitment and preparation, and an ability to tailor a learning experience perfectly to the needs of pupils. At such an extreme of overall quality, one begins to deal with case studies of unique teachers and teaching, rather than a consideration of the general qualities addressed in typical sets of rating scales.

Key classroom teaching tasks

The key tasks involved in classroom teaching can usefully be grouped under three main headings: 'planning', 'presentation and monitoring', and 'reflection and evaluation'. These three groupings form a continuous cycle underlying the teacher's decision-making. *Planning* involves the teacher's decisions about the aims of a lesson, its context, and the learning activities that will effectively achieve its aims. *Presentation and monitoring* involve decisions the teacher makes about the progress of a lesson while it is taking place. *Reflection and evaluation* involve decisions made after a lesson has finished, which feed into future planning activities. These three main groupings of key classroom teaching tasks are reflected in many of the discussions of effective teaching in terms of practical craft knowledge and will be considered here in some detail.

Planning

Good planning is a crucial aspect of effective teaching. Many experienced teachers have a store of wisdom concerning the ingredients of a successful lesson, which enables them to spend much less time in planning than is the case for most younger teachers. However, all teachers need to have clear ideas about the lesson they wish to set up and have carried out the necessary preparation if it is to be successful.

Three main elements are involved in planning a lesson (Butt, 2008; Skowron, 2006). First is the need to consider the general aims and specific educational outcomes the lesson is intended to achieve. The second element, having taken account of the context (e.g. the type of pupils, the school's resources) and desired learning outcomes, is to consider what will be the most effective learning environment, activities and sequencing of these? Third, is the need to monitor and evaluate pupils' educational progress, so that the teacher can assess whether the lesson has been successful. Planning is essential for the success of all lessons. It is also particularly crucial in taking account of important differences between pupils, such as learning difficulties indicative of special educational needs, and in the use of teaching and learning activities designed to combat any problems that may be linked to ability (both high and low), motivation, social class, gender and race. The main questions involved in planning are detailed in Table 6.1.

The most important aspect of planning is to ensure that the learning experience fulfils the three psychological conditions necessary for pupil learning to occur:

- *Attentiveness:* the learning experience must elicit and sustain pupils' attention.
- *Receptiveness:* the learning experience must elicit and sustain pupils' motivation and mental effort.
- *Appropriateness:* the learning experience must be appropriate for the educational outcomes desired.

---

1 What level and range of ability is there in the class?
   What level and type of motivation can I expect?
   What is the composition of the class in terms of ethnic minority pupils, social class and sex?
   Do any of the pupils have special educational needs?
   What do the pupils already know and feel about the subject/topic?
   How have the pupils behaved in previous lessons?

2 What do I want the pupils to learn in this lesson:
   - cognitively (e.g. knowledge, understanding, intellectual skills)?
   - affectively (e.g. interest, attitudes, self-confidence)?

   How does this relate to their present knowledge, feelings and needs?
   How does this relate to the course as a whole (both past and future)?

3 What constraints need to be accommodated:
   - time available for lesson, preparation time available?
   - number of pupils in class, layout of classroom?
   - teacher's knowledge and skills?
   - acceptability of lesson to significant others (colleagues, parents)?

4 Are there any other considerations of note:
   - Has this lesson been successful with a similar class?
   - What time of day, week, term, etc. is it?

5 What teaching method (type of learning tasks, activities and experience) will best foster the cognitive and affective outcomes desired, given the context and the constraints which need to be accommodated (as outlined above):
   - discovery methods, exposition plus practice, individualised learning, work sheets, small group work?

6 Once a particular method and general academic topic for the lesson have been chosen, what sequencing of the tasks/activities/experience, level of difficulty and structuring of the topic, and pace of lessons will be best for the lesson to be successful in maintaining the pupils' attention, interest, understanding and motivation, and achieving the desired cognitive and affective outcomes?

7 What level of pupil performance will be expected, and how will the degree of success of the learning taking place be determined (e.g. questioning of pupils, written work, follow-up tests)?

8 What preparation is necessary before the lesson:
   - Are there sufficient textbooks available, is the equipment in working order, which questions and/or exercises will be set and what are the answers to these?

9 What teacher behaviour is required during the lesson to ensure its success:
   - quality, style and tone of presentation and monitoring?
   - use of questions, reinforcement and feedback?
   - monitoring of general progress and the management of discipline?
   - adjustment to the lesson (e.g. pace, content) as appropriate?
   - helping individual pupils?

10 How will the lesson be perceived and experienced by the pupils:
   - of interest/relevance/importance/difficulty?
   - their comprehension of instructions and task requirements?

11 What problems might arise?

Table 6.1 *Planning a lesson*

Indeed, consideration of these three psychological conditions must underpin all discussion of the key classroom teaching tasks if effective teaching is to take place.

Considering the general aims and specific educational outcomes the lesson is intended to achieve, involves a complex web of concerns. These include tensions between short-term and long-term outcomes, between cognitive and affective outcomes and the fact that different outcomes may be directed at particular pupils within the class. The most important question for a teacher to ask is 'What should pupils have learnt from the lesson?', whether it be in terms of knowledge, understanding, skills or attitudes.

It may be thought that teachers planning for each lesson will follow a three-step logical sequence of: specifying objectives → selecting learning activities → specifying the evaluation procedures to be used during the lesson to monitor pupils' progress and learning outcomes. In general, this is indeed the way student teachers go about planning lessons (particularly as their lesson plans often have to be shown to their school mentors and university tutor). However, this three-step sequence presents too rational a description of how experienced teachers plan lessons. Research studies of how experienced teachers plan lessons, reveal that they give most attention in their planning time to thinking about the content, materials and activities that will be used to make 'a lesson', without explicitly starting with a list of objectives to be achieved. In large measure, this reflects the fact that experienced teachers have internalised the process of planning to such an extent that they can draw heavily upon routines and established practice without the need for much overt conscious reference to lesson objectives themselves.

In considering the selection of learning activities, a useful distinction can be made between content and lesson organisation. With regard to content, the most important consideration is to take account of what pupils already know. The lesson must start 'where the pupils are'. This means not only ascertaining their present knowledge, understanding and skills concerned with the topic in hand, but also building upon any related or relevant knowledge and interests. Of particular importance is the need to check rather than presuppose that pupils have the necessary level of knowledge, understanding and skills that are needed for the lesson to successfully achieve the intended outcomes. If a lesson builds upon work covered in a previous lesson given some time ago, some revision may be necessary, along with an explanation of how the work in hand will relate to the previous work. In most subject areas, each topic is gradually developed and extended by being met periodically within a course. Such a procedure of periodic development linked by revision is particularly effective in allowing the structure of knowledge to be consolidated in the pupil's memory, and it is a common feature of many subject textbooks.

With regard to lesson organisation, a host of concerns are involved during planning. Of prime importance is the need to ensure that the type of activity to be used is right for the type of learning that is desired (Borich, 2007; Good and Brophy, 2003). For example, if the teacher wishes to extend pupils' oral skills, then pupils must be given opportunities to talk. The single biggest danger facing teachers is to slip into an informing mode of teaching when such a mode is not the most effective way to promote the intended objectives of the lesson. Indeed, the fact that pupils learn more effectively by doing rather than listening, indicates that a greater emphasis should be given to pupil involvement and activity across the curriculum than is typical at present.

The planning of a lesson is also an important opportunity to think carefully about the way in which the educational objectives to be achieved may need to be broken down into conceptually appropriate steps, each of which may require practice and consolidation. In terms of the sequencing of activities within a lesson, the most basic sequence for a lesson is one which has a beginning (in which the topic is introduced), a middle (comprising the main learning activities) and an end (which may review the learning which should have occurred). The underlying rationale for the choice of activities and their precise sequencing needs to take account of attentiveness, receptiveness and appropriateness.

Another key point about the planning of lesson organisation is that the outline of a lesson must always be flexible. The ability to extend parts of a lesson further than originally intended, or even to omit certain elements and tasks when appropriate, is essential. Teachers always need to be ready to modify their plans in the light of how the lesson progresses, and to have additional tasks at hand if the work is completed by some or all of the pupils before the end of the lesson.

Finally, in planning lesson organisation, one needs to take account of the learning environment in terms of the tone or atmosphere created. Above all, it needs to be borne in mind that learning, with its risk of failure, is an emotionally charged and high-risk process. Learning thus needs to be carefully nurtured and supported. Some activities are more high risk than others and the teacher needs to be alert to this. The learning environment generated in a lesson is in part a reflection of the style of relationship that develops between teacher and pupils. In order to establish the kind of classroom climate the teacher wants, consideration needs to be given to how the choice of learning activities and disciplinary strategies will influence this. What is important to note here, is that the tone of the learning environment may have a marked impact on the effectiveness of achieving certain educational outcomes in certain contexts.

With regard to planning how the success of a lesson is to be evaluated, a teacher needs to build in strategies that will enable the progress of the lesson to be monitored, and to assess such learning after the lesson. Given the importance of quick corrective feedback to facilitating pupil learning and to ensure that the progress of the lesson maintains its effectiveness, the teacher needs to be continually assessing pupils' learning by checking their work, asking questions and responding to difficulties. More formalised assessment made on the basis of tests and marking homework provides both the teacher and pupils with feedback about progress. A careful match of learning experiences with such assessment is important in the cause of fairness to the pupil and in order to achieve a valid measure of progress.

At this point some attention must be given to the role of lesson notes. Compiling an outline of a lesson in terms of notes about the aims of the lesson, the sequence, timing and type of learning activities to be used and details of the learning materials (including textbooks, worksheets and equipment) serves a number of extremely important functions. First, it forces the teacher to consider the logistics of successfully implementing the plan of a lesson. For example, it becomes immediately apparent whether too much or too little time is available for the intended learning activities. Second, such outlines provide a script to which the teacher can refer during the lesson to check on what should come next. Third, they can alert the teacher to activities and aspects of the lesson that will require preparation in advance, such as the need to ensure that equipment and resources are available. Fourth, lesson notes can usefully include the questions that the teacher intends to ask, the answers expected and the correct answers and results, all of which will enable marking and feedback to progress smoothly. Fifth, they provide the teacher with a record of the lesson that can be referred to and modified for future use.

Making lesson notes is so useful as part of planning effectively, that it is an essential activity for student teachers. Among experienced teachers, however, the use of lesson notes varies extensively, in part because such formalised planning is time consuming and in part because experienced teachers have largely developed the ability to speedily envisage a script for a lesson and to teach as though all was well planned and prepared.

Careful planning is also needed to ensure that effective use is made of teaching assistants, learning support assistants and other adults who may be contributing to the lesson, including team or collaborative teaching with other teachers. A key feature here is on clarifying as much as possible the tasks and roles that the other adults are expected to carry out.

When making use of teaching outside the classroom, such as fieldwork and visits to museums, there is a danger than one can assume that almost all the educational benefit will arise directly from the visit itself. In fact, a significant amount of the educational benefit derives from how well the lessons before and after the visit are planned to prepare for and build upon the visit.

Finally, in planning lessons, one has to make sure that the demands placed on oneself as teacher and on the pupils are sensible and realistic. It may seem odd to state that a staple diet of apparently excellent and exciting lessons would not be desirable. Both teachers and pupils need to have a curriculum that gives opportunities for low-key demands, during which they can take a mental breather, as well as periods when the demands on the teacher and pupils are very high. Such considerations apply not only to the whole-school week, but also to individual lessons. Lessons more than about 40 minutes in length, will certainly benefit from containing a mixture of learning activities and demands in this way, if the mental health of teachers and pupils are to be protected.

Presentation and monitoring

The two key tasks involved in the activity of classroom teaching are presentation and monitoring (Kerry and Wilding, 2004; Ornstein and Lasley, 2004). Presentation refers to all the aspects of lesson organisation and its implementation. Monitoring refers to the ways in which the teacher needs to assess the progress of a lesson to ensure its success. In practice, presentation and monitoring are closely interlinked. Many of the tasks and activities carried out by the teacher during a lesson (e.g. questioning pupils' understanding) are part of both presentation and monitoring. These areas also overlap with issues of classroom management, which in its broadest sense refers to the general management and organisation of pupil learning and discipline. The main characteristics underpinning the task of effective presentation and monitoring are shown in Table 6.2.

In essence, the effectiveness of presentation and monitoring rests on establishing the three psychological conditions necessary for pupil learning: attentiveness, receptiveness and appropriateness. The teacher's classroom teaching *skills* involved in carrying out the *tasks* of teaching, will determine the extent to which these three conditions are effectively realised.

A key factor in presentation is the effective use of time. Pupils should arrive promptly for lessons and lessons should end on time. The speed with which the lesson can commence is helped by establishing well-used procedures, so that pupils are familiar with the routines and conventions linked to one's teaching. This should cover entry to the classroom and the way pupils settle into the rhythm of the lesson presentation. The amount of time wasted at the start of a lesson, by having to settle down latecomers, deal with pupils without pens and waiting for pupils to pay attention, can be minimised by having established clear demands and expectations regarding these problems (e.g. spare pens will be dealt with at the appropriate time by the teacher and should not interrupt the start of a lesson). Time is also saved if there is a clear routine regarding the distribution of materials, including books, worksheets, equipment and other resources.

Once the lesson is underway, time can be saved (or wasted) in a number of ways. Primarily, the teacher needs to organise and present the learning experience in a way that elicits and maintains pupils' attention and engagement. Attention will easily be lost if the work is too difficult, is boring, or appears to lack importance or relevance. In addition, attention will be easily lost if the presentation is poor, for example, if the teacher's tone of voice is monotonous, if the pace of presentation is too fast or too slow, if the whiteboard or materials are unclear, and if the task is passive or too long. Physical conditions can also play a part here, such as if the classroom is uncomfortably

---

In considering those characteristics of presenting and monitoring a lesson which will contribute to its success, the teacher needs to bear in mind that these may well vary depending on the context (e.g. topic, type of pupils); on the particular type of outcomes the teacher wishes to emphasise most (e.g. developing an interest in the topic, ensuring recall of certain facts); and on the type of learning experience or teaching method adopted (e.g. group work, discovery learning).

Nevertheless, a number of characteristics of effective presentation and monitoring apply across a range of lesson types.

1 The teacher appears to be self-confident, is normally patient and good humoured, displays a genuine interest in the topic, and appears to be genuinely concerned with each pupil's progress.
2 The teacher's explanations and instructions are clear, and pitched at the right level for pupil comprehension.
3 The teacher's voice and actions facilitate pupils' maintaining attention and interest.
4 The teacher makes good and varied use of questioning to monitor pupils' understanding and to raise the level of pupils' thinking.
5 The teacher monitors the progress of the lesson and pupils' behaviour, and makes any adjustments necessary to ensure the lesson flows well and that pupils are engaged appropriately.
6 The teacher encourages pupils' efforts.
7 The teacher minimises pupil misbehaviour by keeping their attention maintained on the lesson, and by use of eye contact, movement and questions to curtail any misbehaviour which is developing.
8 Potential interruptions to the lesson caused by organisational problems (e.g. a pupil who has not got a pen) or pupil misbehaviour are dealt with in such a way that the interruptions are minimised or prevented.
9 Criticism by the teacher of a pupil is given privately and in a way likely to encourage and foster progress.
10 Pupil misbehaviour, when it does occur, is dealt with in a relaxed, self-assured and firm manner.

Table 6.2 *Presenting and monitoring a lesson*

hot or cold, or if the seating is cramped or badly arranged. Attention will be most easily maintained by a lively, interesting presentation, linked to a variety of activities that enable pupils to be active for some or most of the time, and where the sequencing and content of the learning activities are intellectually and pedagogical sound (i.e. make intellectual sense from the point of view of the pupils and their perception of the nature of the learning that is taking place).

Lest the impression be given here that saving time is the be-all and end-all of effective presentation, it is important to note that many lessons, particularly those involving apparatus or group work, may be costly in apparent non-learning time, when in fact the processes involved in preparing for the activity and in engaging in it (e.g. waiting for the results in an experiment, or long pauses during discussion) may not only be a worthwhile sacrifice of time, but are in fact of educational value in their own right, in terms of developing a range of important learning skills. Excessive time consciousness by a teacher is a danger if it promotes over-controlled and essentially passive pupil experiences.

Another major task involved in presentation is to ensure that the learning experience offered is intellectually and pedagogically sound, not only in eliciting and maintaining attention (as already noted) but also in fostering the desired educational outcomes. This involves a careful consideration of the steps that the pupils' learning will need to follow in terms of the learning process that need to be utilised (e.g. rote learning, meaningful learning, practice and consolidation, as outlined in chapter 2) and the types of activities that best engage these learning processes (e.g. teacher exposition, writing tasks, small group work and experiential learning, as outlined in chapter 3).

Learning outcomes are most typically discussed in terms of four main elements: knowledge, understanding, skills and attitudes. Promoting each of these involves using an appropriate type and range of classroom activities. The teaching of skills is a particularly interesting area. The essence of a skill is that it relates to the ability to perform a task with a degree of expertise. The emphasis is on doing rather than knowing or understanding *per se*. Thus the teaching of a skill must involve giving the pupil the opportunity to practise and display that skill. Teaching that is mainly expository, where the skill is tested in terms of knowledge and understanding of what the skill involves, is unlikely to develop that skill effectively. Curriculum development in almost all subject areas and in programmes of personal and social education, has led to a much greater emphasis in fostering skills rather than the recall of knowledge. As a result, this has had a major impact on increasing the diversity of teaching methods used in schools. What is important however is not to assume that simply because one uses a variety of teaching methods, one will promote the intended range of learning outcomes. Developing skills, in particular, requires careful monitoring and coaching. It is not true that 'practice makes perfect'. Rather, it is *practice plus feedback* that makes perfect.

The notion that presentation should be intellectually and pedagogically sound requires that the teacher sees the learning experience from the pupils' perspective. This includes not only attempting to judge how one's own performance, teaching materials and learning activities might appear from the pupils' perspective, but also an attempt to ensure that the mental activity in which the pupil is engaged is appropriate. Effective presentation may need to give explicit guidance as to the type of mental and learning strategy that the pupils are expected to use. Many pupils simply do not know how to go about organising their own learning activity on a mental level (e.g. should they be attempting to memorise, make notes, draw upon previous knowledge?). Recognition of this has led to the increasingly widespread development of study skills courses in schools. As was noted earlier, however, too great a degree of spoon-feeding by a teacher may enable a particular lesson to go smoothly, but this may be at the cost of not enabling pupils to develop their own decision-making skills in response to the academic demands made.

Effective presentation goes hand in hand with effective monitoring of the progress of the lesson and of pupils' learning. Indeed, what makes teaching a particularly demanding activity is the need to monitor the whole variety of concerns that need to be taken account of if pupils' attentiveness and receptiveness, and the appropriateness of the learning experience, are to be maintained. Such concerns include the following questions:

- Are pupils becoming bored?
- Has the lesson been pitched at too difficult a level?
- Are some of the pupils completing the set work faster than expected?
- Are pupils encountering problems or making errors?
- Are the materials and resources needed to hand?
- Is the organisation of the lesson leading to problems?

In difficult circumstances, the degree of monitoring required demands a high level of concentration and is likely to leave the teacher mentally exhausted. Clearly, sound planning of a lesson pays handsome dividends if it helps to reduce such concerns.

For inexperienced teachers, the complex nature of such monitoring and decision-making is particularly demanding. However, with time, the teacher becomes more adept at picking up the signals that indicate how the lesson needs to be conducted or modified if attentiveness, receptiveness and appropriateness are to be maintained. Two types of skills, in particular, underpin the teacher's ability to maintain effectiveness in this way.

The first type of skill involves assessing pupils' progress during the lesson, such as checking that they are paying attention and have understood the instructions and explanations, and dealing quickly with any difficulties they encounter. Teachers do this, in the main, by asking questions, using quick tests, moving around the classroom to check on the work being produced, and reading pupils' facial expressions and general behaviour.

The second type of skill is the ability to deal with a number of matters and concerns at the same time (in Kounin's terms 'overlapping'). In most classrooms there are times when to ensure that the flow of progress is maintained the teacher needs to deal with a number of different demands, each of which will hold up progress for one or more pupils if not met. For example, when engaged in teacher exposition, if the teacher notices that a pupil is not paying attention, the teacher can continue the exposition while staring at or perhaps moving close to the pupil in question. In this way, the pupil's inattention is noticed by the teacher and signalled to the pupil, but the flow of exposition, and hence the attention of other pupils, is not interrupted. In a classroom where pupils may be engaged in different activities or progressing through their work at different speeds, dealing simultaneously with their varied demands is essential. This may mean being able to listen to one pupil reading aloud, whilst checking whether another pupil has successfully completed a different task and is ready to move on, and signalling to a third pupil that some further resources are needed for the task in hand. Over and above all this, the teacher may also be considering whether it is time for pupils to start packing away, whether the noise level is too high, and whether there is a need to circulate around the room to check all is generally well. Problems may occur if the organisation of the lesson and activities leads to too many demands being made on the teacher, which therefore cannot be met. This may result in long queues for help and assessment at the teacher's desk or in pupils being able to get away with very little work without being noticed. Effective teaching requires a lesson organisation that can be adequately monitored.

An important part of monitoring involves giving feedback to pupils concerning their progress. This may be done individually, as when a teacher assesses a pupil's work, or collectively, either by making a statement to the whole class based on individual assessments and general monitoring, or by getting pupils to mark their own work by giving the correct answers at the end of the activity. The most important aspects of feedback are that it should be quick (particularly if errors are being made or difficulties encountered), constructive, helpful and supportive. Individual feedback can be tailored to the pupil's particular needs, but there is a limit to how quickly a teacher can circulate and hence the feedback for some pupils may be slow. Collective feedback at least ensures that pupils can note whether they are progressing correctly and, if they are not, they are then aware that they need to review their work or seek help. A mixture of both individual and collective assessment and feedback would seem to be the most effective approach, given the constraints on classroom teaching.

In giving feedback, the teacher needs to first establish the root of the pupil's difficulties. Possible causes may be inattentiveness, not being able to understand the task, a lack of interest in the topic, or use of a faulty learning strategy. Effective feedback needs to diagnose the nature of any problems and, if necessary, go beyond simply giving remedial help. In many cases, pupils may need to be helped to develop better study habits or to have their self-confidence enhanced.

One of the major problems facing effective teaching is how to ensure that those pupils whose progress is less successful than that of their peers do not become discouraged and disheartened. Some forms of learning activity, such as group work, project work, individualised learning and practical work, can do much to mitigate this effect if emphasis is placed on the process of the activity engaged in and on the individual's work as valuable in its own right. For a pupil to say 'I'm no good at history' (or mathematics, or physical education, or science, or whatever) is a tragedy. All pupils ought to be able to enjoy and derive pleasure from all areas of the curriculum. For them not to do so because they do less well than others is unforgivable. This is not to say that pupils should not recognise that others have greater talents in some areas of the curriculum than they do. Rather, it is that such a recognition should not be allowed to undermine their own interest and enjoyment of these areas. The type of feedback and assessment methods used by a teacher is crucial here. To a great extent, the public examination system places major constraints on teachers' room for manoeuvre, since much schooling is ultimately geared to achieving examination success, and the worth of such in our culture is seen very much in competitive terms.

In the quest to improve standards of teaching and learning, some writers have argued that a curriculum that comprises a clear set of objectives in terms of observable performance that can be tested, provides a sharp focus for both pupils and teachers (Gronlund and Tro, 2004). It also provides those who oversee education with data to judge the progress made by pupils and schools in achieving these objectives. The National Curriculum introduced in 1988 was to a large extent based on this viewpoint (DES, 1989). There are clear benefits in adopting an objectives-based curriculum that clarifies aims and helps monitor progress. There are however three major drawbacks with an objectives-based curriculum. First, it can become over-bureaucratic in its specification of objectives. Indeed, the more it attempts to be precise about the objectives, the more burdensome becomes the weight of documentation that teachers need to read and use. Second, it tends to squeeze out many desirable educational objectives that are difficult to measure, such as encouraging pupils to show personal initiative in their work. Third, teachers and pupils tend to focus overmuch on meeting the objectives that are specified and will be tested, to the exclusion of educational breadth or depth. An extreme example of this is focusing almost exclusively on those words and phrases in French lessons that will maximise examination success.

A major challenge facing teachers is how to make effective use of ICT in the classroom (Gillespie, 2006; Somekh, 2007). The use of ICT has many major benefits. First, it has a 'wow factor' that can stimulate and motivate pupils. Second, it can help pupils to develop new ways of working. Third, it can help pupils to develop their familiarity and use of ICT in a range of settings. However, it is extremely important for teachers to recognise that making use of ICT in the classroom for these three reasons (what I call 'stage 1 ICT use'), worthy as they are in their own right, is only part of the story. Teachers also need to make use of ICT in ways that genuinely enhance the quality of pupils' learning and understanding of the topic area in hand (what I call 'stage 2 ICT use'). Some studies have indicated that the ways teachers use ICT in their teaching and the ways in which pupils are asked to engage in using ICT in their learning are too often limited to stage 1 use, and that more needs to be done to support teachers and pupils to extend teaching and learning involving ICT to stage 2 use.

In discussing the major aspects of presentation and monitoring little has been said here regarding the rapport and relationship between teacher and pupils that develops in a lesson, and that establishes the tone and climate of the learning environment. In addition, little has been said of the role of teacher authority in establishing discipline and in dealing with misbehaviour. In fact, these questions are so important and fundamental to effective teaching that they will be explored fully in the next two chapters. Suffice to say here that presentation and monitoring are inextricably bound up with these very questions.

Reflection and evaluation

Reflection and evaluation after a lesson are essential if the teacher is to continue to improve the quality of the learning experience offered. Two main tasks are involved. First, to consider whether the lesson has been successful and to act on any implications for future practice. Second, to assess and record the educational progress of the pupils. The key questions underlying reflection and evaluation are listed in Table 6.3.

Assessing the success of a lesson involves considering a whole range of concerns. At one level, the teacher needs to consider whether the intended learning outcomes have been effectively achieved. At another level, the teacher also needs to consider a whole host of very practical issues that largely focus on whether the lesson went as planned. It would be naive to believe that a teacher's reflection on a lesson is purely a matter of whether intended learning outcomes have been achieved. As was noted in the earlier discussion of planning, teachers are equally concerned, on a day-to-day basis, with whether the organisation of different tasks and activities in a lesson was successfully implemented, in terms of simple logistics. In effect, did the pupils do more or less what I envisaged for the lesson, in the manner I had intended? In terms of reflection and evaluation, the question of what learning took place is often secondary to the question of whether the lesson organisation was successfully implemented in terms of the envisaged script.

However, a major danger regarding an emphasis on implementation rather than learning outcomes is that it is all too easy to infer that because a lesson has been successfully implemented (i.e. went as planned), effective teaching has taken place. Indeed, some teachers' aims for a lesson may explicitly refer to lesson content and organisation (e.g. pupils will undertake a group work task looking at racial prejudice) rather than the intended learning outcomes (e.g. pupils will be able to distinguish between different categories of racial prejudice). Nonetheless, the teacher will usually have in mind, albeit implicitly, some notion of the ways in which successful implementation fosters intended learning outcomes.

Reflection and evaluation regarding one's teaching is crucial for the continuing development of teaching skills in general, and for specific knowledge about how a particular lesson could have been improved (with implications for similar lessons). Each teacher has intentions about their own teaching; teachers may differ in respect of both the educational outcomes they wish to emphasise and the types of learning experiences they wish to use. In this respect one teacher may feel a lesson has gone well, whilst an observer may well feel that other educational outcomes or learning experiences could more usefully have been involved. Periodically, teachers need to reflect on the general character of their teaching and relate this to curriculum developments aimed at improving the quality of education.

The following questions form an outline agenda for reflection and evaluation. Each can usefully be elaborated in a number of ways.

1 Did this lesson go well?
   - Were the learning activities envisaged successfully implemented?
   - What did the pupils learn in the lesson?
   - How can I be sure such learning occurred?
   - Did the lesson and learning reflect my intended aims?

2 Did any pupil or group of pupils fail to benefit (e.g. able pupils, average pupils, less able pupils, shy pupils, a pupil who missed previous lessons, a disruptive pupil)? If so, could this have been avoided?

3 What changes can I usefully make before giving a similar lesson to another class?

4 What have I learnt about this class, or particular pupils, that might influence future lessons with this class?

5 What have I learnt about this topic or subject matter that might influence future lessons?

6 Are there any immediate actions I should take following this lesson (e.g. did any pupil appear to indicate some special educational need?)?

7 Am I satisfied with my general planning of this lesson, and its presentation and monitoring? Did the lesson sustain pupils' attention and interest, and did it appear to be intellectually and pedagogically sound?

8 Did any problems occur in the lesson that I should take note of?

9 How can I consolidate the learning which occurred and relate it to future demands and applications?

10 How did this lesson fit in with the teaching in the department and school, and with curriculum developments concerning teaching in this area?

Table 6.3 *Reflection and evaluation*

In thinking about the successful implementation of a lesson, the teacher needs to be alert to the strategies and techniques pupils use to give the appearance of attending, understanding and meeting academic demands, without in fact being engaged in the learning activities in the way assumed and intended by the teacher. For example, pupils are adept at not paying attention during teacher exposition until they notice a change in the pitch of a teacher's voice that denotes that someone is about to be asked a question. In addition, when answering a question, pupils are skilful at giving non-committal answers and using prompts from the teacher (including facial expression and tone) to work towards the answer required. In a way, both teacher and pupils have a vested interest in the smooth running of a lesson. Thus, if a teacher suspects that a pupil has not been paying attention, it is tempting to avoid asking that pupil to answer a question. If a pupil does little work, but keeps a low profile, it is an easy option to ignore the pupil's lack of progress. If a pupil does not appear to understand the work, it is tempting to simply give the pupil the correct answer, rather than spend time helping the pupil to understand the process involved. As such, throughout teaching and learning, both teachers and pupils are often tempted to take the easy path and engage in a degree of collusion to avoid 'making waves' or expending additional effort. It requires great integrity for a teacher not only to resist such temptation when it occurs, but to actively seek, through the teaching activities used, to identify and overcome such classroom processes. In this respect, the teacher's sensitivity in being able to take account of each pupil's perspective of a learning activity is an essential aspect of the effective monitoring of pupils in the classroom and vital to subsequent reflection and evaluation of the lesson.

Of course, the formal assessment of learning, ranging from marking classroom work and homework to the use of tests and examinations, also provides the teacher with regular and essential indices of educational progress (Black *et al.*, 2003; Gardner, J., 2006). Although such assessment will inevitably focus on academic attainment rather than other educational outcomes (e.g. study skills, motivation, moral values), the latter may be to some extent involved in, or inferred from, particular types of assessed pieces of work. In the context of effective teaching, formal assessments serve a number of important functions. They provide both teacher and pupils with feedback concerning the pupils' attainment. They also form a vehicle whereby the teacher can diagnose difficulties and problems, which can then be remedied by feedback accompanying the marking and specifically addressed in future lessons. In addition, formal assessments enable the teacher to maintain a record of the pupils' attainment, which can serve as a basis for future planning of courses, for monitoring whether a pupil's progress has declined over a period of time and for incorporation into reports both internal to the school (e.g. as used in discussion of possible special educational needs) and available to those outside the school (such as those made out when a pupil transfers to a new school) and sent to parents, employers and other educational institutions.

In discussing formal assessment, it is important to note the effects on pupils of such assessment. On the one hand, the evaluation of their work and attainment needs to provide pupils with helpful feedback about the standards expected and how the work presented could have been improved. On the other hand, it must also help pupils maintain motivation and positive attitudes towards learning, rather than discourage and undermine their self-esteem. To achieve both these aims is essential but by no means easy and is one of the major challenges facing teachers. Teachers need to provide feedback to pupils that has a balance of both these elements, rather than an undue emphasis on one at the expense of the other.

The phrase 'assessment for learning' has been increasingly used to refer to the ways in which pupils and teachers can make use of assessment activities to gain a clearer understanding of the learning that has taken place to date and how their future learning can best progress (Black *et al.*, 2003; Fautley and Savage, 2008; Gardner, J., 2006). A particularly noteworthy example of this approach is the way in which teachers frequently share with pupils the criteria that are used to assess pupils' performance; this may include asking pupils to discuss with each of these criteria and to have a go at marking a piece of work themselves using these criteria.

Assessment for learning builds upon and extends the notion of formative assessment and was included by the DfES (2005a,b) as an important strand of 'personalised learning'. Personalised learning refers to how a school can tailor the curriculum and teaching methods to the specific learning needs of each pupil, and offer each pupil the type of personalised support that will enable them to develop the skills needed to access learning activities to better effect (Courcier, 2007; DfES 2005a,b, 2007).

Strong links have also been made between assessment for learning and personalised learning as part of the 'Every Child Matters' agenda that has been developed by the DfES (2004a) to promote pupil achievement to schools (Cheminais, 2006).

Some types of pupil evaluation do include wider forms of assessment. One major development in secondary schools has been the issuing of 'Records of Achievement' to pupils at the age of 16 or later as part of the 16–19 curriculum, which is intended to provide a much broader record of pupil achievement than can be covered by reference to their public examination results alone (Broadfoot, 2007). Such records typically include four main elements:

- The expected results of public examinations.
- Other academic successes, including proficiency in basic subjects.
- A record of achievement compiled by the pupil, including out of school achievements.
- An assessment of the pupil's personal qualities.

Such records have highlighted an important distinction between two main types of assessment: *summative* and *formative*. A summative assessment focuses on providing a statement of a pupil's level of attainment, either relative to others or in terms of specified objectives that have been met. This normally takes the form of a grade or mark. Formative assessment focuses on giving feedback to pupils during a course, aimed at promoting self-understanding and motivation, and which will help them improve the standard of their work. Such feedback tends to be diagnostic in emphasis and may include specific advice regarding how best to approach future tasks. Advocates of the use of records of achievements argue that they provide a much more useful and meaningful summary of pupils' achievement (summative assessment), which is more helpful to potential users such as employers and post-16 education admission tutors than are examination results alone. In addition, they also encourage formative assessment to occur more often, by making use of periodic review meetings between pupils and teachers in which pupils can discuss their progress and how this will eventually relate to their final Record of Achievement document. Such discussions will typically include encouraging pupils to participate in a wide range of activities, both in school and outside school (such as in the areas of sports, music and community work), and also to consider how they can develop and display certain personal qualities.

The teacher's ability to reflect upon and evaluate their lessons and their teaching in general is a key task of effective teaching (Dillon, 2007). Whilst all teachers reflect on their teaching, the degree of time and effort devoted to this varies immensely from teacher to teacher. For some, it forms an important part of their thinking about their lesson organisation and use of teaching methods. Indeed, it may even form the basis of small-scale research studies, often referred to as 'practitioner research' or 'teacher action research' (Koshy, 2005; Somekh, 2006). For others, such reflection appears to be more cursory. Over the years, many writers have argued that teachers need to develop their ability to reflect critically on their own classroom teaching with a view to developing and maintaining its effectiveness, and have argued that it is important for both initial teacher education and in-service professional development activities to help teachers to develop this reflective stance towards their own practice. The introduction of teacher appraisal and performance management in schools is in part a recognition of the importance of the need for teachers to spend more time reflecting upon and evaluating their own teaching, and an attempt to encourage teachers to do so more effectively as a regular feature of their classroom practice (Jones et al., 2006; Middlewood and Cardno, 2001).

Summary

In this chapter, the key teaching qualities and tasks underpinning effective teaching in the classroom have been discussed. The unifying theme has been that effective teaching needs to sustain pupils' attentiveness and receptiveness and must be appropriate for the educational outcomes desired. The key classroom teaching qualities and tasks outlined here in effect serve as a set of agenda items that enable the major issues and skills involved in effective teaching to be discussed. Reference to such qualities and tasks thus provides a framework for applying the earlier discussions of chapters 2–5 to the raw stuff of the activity of teaching. However, the discussion does not conclude here, for two aspects of key teaching qualities and tasks are so important that they warrant attention in their own right. These are teacher–pupil relationships and dealing with pupil misbehaviour. These will be dealt with in the following two chapters.

Discussion questions

1 What are the key qualities displayed in a lesson that lead to effective pupil learning?

2 What are the key features involved in effective planning and preparation?

3 How can a teacher best monitor the effectiveness of a lesson whilst it is in progress?

4 How should feedback to pupils be given in order to elicit and sustain their progress?

5 How can teachers' reflection on the success of a lesson help improve their teaching in future?

6 What are the main purposes of assessing pupils' work?

Further reading

Butt, G. (2008). *Lesson Planning*, 3rd edn. London: Continuum. An excellent, succinct and clear overview of the key issues involved in lesson planning.

Gardner, J. (ed.) (2006). *Assessment and Learning*. London: Sage. This book presents a good overview of the ways in which assessment can be used to unpin effective teaching.

Gillespie, H. (2006). *Unlocking Learning and Teaching with ICT: Identifying and Overcoming Barriers*. London: David Fulton. A very helpful introduction to the use of ICT to support teaching and learning in schools, highly informative and written in a very accessible style.

Kyriacou, C. (2007). *Essential Teaching Skills*, 3rd edn. Cheltenham: Nelson Thornes. This book focuses on the key skills involved in effective teaching, such as planning and preparation, lesson presentation, lesson management, classroom climate, discipline, assessing pupils' progress, and reflection and evaluation, and how these provide a sound basis for effective teaching.

Petty, G. (2006). *Evidence Based Teaching: A Practical Approach*. Cheltenham: Nelson Thornes. This books draws on research evidence to consider the practices that appear to have the most impact on pupils' learning.

7

Relationships with pupils

Objective

To consider how teachers establish sound relationships with pupils and the discipline necessary for effective learning to proceed.

The relationship between teachers and pupils is of fundamental importance to effective teaching. It will be argued here that a sound relationship between teacher and pupils needs to be based on two qualities. The first of these is the pupils' acceptance of the *teacher's authority*. The teacher's prime task is to organise and manage pupils' learning. This involves exerting control over both the management of learning activities and the management of pupils' behaviour (including the maintenance of discipline). Unless pupils accept the teacher's authority to organise and manage in this way, effective teaching is likely to be undermined. The second quality that is required for a sound relationship is *mutual respect and rapport* between the teacher and pupils. This refers to the teacher and pupils recognising each other as individuals, holding each other in esteem, and treating each other in a manner consistent with such esteem. These two qualities are inter-related in a number of ways. Behaviour contributing to one will, inevitably, influence the nature of the other. What is important is the need for both to be established in an acceptable form.

The first part of this chapter will focus on the way that the teacher's authority is established and the basis for developing mutual respect and rapport. In the second part, attention will focus on two aspects of effective teaching that encapsulate the qualities underpinning sound teacher–pupil relationships. The first of these is 'classroom climate', which refers to the emotional tone of teacher–pupil relationships in the classroom. Classroom climate is concerned with how the teacher and pupils feel about each other and the learning activities in hand (Campbell *et al.*, 2004; Chaplain, 2003; Watkins, 2005). Of particular interest regarding classroom climate is the subtle way in which, by their behaviour (most notably their use of language), teacher and pupils can communicate a rich collection of messages to each other. The precise choice of words and phrases used, their tone, and accompanying body language, often communicates a deeper message, sometimes unintended, about how pupils and teachers feel about each other and the work in hand.

The second aspect of effective teaching that will be considered is that of 'pastoral care'. In essence, pastoral care is explicitly concerned with the welfare and wellbeing of the pupil. Although all secondary and many primary schools have a formalised pastoral care system of some sort, the pastoral care role of the classroom teacher forms part of a sound teacher–pupil relationship.

The teacher's authority

An essential task involved in effective teaching is the need for a teacher to establish and maintain authority over the organisation and management of pupils' learning. Such authority can be established and maintained in a number of ways. How this is done will reflect the teacher's personality, character and general approach to teaching on the one hand, and the context (e.g. the type of pupils, subject matter, school ethos) on the other hand. In establishing and maintaining authority, the teacher needs to create a tone of purposefulness during lessons, as well as sustaining pupils' attention and motivation, and ensuring the appropriateness of the learning activities, so that his or her authority is in large measure taken for granted by the pupils. Basically, the teacher's authority needs to be based on effective teaching rather than on coercion. This is not to say that disciplinary techniques are not important in establishing authority. Rather, it is to stress that if the exercise of disciplinary techniques is used to control problems arising from poor teaching, such problems will persist and undermine the quality of the learning that will occur.

There are four main factors involved in establishing and maintaining authority:

- Status.
- Teaching competence.
- Exercising control over the classroom.
- Exercising control over discipline.

Whilst these sources are interrelated in some respects, they each make a separate and identifiable contribution to the teacher's authority.

Status

The teacher derives a certain amount of status from being a teacher and from the respect that teachers hold in the eyes of society as a whole, and in the eyes of their pupils' parents in particular. Pupils who come from homes where the child's relationship with parents and other adults has been sound and where a respect for teachers has been fostered, will often hold teachers in high esteem and unquestioningly accept their authority. Here, teachers will derive some status simply from being adults. Unfortunately, the converse is also true. Where pupils' homes have not fostered such respect for teachers and other adults, the teacher will derive little such benefit.

Within the context of the school, a teacher's status is linked with his or her position. Being a headteacher or head of department will confer additional status related to the pupils' perceptions of the teacher's seniority within the school. Pupils are aware that senior teachers can exercise more power and control and this will induce more compliant behaviour.

Robertson (1996) has drawn particular attention to the way in which teachers can use behaviour, which signifies their status to establish their authority. In effect, if one behaves like a person who has status, a degree of authority will be assumed. The key examples of how such status is conveyed through behaviour are:

- *By appearing to be relaxed and self-assured.* Tone of voice, facial expression, use of eye-contact and even posture, all serve to convey an impression of ease and self-assurance, as opposed to anxiety and uncertainty.

- *By exercising rights of status*. High-status individuals can typically move around freely in the territory of others, can initiate conversations and terminate them, and can touch others and others' property. In the classroom this is typified by teachers moving freely around the room and conversing with pupils. Such rights are denied to pupils except by explicit permission.

- *By communicating an expectation of imposing one's will*. The tone of delivery of instructions and control over who speaks and when, will all strongly imply an expectation that pupils have accepted the teacher's authority. The exercise of one's will is a key element in exercising status, and is exemplified by pupils fitting in with the teacher's intentions rather than vice versa. An example of this is the teacher not allowing the introduction of a lesson to be side-tracked by pupils requesting pens.

If one behaves as though one has authority, it is surprising how far this attitude exerts a momentum of its own, leading pupils to behave accordingly. A need to deal frequently with problems of discipline implicitly indicates a lack of authority. Effective teachers are adept at pre-empting misbehaviour so that it does not have to be 'dealt with'.

Exercising status is in a sense a game of bluff and counter-bluff. Effective teachers are able to take account of subtle signals and cues to know when a clash of wills with a pupil should be engaged in and when averted. The classroom is rich with such signals. For example, if, as the teacher moves around the room, a pupil remains slouched in his or her seat, a signal is being sent about how this pupil feels about the teacher's authority. If the teacher ignores this signal, some degree of authority is lost. Alternatively, a glance at the pupil with a raised eyebrow is likely to be sufficient for the pupil to sit up properly. If this is not sufficient, the teacher may move closer to the pupil, or may quietly ask the pupil if the work required is clear. Only if such low level signals are unsuccessful, need the teacher explicitly ask the pupil to sit up properly.

There are, however, potential dangers in exercising status, particularly regarding touching pupils and taking pupils' property. The need to know one's class well is thus of paramount importance in being able to judge how to exercise status and avoid unnecessary confrontations.

Teaching competence

There are three main elements involved in teaching competence that contribute to the teacher's authority:

- Subject knowledge.
- Interest in and enthusiasm for the subject.
- The ability to set up effective learning experiences.

Many pupils will accept the teacher's authority to manage and organise their learning, in part because they know that the teacher has expertise in the subject being taught. Indeed, it is interesting to note how often pupils will attempt to explore, through casual conversation with teachers, details of how they became teachers. Clearly, teachers who have difficulties with the academic tasks demanded by the subject may well find their authority undermined. In some respects, this may explain why teachers are often anxious about teaching in areas outside their own expertise, which inevitably arises with developments in the curriculum and its content, particularly if there is a risk that pupils will ask difficult questions. However, there is a danger in being too defensive about subject expertise, since there is also educational value for pupils to appreciate that teachers have more to learn too! Nevertheless, a reasonable degree of expertise is important if subject credibility is to be established.

Interest in and enthusiasm for the subject is a major contributor to establishing authority. Interest and enthusiasm is infectious and helps to create a climate within the classroom that emphasises the worthiness of the learning activities. However, it is important to stress that this interest and enthusiasm must be shared with pupils, not merely demonstrated in a way that pupils observe but find difficult to understand. Learning activities should be presented in a manner that will elicit pupils' interest and enthusiasm. Teachers should not simply hope that their own interest and enthusiasm is sufficient. At the other extreme, a lack of interest and enthusiasm not only acts as a poor model, but actually undermines the quality of presentation (e.g. through the teacher's tone of voice being harder to pay attention to). Each lesson requires a performance from the teacher which, at its best, will be fresh and authentic for the pupils. When the teacher asks a question, his or her tone of voice will communicate that the teacher is interested in the pupil's reply, and the reply will be listened to and taken account of. When the teacher monitors pupils' progress, his or her delight in good work and helpful concern for those having difficulties will sound genuine.

The ability to set up effective learning experiences is at the core of the teacher's ability to teach. If the teacher's exposition is hard to understand (either because it is spoken inaudibly or because the points are poorly made), if the work set is consistently too easy or too difficult, if the work set does not prepare the pupils properly for the learning they perceive is required, then they are likely to become frustrated and discouraged, and the teacher's authority will be at risk. The vast majority of teachers are more than adequately skilful in this respect, but it is important that they keep abreast of the changing nature of teaching and learning in schools, so that effective teaching can be sustained.

Each generation of pupils grows up in a new context of patterns of interacting with others and in dealing with information. For example, pupils are inevitably influenced by new technologies and changes in how adults interact with children outside school. Such influences will shape their expectations of how they expect to be taught in school. Teaching methods and content which were successful in the past, may not be acceptable now. The learning experiences set up by teachers now must be tailored to the needs of pupils as they exist now. Otherwise, there is a danger that school will be experienced as an unreal world with outdated activities. Feedback from pupils in the form of lack of interest and motivation provides schools with a continuing critique of the quality of the match between learning experiences and pupils' needs and expectations. Many curriculum developments, although advocated on educational grounds, are in a real sense a reaction to the fact that what they replaced simply was not working. Perhaps the clearest example of this is the move away from didactic teaching, where pupils are essentially passive, towards greater use of learning experiences where pupils are more active and have some control over the course of the learning taking place.

This aspect of teaching competence is thus not something a teacher achieves at one moment in his or her professional career and then maintains in that same form thereafter. Rather, it is an ever-changing requirement based on continuing professional development and critical reflection about one's own teaching.

One final important element in setting up effective learning experiences is the quality of corrective academic feedback pupils receive. Pupils are very sensitive to the speed and care with which teachers monitor and assess their educational progress. Written work that is carefully marked and quickly returned is not only effective in increasing pupils' understanding, but also in communicating to pupils the teacher's concern with their work. Similarly, giving helpful and constructive feedback during the lesson to pupils having difficulties and ensuring that those finding the work easy are extended, will enhance the pupils' perception of the teacher's competence in teaching.

Exercising control over the classroom

An important aspect of the teacher's authority is his or her control over classroom activities. In order to ensure that such activities do not lead to chaos and conflict, a number of rules and procedures need to be adopted. These are essential if the smooth running of teaching is not to be frequently interrupted. Smith and Laslett (1992) identified four key rules of classroom management as 'Get them in, get them out, get on with it, get on with them'!

Undoubtedly, how lessons are commenced and ended has major significance for establishing authority. It is an advantage for the teacher to be present when pupils arrive for a lesson, and to ensure that entry into the classroom is orderly and reasonably quiet. Squabbles over seating are often used as an opportunity to test out the teacher's authority and, as such, need to be dealt with quickly and firmly. It is also important for lessons to start quickly. Pupils should be dealt with effectively if they come late, so that they are not habitually late, and teachers should ensure that the start of the lesson is not delayed by matters that could easily be dealt with at some other time. Pupils' remarks at the start of a lesson are important in this respect. While it is part of good rapport between teacher and pupils for some social interchange to take place, the need for the teacher to quickly establish order and to start the lesson promptly, must take precedence. Indeed, pupils may often attempt to take the initiative in this respect by some social remark, and this may have to be ignored or dealt with quickly by the teacher if control is to be retained. Similarly, it is important for lessons to end on time (neither too early nor too late), and for pupils' exit from the classroom to be orderly and reasonably quiet. The simplest way to ensure this is by establishing a routine governing how pupils leave the room. The final few remarks made by a teacher at the end of a lesson are particularly telling. These remarks should be positive and refer to good work and what has been achieved and learnt, rather than negative and reflecting mutual relief from each other's company!

During the lesson itself, the teacher needs to effectively regulate classroom activities and teacher–pupil interaction, including the circumstances under which pupils can speak and move from their seats. This may sound authoritarian, but it merely reflects the need to have ground rules operating in any social situation where a large number of individuals interact. A number of studies have identified the type of classroom rules used by teachers, either explicitly set down by them or implicitly inferred by the way teachers deal with pupils. These typically include the following:

- No talking when the teacher is talking.
- No disruptive noises.
- Rules for entering, leaving and moving in classrooms.
- No interference with the work of others.
- Work must be completed in a specified way.
- Pupils must raise a hand to answer, not shout out.
- Pupils must make a positive effort in their work.

- Pupils must not challenge the authority of the teacher.
- Respect must be shown for property and equipment.
- Rules to do with safety.
- Pupils must ask if they do not understand.

A very interesting study conducted by Thornberg (2008) in Sweden looked at primary school pupils' views of school rules and identified five rule categories:

- *Relational rules:* how to behave towards others (e.g. don't tease others).
- *Structuring rules:* how to behave in a way that supports learning activities (e.g. put your hand up before you answer).
- *Protecting rules:* how to behave safely (e.g. don't run in corridors).
- *Personal rules:* how to reflect on one's own behaviour (e.g. think before you act).
- *Etiquette rules:* how to behave in line with social expectations (e.g. don't use bad language).

This study highlighted how school rules underpin the value system that operates within the school, and thereby forms an important part of the school's hidden curriculum. Thornberg argues that for school rules to have a positive impact on helping pupils to develop self-discipline, teachers need to enable pupils to understand the purpose of school rules, rather than attempt to foster a blind compliance.

Effective teaching is greatly facilitated if clear classroom rules are laid down and enforced, so that pupils act in accordance with them almost as second nature. A study by Kyriacou *et al.* (2007) of the views held by student teachers regarding effective strategies for dealing with pupil misbehaviour found that the student teachers viewed the establishment of classroom rules as one of the most effective strategies.

Establishing such rules clearly and consistently is an essential aspect of the teacher's authority. Pupils are very sensitive to the teacher's ability to establish such rules and will often test out how a teacher will cope with an infringement in order to clarify the rules and how they will be operated. In fact, almost every classroom activity has a potential for pupils to challenge the teacher's authority and control over their behaviour. Handing in or giving out books, moving furniture about, collecting equipment, closing a window and even sharpening a pencil, could all be done by pupils in a manner or at a time that tests the teacher's control. In all such cases, well-established norms and procedures will limit the scope for potential problems occurring. Unpredictable events, such as the appearance of a window cleaner, or a wasp flying about the room, can pose particular problems, although a touch of humour in such situations is often useful.

One major issue related to control concerns the level of classroom noise. The teacher must be able to establish silence before addressing the class, or when pupils are asked to speak. Having asked pupils to pay attention, it is important to wait momentarily for quiet before commencing the verbal exchange, so that no one has to speak loudly to be heard over a level of background noise. The level of background noise which occurs while pupils are working is a particularly sensitive issue for most teachers, in part because it may disrupt other pupils in the class and disturb neighbouring classes, but also because it is often taken to be indicative of a teacher's degree of control or lack of it. This sometimes leads teachers to be somewhat over-strict about noise levels. Some background noise reflecting cooperative talking or group work should not be inhibited by an unnecessary emphasis on low noise levels, but background noise should be kept to a reasonable level if concentration and a climate of purposefulness are to be sustained.

Finally, control over classroom activities requires vigilance. The teacher needs to continually monitor pupils' behaviour, as it is easier to regain control if one acts quickly rather than tackling undesirable behaviour that has been going on for some time. Vigilance is also required to ensure that rules and procedures are effective. For example, if pupils have to put up their hand to gain the teacher's attention, the teacher should be looking around periodically to notice this. Such vigilance is facilitated if the teacher stands centre-stage where the teacher and pupils can clearly see each other, whilst at the same time this helps to establish the teacher's presence.

Exercising control over discipline

Discipline refers to the maintenance of order and control necessary for effective learning. In essence, this involves pupils acting in accordance with the teacher's intentions for their behaviour, be it listening, talking or undertaking the academic work in hand. Unfortunately, most discussion of discipline tends to centre on overtly disruptive pupil behaviour such as noisy non-work-related talking, rowdy behaviour or insolence. Such discussion tends to imply that exercising control over discipline is solely concerned with how to deal with pupil misbehaviour. In fact, discipline is much more concerned with sound planning, presentation and monitoring of learning experiences, all of which enable the teacher to elicit and sustain the pupils' attention and motivation, thereby minimising the occurrence of misbehaviour. Clearly, however, the teacher does have to adopt a range of techniques for pre-empting and dealing with misbehaviour, and these will be outlined in the next chapter.

In terms of the teacher's authority, the central issue of concern here is the contribution that control over discipline makes to such authority. It has been argued thus far that the teacher's authority derives in large measure from status, teaching competence and the ability to exercise control over the classroom. Periodically, however, teachers need to impose their will over pupils in the face of opposition. Success in such a clash of wills lies at the core of exercising control over discipline. Such a clash of wills is manifest in the case of overt disruptive behaviour. However, it also occurs less overtly, whenever a pupil fails to pay attention, or apply adequate effort to the work in hand. The teacher needs to exercise control over discipline whenever the teacher's intentions are being opposed or frustrated by pupils in some way, either overtly or covertly. Examples of such covert opposition will include what might appear to be quite trivial problems, such as pupils trying to engage the teacher in social conversation when the teacher is anxious to start the lesson promptly, or expressing reluctance to make a contribution when the teacher is trying to promote classroom discussion. Such covert disruptive behaviour can have a subversive quality about it, in that they are not overt acts of misbehaviour, but they do prevent or interfere with the smooth progress of the lesson. Indeed, it is the need to continually monitor pupils' work, encourage those pupils with poor attitudes towards work, and deal with such low-level inferences, which makes the task of teaching so demanding.

Exercising control over discipline concerns those actions that teachers take to impose their will in such circumstances. Such actions can be categorised into two main groups. The first group consists of *task-oriented actions*, which the teacher can take during the lesson regarding the learning experience that will re-establish pupils' attention, motivation and ability to meet the academic demands in hand. Such actions might include introducing an interesting anecdote or application of the topic, moving on to a different type of activity such as oral work or a written task, and giving individual help. The second group consists of *power-oriented actions* where the teacher exercises power in a dominant manner, such as using coercion, threats, intimidation, reprimands and punishments. A firm raised voice, together with an imperative command such as 'get on with your work', 'pay attention', 'get back to your seat now', together with an assertive tone, posture and facial expression, are typical of such actions.

It is argued here that task-oriented actions are more important for effective teaching *per se*, but there are inevitably circumstances where power-oriented actions come into play. What is essential is that the teacher is able to distinguish which type of action is more appropriate for a particular set of circumstances. The major danger is to rely on power-oriented actions, when problems stem essentially from ineffective teaching. Effective teaching must win the hearts and minds of pupils if the learning experience is to involve intrinsic motivation, curiosity, interest and a proper educational engagement. Such a state cannot be achieved if the teacher's authority rests heavily on the exercise of power. Indeed, teachers frequently express dissatisfaction with aspects of the school curriculum that seem to have little relevance to pupils' interests, needs or lives, precisely because they have to frequently exercise power to maintain progress. Teachers, and schools, are thus continually striving to develop a curriculum, both in terms of content and teaching methods, which requires more task-oriented and less power-oriented control to support progress.

The frequency and extent to which the teacher exercises power in a dominant manner is a major issue in a consideration of how best to establish authority in the classroom. On the one hand, if this is excessive, it will almost certainly undermine the mutual respect and rapport necessary for sound teacher–pupil relationships and may contribute to an expectation that pupils need to be coerced into working at all times. On the other hand, a teacher who frequently ignores taking action whenever a clash of wills occurs will soon find that discipline is undermined. Clearly, a balance of action between these two extremes is required. If disruptive behaviour occurs frequently and is widespread, it is clear that the teacher has failed to establish their authority. Effort spent in carefully monitoring pupils and skilfully exercising control over discipline will thus pay handsome dividends in contributing to effective teaching.

Mutual respect and rapport

The importance of mutual respect and rapport between teacher and pupils cannot be over-estimated. In their consideration of 'good teachers' Ofsted regularly make reference to the importance of teachers commanding the respect of their pupils, not only by their ability to teach well, but also by the respect they show for pupils, and their genuine interest and curiosity about what pupils say, leading to a two-way passage of liking and respect in which pupils can flourish (e.g. Ofsted, 2007).

In our consideration of the teacher's authority, it was noted that such authority derives from four main sources: status, teaching competence, exercising control over the classroom, and exercising control over discipline. The skill of the teacher in each of these four areas will of itself help earn the pupils' respect, or, if inadequate, contribute to undermining such respect. Studies of pupils' views of teachers and teaching (e.g. Cullingford, 2003; Haydn, 2007; Pollard *et al.*, 2000; Rudduck and McIntyre, 2007) show that pupils have clear ideas about the teacher's role and the demands and expectations they have of a teacher who is fulfilling that role effectively.

For example, a study by Rudduck and McInytyre (2007) of pupils' views of teachers, teaching and teacher–pupil relationships grouped pupils' views of good teachers in terms of four central assertions:

- Good teachers are human, accessible, reliable and consistent.
- Good teachers are respectful of pupils and sensitive to their difficulties.
- Good teachers are positive and enthusiastic.
- Good teachers are professionally skilled.

In their analysis of teacher–pupil relationships, Rudduck and McIntyre noted that as well as recognising the importance of 'mutual respect', pupils also recognised the importance of 'mutual trust'.

Much pupil misbehaviour is often simply a reaction to ineffective teaching or to behaviour by the teacher that is felt to be unfair, which serves to undermine their respect for the teacher. However, teachers who are reported to be 'firm but fair' (can keep order without being too strict, are consistent, and have no favourites) and can teach well (can explain clearly, give help, are patient and friendly, and make lessons interesting), are generally well liked by pupils.

Effectively establishing one's authority, therefore, can do much to earn respect from pupils. However, it is essential that the manner in which the teacher attempts to establish such authority does not undermine the development of good rapport. Good rapport between the teacher and pupils refers to their having a harmonious understanding of each other as individuals and is based on mutual respect and esteem. Behaviour by a teacher which indicates that he or she has little respect or esteem for pupils will inevitably undermine the development of good rapport.

The development of good rapport is based on three qualities in the teacher's interaction with pupils:

- The teacher shows genuine care for each pupil's progress.
- The teacher shows respect for pupils as learners.
- The teacher shows respect for pupils as individuals.

Caring for pupils' progress shows itself in a number of ways. First, in a concern to tailor the learning experiences as accurately as possible to meet the pupils' needs and level of understanding. Second, by carefully monitoring pupils' understanding and progress, identifying difficulties, and giving additional help (either individually or to the class as a whole) in a constructive, helpful, supportive and patient manner. Third, by the care and attention given in preparing lessons and in marking work. Fourth, by dealing with a lack of progress in a concerned manner, which emphasises both a belief in the importance of the pupil doing better, and a belief that the pupil is capable of doing better. Fifth, by giving praise and valuing good work and achievements.

Respect for pupils as learners requires setting up learning experiences where the views and opinions of pupils can be heard, developed and elaborated, and where the pupils are given a large measure of control in shaping and carrying out learning activities. A more active role for pupils (often called 'active learning') not only makes sense in terms of effective learning, but is extremely important in fostering pupils' self-esteem regarding themselves as learners and helping them develop and practise those skills, both practical and intellectual, which are required in exercising control over a learning activity. Of course, this will inevitably result in time apparently being wasted as pupils begin to develop these skills and make mistakes or poor judgements. In addition, less is likely to be covered than would be the case where teacher control over the activity was tight and more didactic. However, the broad educational benefits of an active learning role for pupils make this well worthwhile.

Respect for pupils as learners lies at the heart of the hidden curriculum operating in the classroom. The interaction that takes place between teacher and pupils during the lesson communicates their respective perceptions of each other's role. As well as the overt message of what is said, the way the teacher responds to pupils' answers to questions, whether pupils can initiate questions, and whether the teacher exerts unequivocal control over the learning experiences, all serve to indicate to pupils hidden messages about knowledge (e.g. all knowledge resides in the teacher versus knowledge is gained by exploration of learning activities), about the pupil's role as learner (e.g. active and enquiring versus passive and receptive), and about the status of pupils' knowledge, views and experience (e.g. pupils have knowledge, views and experience worthy of attention and consideration versus such knowledge needs to be tightly constrained, directed, modified and controlled by the teacher before it is of value). Such hidden messages have a fundamental influence on the classroom climate that develops, and this will be explored later in this chapter.

Of the three qualities being considered here, respect for pupils as individuals is perhaps the most important contributor to good rapport. Such respect involves an interest in pupils' lives, both within school (outside the subject area of the teacher) and outside the school. In effect, the teacher needs to get to know the pupils as individuals. At the outset, this certainly involves learning their names as quickly as possible. Opportunities for social conversation at the beginning or end of lessons, in the corridor, during registration periods, and through extra-curricular activities, enable the teacher to get to know pupils in a more personal context. Such remarks as 'anyone go to the match on Saturday?', 'I enjoyed your performance in the school concert', 'Saw you in town last night', are all indicators of good rapport. Such exchanges also need to be a two-way process, with the teacher as an equal, freely mentioning his or her own interests and activities relating to the exchange. Of course, pupils may take advantage of such personal interaction to either ask deliberately embarrassing questions or to adopt a disrespectful attitude towards the exchange. However, if the teacher's authority is well established and secure, such exchanges serve to enhance and develop mutual respect and rapport rather than to undermine such authority.

A study by Pye (1988) gives evidence of how much pupils valued teachers who seemed to treat them as individual persons during lessons. What is interesting about such teachers is that almost all the pupils in the class come to feel that their individuality had been recognised, and that the teacher acknowledged each of them. It is not a case of the teacher having a selected few favourites who are treated in a special way.

At this point it is important to acknowledge that friendly relationships between teacher and pupils need to be treated with caution. The development of good rapport needs to be kept separate, to some extent, from the teacher's role in effective teaching. When teaching, the teacher must continue to periodically exert control over classroom activities and discipline in order to maintain an effective learning environment. This inevitably requires teachers to be able to quickly distance themselves when needing to exercise such authority. Certain conventions are employed by some teachers to facilitate such distancing. The most widespread example of such a convention is that teachers must be addressed as 'Sir' or 'Miss' and not by the first names.

In addition, teachers need to be sensitive to the strong affection for them that some pupils may develop. In the primary school, this may involve teachers being regarded as a parent and pupils may sometimes inadvertently call the teacher 'Mum' or 'Dad'. In the secondary school years, however, a particular problem may arise concerning sexual attraction and fantasies. For this reason, teachers need to be careful about using ambiguous cues signalling sexual intimacy, particularly touching in an affectionate manner. In general, especially during the adolescent years, unnecessary touching is best avoided, despite the fact that some teachers can develop excellent rapport based on a strong 'parental' relationship.

Teaching in inner-city schools serving areas of social disadvantage can be particularly demanding. A number of studies have looked at the qualities of effective teaching in schools containing a high proportion of potentially difficult pupils, and found that the most successful teachers were not authoritarian pedagogues, but rather were very skilful at developing good rapport with pupils. Such teachers often held pastoral care posts within the school. This overlap between the qualities involved in effective teaching and in pastoral care activities is an important one. Effective teachers are also often regarded by pupils as being approachable, which is a key quality of good pastoral care. The role of pastoral care will be considered later in this chapter.

Classroom climate

From the discussion so far in this chapter it is clear that teacher–pupil interaction during the lesson involves a very rich flow of information concerning their perceptions, expectations, attitudes and feelings about each other and the learning activities in hand. The notion of classroom climate draws explicit attention to the emotional tone and atmosphere of the lesson, and how this is shaped by teacher and pupil perceptions.

An effective classroom climate is one in which the teacher's authority to organise and manage their learning activities is accepted by the pupils, there is mutual respect and good rapport, and the atmosphere is one of purposefulness and confidence in learning (Campbell *et al.*, 2004; Watkins, 2005). In discussing classroom climate here, attention will be paid to the ways in which the teacher's behaviour may facilitate or undermine the establishing of an effective classroom climate. A key consideration is the extent to which the teacher is able to foster favourable perceptions towards learning among pupils, most notably by establishing in pupils self-respect and self-esteem regarding themselves as learners.

A study by Kunter *et al.* (2007) looked at the impact that classroom management can have on pupils' interest in the subject being taught. This study looked at two particular aspects of classroom management: rule clarity and monitoring. They reported that pupils who felt closely monitored by their teachers and who perceived that the rules set in the classroom were transparent tended to become more interested in the subject. Kunter *et al.* argue that this effect appears to have come because a well-managed class promotes pupils' feelings of success and competence.

The writings of Carl Rogers have been particularly inspirational in advocating how a humanistic classroom climate can facilitate learning (see Rogers and Freiberg, 1994). The *humanistic approach* to teaching and learning can be summarised in terms of four main principles:

- An emphasis on the 'whole person' (a holistic of mind, body and feelings).
- An emphasis on personal growth (the tendency of moving towards higher levels of health, creativity and self-fulfilment).
- An emphasis on the person's awareness (the person's subjective view about themselves and the world).
- An emphasis on personal agency (the power of choice and responsibility).

A humanistic classroom climate will be in large measure based on the teacher display-ing a positive regard for pupils and giving them marked control over their learning through the use of active learning.

A study by Kyriacou and Cheng (1993) asked 109 student teachers at the beginning of their teacher training course to rate the strength of their agreement with 20 statements regarding the humanistic approach to teaching and learning. A sample of the student teachers were interviewed later in the year after they had completed a block of teaching practice in schools. The study reported that the vast majority of the student teachers agreed with the humanistic approach, but that those interviewed after their teaching practice said they had found it hard to put these qualities into practice. For example, they found it difficult to maintain a positive regard towards all their pupils and also to allow pupils a marked degree of control over their learning activities. These findings accord with other studies indicating that most teachers hold such humanistic views as 'ideals' but feel that the constraints and realities of classroom life and pupils' attitudes often make it difficult to sustain these in practice. Despite these difficulties, the class-room climate in schools has become much more humanistic in its tone over the years.

A major influence of the classroom climate is the physical appearance and layout of the classroom itself. The move towards more informal teaching styles in schools has had a marked impact on this, particularly in primary schools. The increased emphasis on an active role for pupils through discovery and exploratory learning and group work shows itself in the use of different activity areas within the classroom, the use of tables set up for group work rather than for individuals sitting in rows, and relatively free access for movement to and from resource areas. In addition, the use of wall displays of pupils' work contributes to a positive atmosphere indicating pride and esteem in the work produced in lessons.

Without doubt, the most important aspect of classroom climate is the hidden curricu-lum and how the teachers' expectations and behaviour convey this. What is particularly interesting about the hidden curriculum is the extent to which much of the information signalled to pupils may be unintended by the teacher, and may indeed serve to under-mine the effectiveness of the teaching. Particular attention in this respect has been paid to the use of language. Who says what, when and how, lies at the heart of the hidden curriculum. In terms of classroom climate, the use of 'spoken' language by teachers and pupils has received the greatest attention. It has been widely observed that the classroom tends to be dominated by teacher talk. When pupils are allowed to speak, it tends to be in a context highly constrained by the teacher, such as in answer to ques-tions. Comments and observations by pupils tend to be drawn back into the line the teacher has envisaged for the dialogue. This not only fails to foster pupils' language skills, but also tends to undermine their self-esteem as learners.

A number of studies of classroom discourse has illustrated clearly how teachers chan-nelled pupils' contributions along pre-determined lines, which resulted in pupils' com-ments being rejected as unacceptable or incorrect, not because the pupils' comments did not make sense, but because they did not fit closely enough to the teacher's require-ments (Mercer and Sams, 2006; Myhill et al., 2006). From the pupils' perspective, the overriding message was that their contributions needed to match what the teacher wanted. Hence, pupils are led to search for clues to the right answers required, rather than to genuinely enter into intellectual dialogue with the teacher. Barnes also noted that teachers seemed to place undue emphasis on pupils using the correct terminology in their contributions, rather than to the intellectual quality per se of what they were saying. As such, much attention is now given to ways in which teachers can make more effective use of oral work in the classroom to encourage pupil involvement and critical thinking (e.g. Mercer and Sams, 2006; Myhill *et al.*, 2006).

Effective teaching thus requires that the teacher gives pupils plenty of opportunities to contribute and elaborate their own ideas, and that he or she genuinely listens to what pupils say (or are trying to say), and attempts to consider this from the pupils' perspective. To some extent this means that the teacher needs to accept the value of each pupil's contribution and the relevance of the pupil's experience. Of course, if carried to extremes, such a policy would pose difficulties and would undermine realistic feedback. What is being argued here is the need to maintain a balance between teacher talk and pupil talk, which is less markedly weighted in favour of the teacher than is typically the case. Fortunately, the trend in many schools over the years has been towards this more desirable state of balance.

A particularly difficult issue concerning pupils' language is the teacher's response to strong regional and ethnic accents and dialects. On the one hand, it is important for all pupils to be accepted as they are. On the other hand, there is also a need for all pupils to be able to communicate acceptably in Standard English. To some extent, the 'more correct' speech of teachers in schools may contribute to some pupils viewing school as an alien environment. There is no easy solution to this problem. However, attempts have been made, most often in English lessons, to look at such differences in speech with a view to recognising these as different rather than as intrinsically inferior to Standard English. The most important point is that an undue emphasis on correct speech should not be allowed to inhibit and restrict pupils elaborating on their own ideas. Somehow, a balance of concerns needs to be maintained here.

A very important aspect of classroom climate derives from the choice of words a teacher uses in his or her communication with pupils. Every utterance that a teacher makes during a lesson involves a choice of words. The particular choice made will convey a clear message to pupils, over and above its actual content, concerning the teacher's underlying feelings and expectations. This is particularly evident in how teachers react to pupils' incorrect contributions and how they reprimand misbehaviour. In both these contexts, it is important that the teacher comments on the contribution or behaviour rather than on the pupil. This indicates that it is these rather than the pupil that are at fault. For example, saying 'I might have known you would not have the right answer,' or 'You are an insulting little boy,' are in effect 'character attacks', which are best avoided. Dealing with the nature of the answer or misbehaviour itself, without reference to the pupil's character, is much less likely to undermine mutual respect and rapport. The key rule here is to try to criticise the behaviour rather than the person.

Another important aspect of classroom climate is the way in which the teacher's choice of words may contribute to the effects of *labelling* pupils. Labelling refers to the process by which pupils come to see themselves and act more in accordance with the labels that teachers typically use to describe them. As well as overt examples of such labelling, for example when a pupil is described as 'thick' or a 'trouble maker', there are also covert examples, such as when a pupil is never invited to make a contribution to class discussion or expected to do better. Labelling also arises from organisational characteristics of the school. For example, being in a low set appears to foster underachievement through its effects on pupils' attitudes and self-esteem. Overall, it would appear that teacher labelling does have an influence on pupils, but it is extremely difficult to separate out the influence of the teacher's behaviour on the pupil from that of the pupil's behaviour on the teacher.

The crucial question for effective teaching is to what extent a teacher's avoidance of negative labelling behaviour in the classroom can mitigate against the gradual erosion of low-attaining pupils' attitudes towards themselves as learners. In a school with an ethos of concern for attainment based on comparisons between pupils, the teacher has an uphill struggle. In a school adopting more pupil-centred teaching, emphasising the process of learning rather than merely products, and where attainment is based on individual progress rather than comparisons with age-norms, the teacher has much more opportunity to mitigate such effects.

It also needs to be noted that learning is an emotionally charged and high-risk activity for pupils. When they encounter difficulties, it is all too easy for this to undermine their self-esteem and attitudes towards making an effort in future. As such, an important aspect of an effective classroom climate is that is provides continual support and encouragement for pupils when they encounter difficulties and make mistakes.

Written comments by teachers are also important in the same way. Here too, a code seems to operate whereby more is signalled by the comments than is apparent at its face value. Marking pupils' work involves more than assessment. It also involves giving pupils feedback about how their work could have been improved. Comments such as 'hopeless' or 'inadequate' are likely only to discourage, whereas positive guidance such as 'this essay would have been better if more material had been covered' or 'always calculate the length of the sides first' is more helpful to pupils. An important aspect of classroom climate is the standard of work expected by the teacher. There is, however, a problem if the standard is set so high that most pupils experience prolonged failure (in the form of low marks). On the other hand, too low a standard of expectation may create a false sense of progress, so that the pupil is shocked to find that after a year of apparent success they are likely to gain a low attainment grade. In this respect, comments made in school reports are of particular interest, both in terms of their typical ambiguity regarding progress and of the meaning to be attached to various phrases commonly used, such as 'could do better'.

It is interesting to note here that a study by Rubie-Davies (2007), which compared the classroom practices of teachers categorised as having high expectations compared with teachers categorised as having low expectations, reported that teachers with high expectations spent more time providing a framework for their pupils' learning, provided their pupils with more feedback, questioned their pupils using more higher-order questions, and managed their pupils' behaviour more positively. In effect, it appears that teachers with high expectations are purposively more committed through their teaching to creating a classroom climate within which pupils may make greater progress.

Generally speaking, the most effective classrooms appear to be those in which the atmosphere is task-oriented but where at the same time the social and emotional needs of the pupils are met by establishing mutual respect and good rapport. There is clearly an overlap between the notion of classroom climate and school climate, which have implications for and links with each other. Studies of the ways in which the school climate influences pupil learning have typically shown that it is far easier to be an effective teacher in some schools than in others. The overall ethos of the school draws on the expectations and norms of teachers and pupils at the school. A positive school ethos can provide a large measure of support that facilitates effective teaching, in which positive expectations towards working well are mutually reinforcing among both teachers and pupils. Conversely, a negative school climate acts as a barrier for effective teaching and for pupil motivation. Such studies have shown that certain features of school organisation and management, such as effective leadership from the head-teacher, can have a marked impact on establishing a positive school climate, even in schools serving very disadvantaged communities.

Indeed, a report by Ofsted (2008a) looked at a sample of schools that had been judged to be performing below an acceptable standard and placed in 'special measures', and which had subsequently improved and sustained that improvement. The report identified a number of key factors involved in bringing about this improvement. One of the key factors was strong leadership by the headteacher in establishing productive working relationships between teachers and pupils in the classroom based on mutual respect, and establishing among pupils a greater engagement in school life, thereby enhancing their identity and sense of belonging. An important aspect of this involved improving teachers' skills in dealing with challenging behaviour in order to stabilise pupils' behaviour and create a calm classroom climate.

Pastoral care

Over the years increasing attention has been paid to the importance of pastoral care in schools (Crow, 2008; Wortley and Harrison, 2008). The interface between academic teaching and pastoral care roles of schools has been markedly enhanced by the introduction of the *Every Child Matters* agenda (Cheminais, 2006; DfES, 2004a), which views pupil performance and pupil wellbeing as going hand in hand, and identifies five outcomes for children:

- *Being healthy:* helping pupils to adopt healthy lifestyles, build their self-esteem, eat and drink well and lead active lives.
- *Staying safe:* keeping pupils safe from bullying, harassment and other dangers.
- *Enjoying and achieving:* enabling pupils to make good progress in their work and personal development and enjoy their education.
- *Making a positive contribution:* ensuring that pupils understand their rights and responsibilities, are listened to, and participate in the life of the community.
- *Achieving social and economic wellbeing:* helping pupils to gain the skills and knowledge needed for future employment.

In essence, pastoral care focuses on the concern for the individual wellbeing of each pupil. This concern attempts to ensure that each pupil is able to take advantage of what schools have to offer, and involves four main aspects of schooling:

- Academic progress.
- General behaviour and attitudes.
- Personal and social development.
- Individual needs.

In most secondary schools, the pastoral care system is usually formalised in terms of a house system or year-group system with tutor or form groups, where individual teachers (ranging from the head of house or year to the form tutor) are given particular pastoral care roles and responsibilities. In addition, other members of staff, including the headteacher, deputy heads, and classroom teachers, will also be involved in pastoral care responsibilities. Most primary schools use less formalised systems, but still need to cater for the same range of concerns and needs.

Concern with academic progress involves rewarding success as well as exploring the reasons for marked underachievement. In some schools, subject choice and vocational guidance are also included within the responsibility of the pastoral staff. General attitudes and behaviour, particularly misbehaviour in lessons, may be referred to the pastoral care staff if particular guidance and counselling, or contact with parents is felt to be appropriate. The fact that the same teacher may have to fulfil both a classroom teaching role and a pastoral care role can sometimes produce tensions, such as when the teacher is torn between trying to exert firm discipline and showing a sympathetic understanding of a pupil's worries.

The concern with personal and social development has led to the development of a pastoral curriculum, or personal, social and health education (PSHE) programme, within schools. This refers to those learning experiences set up within the school that aim to foster personal and social development, often explicitly linked to pastoral care. Such teaching can include almost anything that has a pastoral connection: moral education, religious education, life and social skills teaching, sex education, and study skills. In many schools the PSHE programme is delivered during extended registration periods, whilst in other schools it is treated as a separately timetabled subject area. Such programmes often make particularly heavy use of active learning and include innovative forms of teaching, which can gradually permeate into the teaching of traditional subject areas.

The nature, content and purpose of the PSHE programme in schools is a fast-moving field, in part because it is seen to be the part of the school curriculum that can respond most rapidly to major concerns 'of the day' regarding pupil welfare and preparation for adult life. One major benefit for teachers of web-based resources, is that major initiatives within the PSHE programme for schools are now typically accompanied by designated websites, together with downloadable resources. For example, the initiative on 'Social and Emotional Aspects of Learning' (SEAL), which aims to promote 'the social and emotional skills that underpin effective learning, positive behaviour, regular attendance, staff effectiveness and the emotional health and wellbeing of all who learn and work in schools' (DCSF, 2007b), is accompanied by teaching resources to support five social and emotional aspects of pupils' learning: self-awareness, managing feelings, motivation, empathy and social skills. In addition, 'personal wellbeing' is one of three non-statutory programmes of study (alongside 'religious education' and 'economic wellbeing and financial capability') in the secondary school curriculum from September 2008 (QCA, 2007). Crow (2008) has argued that there is now a 'wellbeing imperative' in schools, where pupil wellbeing is seen to be a critical partner in raising standards and achievement. Crow argues that successfully linking the school's pastoral care systems with the effective teaching of PSHE is increasingly being viewed as a crucial aspect of school effectiveness.

A concern with individual needs involves a consideration of personal problems threatening the pupil's wellbeing in some serious way. These may include extremes of poor attainment and disruptive behaviour, as well as other problems, such as juvenile delinquency, truancy, physical illness, incest, emotional disturbance and being bullied (Kyriacou, 2003).

Given the range of concerns involved in pastoral care together with the fact that these are discharged by both teachers designated as pastoral staff and by others discharging a pastoral duty within some other context, an adequate description of the pastoral care system within a particular school will inevitably be complex. Indeed, there are also many areas of activity, such as the delivery of special educational needs and the development of record of achievement documents, which have served to blur the distinction between pastoral care activities and other aspects of school life.

In the context of effective teaching, it is worth noting that effective teaching is in itself the highest form of pastoral care, since it stems from a duty of care by the teacher for the pupil's educational progress. Effective teaching conveys a message to pupils that their progress is important and worthwhile, and that time and effort has been devoted to making the teaching effective in order to achieve this. In part, this also explains why pupils find ineffective teaching 'hurtful', because it contains a covert message that they are not worthy of being taught effectively.

One of the problems with the way in which pastoral care operates in many schools, is that the dominant academic ethos of the school places major constraints on what pastoral care staff can do to help meet the needs of the less able and the more disadvantaged pupils. By and large, pastoral care staff are heavily constrained to support the *status quo* of school life, by encouraging such pupils to accept their relative failure and to not protest in the face of either boring teaching or a curriculum that seems to have little relevance to their lives, no matter how much they may sympathise with pupils' feelings regarding these. For such pupils, school is almost like a prison sentence, in which they look forward to their day of release. In an ideal world, schools would be flexible enough and well-resourced enough to ensure that they offered something to everyone. However, the dominant academic ethos in school ensures that some pupils will want to react against school life, and the main role of pastoral staff will be to encourage such pupils to conform to this ethos as it is ultimately in their own best interests to do so.

There are many ways in which pastoral care may support effective teaching. The most important of these is in giving pupils a feeling that the school cares about their educational progress and wellbeing on a one-to-one basis. The pastoral care system adopted in a school should ensure that this message is conveyed to each pupil whenever appropriate. General comments to groups of pupils in, for example, school assemblies or form group meetings, are important, but the message must also be reinforced on an individual basis at moments of crisis and when particular problems arise. In the primary school, the class teacher will almost certainly discharge this pastoral responsibility. In the secondary school, with its typically formalised system of pastoral care, a number of teachers may act in this way.

Indeed, in secondary schools a particularly important function of the pastoral care system is that of coordinating information about a pupil that crosses subject boundaries and involves other agencies. This enables the pastoral staff to build up a much fuller picture of each pupil's progress, as well as possible problems, than the individual class teacher can have, which makes it possible to plan a more effective strategy to meet that pupil's needs.

The crucial features of effective teaching lie in the learning experiences set up by the teacher and the type of learning outcomes desired. In the past, pastoral care was largely distinguished from the explicitly academic and instructional aspects of classroom teaching in normal circumstances. However, this distinction has become increasingly blurred, with pastoral care staff playing an active role in offering advice to colleagues in terms of how their classroom practices can be developed to combat pupil disaffection. This healthy dialogue between staff at school lies at the heart of many important curriculum innovations that have attempted to better prepare pupils to meet the academic demands made on them.

The role of pastoral care in dealing with pupil misbehaviour has been highlighted in many studies. One of the main advantages of teachers having an identifiable pastoral care role within the school is that it can offer pupils an opportunity to outline their worries and concerns to someone other than their normal class teachers. The pastoral care staff can then sometimes take a fresh and more detached view of the pupil's perspective, which can then form a basis for planning how best to deal with the situation. Unfortunately, in some schools, pastoral care staff are often used as 'trouble shooters' who act as discipline specialists and who see their prime task as exerting discipline in an effort to support class teachers. Whilst it is important that pastoral care staff are supportive of colleagues, it is better on the whole for them to retain a sympathetic counselling role on behalf of the pupils referred to them, so they can broker a positive outcome to deal with the pupil's problems, which meets the needs of the pupil whilst not undermining the complaints of the normal class teachers.

What is extremely important here is that when a class teacher encounters discipline problems, these should not be seen as needing to be referred automatically to a more senior colleague, nor be seen as a matter for pastoral care staff. In the first instance, all teachers have a pastoral care role and it is part of effective teaching that teachers can develop their relationship with pupils to include both an instructional role and a pastoral role. Indeed, studies of pupils excluded from schools for misbehaviour indicate that exclusion rates are far lower in schools where the class teacher exerts a pastoral concern in dealing with difficult pupils and is supported by the school to cope with such problems at the class level compared with schools where class teachers quickly refer difficult pupils to more senior teachers to deal with (Kyriacou, 2003; Vulliamy and Webb, 2003).

Another important aspect of pastoral care is to specifically combat the development of groups of pupils within the school creating an anti-school subculture. As well as using counselling to encourage pupils to develop positive attitudes towards schooling, pastoral staff can also act to break up such groups by moving key pupils within the group to different forms and classes. Indeed, one argument in favour of mixed-ability class groupings is that they help undermine the development of such anti-school peer groups. Success here appears to lie not only in breaking up such a group, but also in the fact that mixed-ability groups mean that teachers and pupils are less likely to form stereotyped views about the class and its status than when the class is in sets or streamed.

Finally, attention needs to be paid to the way in which pastoral care can help deal with pupils' worries and anxieties, ranging from worries about their academic worth and progress, to coping with the demands of school life in general. Particular worries occur when starting a new school and most schools certainly do a lot to make sure this is much less traumatic than it was in the past. Another area where attention has been paid is that of helping pupils to organise themselves better to cope with coursework deadlines and examination stress. Other pupil worries and anxieties may be the result of reactions to crises at home, such as the death of a parent or marital disharmony, or may be school-based, such as being bullied. Teachers need to be continually sensitive to problems arising from such worries, and in this respect the class teacher and form teacher are in a key position to identify a possible cause for concern. Part of the importance of a sound teacher–pupil relationship is that it allows teachers to get a sense of any changes in the pupil's behaviour that may be attributable to an acute worry of some sort.

Summary

In the discussion here of teacher–pupil relationships, it is apparent that such relationships underpin a number of different activities and situations arising in the school. The challenge facing teachers is to establish and sustain the appropriate type of relationship for the particular activity and situation, whether it be the need to exert authority, guiding a pupil with a learning difficulty, or counselling a pupil with a personal problem. The most important quality of such relationships advocated here is that of mutual respect and good rapport. From the discussion of classroom climate and pastoral care, it will be evident that sound teacher–pupil relationships lie at the heart of effective teaching.

Discussion questions

1 How should teachers establish their authority in the classroom?
2 What would be a reasonable set of classroom rules that pupils should be expected to follow?
3 What role should mutual respect and rapport play in teacher–pupil relationships?
4 What are the key features of a positive classroom climate?
5 How does the teacher's use of language influence pupils?
6 How should a teacher's pastoral care role influence their relationship with pupils?

Further reading

Campbell, J., Kyriakides, L., Muijs, D. and Robinson, W. (2004). *Assessing Teacher Effectiveness: Developing a Differentiated Model*. London: RoutledgeFalmer. This book identifies the values held by teachers regarding teaching and learning and how these values impact on the type of classroom climate they seek to establish.

Chaplain, R. P. (2003). *Teaching Without Disruption in the Primary School: A Model for Managing Pupil Behaviour*. London: RoutledgeFalmer. This book looks at how teachers can develop a positive classroom climate. A companion version of this book focuses on secondary schools.

Kyriacou, C. (2003). *Helping Troubled Pupils*. Cheltenham: Nelson Thornes. An analysis of seven adverse circumstances (bullying, truancy, exclusion, stress, abuse, bereavement and delinquency) and the role that teachers can play in helping pupils cope with the situation they find themselves in.

Rudduck, J. and McIntyre, D. (2007). *Improving Learning through Consulting Pupils*. London: Routledge. An insightful analysis of how pupils view teachers, teaching and teacher–pupil relationships, which informs how effective teaching can take account of pupils' views.

Watkins, C. (2005). *Classrooms as Learning Communities: What's in it for Schools?* London: RoutledgeFalmer. A readable overview of the teaching skills involved in eliciting and sustaining a high level of pupil engagement and a sense of belonging.

8 Dealing with pupil misbehaviour

Objective

To consider how teachers can deal effectively with pupil misbehaviour.

The dominant theme of this book has been the importance of ensuring that the learning experience set up by teachers is effective in terms of maintaining pupils' attentiveness and receptiveness and in terms of being appropriate for the learning outcomes intended. This, along with sound teacher–pupil relationships (as outlined in the previous chapter), can do much to minimise pupil misbehaviour. It cannot be stressed too strongly, that the first concern of a teacher faced with frequent pupil misbehaviour must be to take stock of his or her teaching, rather than to seek to establish discipline and control by recourse to the frequent administration of reprimands and punishments.

Of course, all teachers, no matter how effective, will need to deal with pupil misbehaviour from time to time. Being able to deal with such misbehaviour is extremely important in complementing their ability to set up and sustain effective learning experiences. If the techniques and skills involved in dealing with pupil misbehaviour are not coupled with effective learning experiences, they will, at best, serve only as damage limitation exercises, aimed at establishing some sort of truce between teacher coercion and pupil resistance. At worst, there will be no truce, but a continuing saga of friction, hostility, frustration and mutual resentment.

A great deal has been written about dealing with pupil misbehaviour, ranging from practical advice given by experienced practitioners to sophisticated research studies (e.g. Cowley, 2006; Evertson and Weinstein, 2006; Rogers, 2006). Such writing generally stresses the importance of:

- sound preparation and presentation
- good teacher–pupil relationships
- good classroom teaching skills
- pre-empting misbehaviour before it starts
- avoiding confrontations
- making sure any punishments are in line with school policy.

What is noteworthy here is that experienced teachers recognise that the key to success is not how you deal with misbehaviour but rather how you prevent misbehaviour occurring to start with. Perhaps the single most important piece of advice concerning a discipline problem is 'Try to think out *why* the problem arose in the first place'.

The nature and causes of pupil misbehaviour

Pupil misbehaviour refers to any behaviour by a pupil that undermines the teacher's ability to establish and maintain effective learning experiences in the classroom. In a very important sense, pupil misbehaviour lies in the eyes of the beholder and each teacher will have his or her own idea of what constitutes misbehaviour. While there is a large consensus among teachers regarding some forms of misbehaviour (e.g. refusal to do any work, hitting another pupil), there are many areas where there is a high degree of variation in teachers' judgements (e.g. the degree of talking that is allowed). In addition, a particular teacher's judgements may well vary from class to class, and from pupil to pupil within the same class. Equally, each teacher has his or her own notion of the *ideal pupil*. Most usually this is a pupil who is very attentive, highly motivated and interested in the work at hand, and who is able to remain solely concerned with the learning activities being undertaken. Ironically, a danger for teachers faced with such ideal pupils is that they are over-tolerant of ineffective teaching, and can induce a teacher to allow the quality of their teaching to slip.

Each teacher must decide, for each individual class and pupil, at what point any deviation from this ideal constitutes misbehaviour. Furthermore, the teacher must judge what degree of such misbehaviour can be tolerated (in as much as it will not undermine learning or is unrealistic to attempt to modify) and what degree requires action. There are thus two grey areas here: firstly, the point at which misbehaviour is deemed to have occurred, and secondly the point at which such misbehaviour requires action. Because the notion of misbehaviour inherently involves such ambiguities, an essential feature of effective teaching is that the teacher's expectations and requirements in this area are made explicit and applied consistently. All pupils wish to know exactly where they stand in relation to a teacher's judgements of misbehaviour. Teacher action based on a lack of fair warning and which is inconsistent will invariably cause resentment.

Pupil misbehaviour can range from simple non-compliance (e.g. not paying attention) to overt disruptive behaviour (e.g. throwing a missile across the room). Obviously, such overt disruptive behaviour gives teachers the greater immediate cause for concern, but it will be evident from the discussion of effective teaching throughout this book, that it is the teacher's ability to keep pupils engaged in the learning experiences that is of fundamental importance for maintaining discipline.

Studies of pupil misbehaviour (e.g. Evertson and Weinstein, 2006; Kyriacou et al., 2007) have shown that the vast bulk of pupil misbehaviour is quite minor in nature. It largely consists of noisy or non-work-related talking, not getting on with the learning activity, and mild misdemeanours and transgressions such as eating, being out of one's seat and fidgeting. Serious misbehaviour, including direct disobedience, physical aggression, or damage is much less frequent. Most pupil misbehaviour occurs much nearer to the non-compliance end of the continuum than to the disruptive end. Nevertheless, in a number of schools, serious disruptive behaviour occurs sufficiently frequently to be a major source of concern for the schools, and this has given rise to a steady stream of major reports concerning the state of discipline in schools (e.g. the Steer Report, 2005).

Approaches to dealing with serious disruptive behaviour in schools are varied. Some schools, particularly those serving inner-city areas with a particularly disadvantaged intake, have established school-based units on the school site where disruptive pupils can be sent for short 'cooling-off' periods or for longer periods (such as one or two weeks) where they may receive individual tutoring in particular subjects. Some LAs have established offsite centres to cater for disruptive pupils and truants serving a number of schools in an area. Such offsite centres often include ambitious programmes of counselling and academic support with a view to helping such pupils return to mainstream schooling.

One major difference between schools is the degree to which the school takes a stance that with counselling and support, the school may be able to help the pupil improve their behaviour to a level that is acceptable, or at least can be tolerated if a sympathetic stance towards helping the pupil is maintained. In such schools, a strong pastoral care ethos is evident. In contrast, there are schools that take a much more forceful line in seeing the pupil's misbehaviour as a problem that rests fairly and squarely with the pupil, and if the pupil is not willing to conform to an acceptable standard of behaviour, the school (to be fair to its reputation and to the needs of its other pupils) cannot be expected to keep the pupil on its roll, and further misbehaviour is likely to result in permanent exclusion from the school.

A number of studies have shown that schools serving a similar catchment area of pupils vary markedly in their exclusion rates (Kyriacou, 2003; Munn and Lloyd, 2005). One of the main reasons for this relates to the school's stance towards pupils as outlined above. Schools with relatively lower rates of exclusion tend to try to deal with misbehaviour at the classroom level, with support as necessary from pastoral care staff. Schools with higher rates of exclusion tend to refer misbehaviour quickly from the classroom level to senior management and the headteacher, often coupled with an implicit or explicit message to the pupil, and to his or her parents, that the pupil either behaves acceptably in future or goes.

Studies of the misbehaviour cited by schools as being the cause for exclusion highlight two main patterns of misbehaviour that result in exclusion (Kyriacou, 2003; Munn and Lloyd, 2005; Vulliamy and Webb, 2003). The first pattern relates to the occurrence of extremely serious incidents, which result in themselves in immediate exclusion, such as attempting to sell drugs to others pupils, or assaulting a teacher. The second pattern relates to a gradual build up of problems, which eventually reaches a point where the headteacher feels exclusion is necessary, although the precipitating incident itself may not be very serious when taken on its own. The most frequent precipitating incidents cited by schools fall into five categories:

- *Physical abuse*, including assaults on children, teachers and other adults.
- *Verbal abuse*, including insolence, swearing and disobedience to staff, and abusive language to other pupils.
- *Disruption*, including disruption in lessons, refusal to accept punishments, breaking contracts, and misbehaviour that disrupts the smooth running of the school.
- *Criminal*, including drug-related activities, vandalism and theft.
- *Truancy*, plus other attendance problems including absconding.

In discussing the nature of pupil misbehaviour, it is clear that a wide variety of behaviour is involved, ranging from failure to pay attention, to truancy. Where serious and persistent misbehaviour occurs, the pupil may need to be assessed to ascertain whether the pupil is deemed to have special needs as a result of an 'emotional and behavioural disorder', for which additional support and provision may be made either in school or by placement in a special school. In general, emotional or behavioural disorder applies when a pupil's behaviour is so disturbing (either in terms of being detrimental to themselves or to others) that special provision is sought. A distinction may be made between an emotional disorder and a behavioural disorder underlying a pupil's learning difficulty. The former relates to emotional problems, such as anxieties, phobias, depression and extreme withdrawal, which in extreme cases may constitute a psychiatrically diagnosed neurosis or psychosis. The latter refers to behaviour problems, such as anti-social behaviour, truancy, stealing and violence towards others, which in extreme cases may constitute as psychiatrically diagnosed conduct disorder.

During the primary school years, such disturbing behaviour may well result in placement in a special school. During the secondary school years, however, the difficulties in arranging assessment and subsequent special provision (either at a mainstream school or at a special school), often results in such pupils remaining unassessed, frequently truanting, or being located in offsite centres for disruptive pupils. Indeed, the way in which the education system deals with such pupils has been a continuing cause for concern, both in terms of the procedures in place for assessing their needs, and in terms of the quality of educational provision such pupils typically come to receive.

Given the range of pupil misbehaviour, the discussion of its causes could easily form the basis of an entire book. Indeed, each particular form and type of misbehaviour has received its own specialist attention, whether it is vandalism, drug abuse, truancy or bullying. Clearly, many interrelated factors influence the degree and type of misbehaviour that occurs. However, a particularly helpful distinction can be drawn between those factors outside the classroom, which may predispose or increase the likelihood of misbehaviour, and those factors operating within the classroom, which trigger off the actual misbehaviour.

In looking at the outside factors that contribute to the likelihood of misbehaviour in the classroom, we need to consider a whole range of influences that facilitate or hinder socialisation of the pupil into the ideal pupil role (i.e. attentive, highly motivated, interested in learning, and able to remain solely concerned with the learning activities at hand). Probably the main influence here is the family and its circumstances. One may contrast those child-rearing practices and family circumstances that contribute to children's intellectual development and self-confidence in themselves as learners with those that undermine such development. There is little doubt that children's experiences of schooling in the first few years in the infant school are of crucial importance to their later educational progress, for it is here that children begin to form an image of themselves in the pupil role and lay the foundations for how they will accept and cope with, or react against, the demands that will be made on them.

An important feature of the pupil role is the ability to deal with frustration that occurs over difficulties in meeting the demands that the school makes, both academic and non-academic in nature. The development of impulse control is critically important for the pupil's adjustment to schooling, and such control is essentially learnt socially and is heavily influenced by child-rearing practices (Smith *et al.*, 2003). A notable aspect of such development is 'delayed gratification', which refers to the ability to behave in a way that will achieve a greater reward in the future rather than a lesser but more immediate reward. In many ways, this is a key feature of being socialised into the ideal pupil role. Those pupils who see educational attainment as an important requirement for their future (adult) lives are much more likely to strive to meet the demands of school life (including toleration and acquiescence where appropriate) than their peers who have not adopted such values or aspirations. Furthermore, where such motivation does exist, pupils nevertheless differ in their ability to emotionally sustain delayed gratification, as is evidenced by those who display strength of character and perseverance to sustain school learning in the face of temptation such as watching television, or adversity such as family discord. It is worth noting here that such behaviour is also influenced by other aspects of the social-cultural milieu, and also, to some extent, by genetic factors that influence personality development.

Whilst such outside factors are clearly important, attention must also be paid to those aspects of pupils' experience of schooling that increase the likelihood of misbehaviour. Studies based on interviewing pupils about when and why they misbehaved in school indicate how what appeared to teachers to be quite senseless misbehaviour were, when seen from the pupils' perspective, meaningful and understandable reactions to their circumstances and to the teacher's behaviour towards them (Blair, 2001; Munn and Lloyd, 2005; Wright *et al.*, 1999). Such studies have highlighted four situations that pupils particularly felt 'provokes' them into misbehaviour. These are:

- teachers being boring
- teachers who could not teach
- teachers whose discipline was weak
- teachers who made unfair comparisons.

In these situations, the pupils often report that they found the teacher's behaviour insulted them in some way and that their misbehaviour was in large measure an attempt to maintain their sense of self-dignity in the circumstances that confronted them.

Indeed, many studies that have focused on pupils' views of teachers and teaching have shown just how sensitive pupils are to how teachers behave towards them, and it is easy to see how some pupils may see their own misbehaviour simply as a fair and legitimate reaction to the teacher's teaching. As such, all teachers need to be aware of how their behaviour can serve to hinder rather than facilitate good discipline in the classroom.

Overall, the most common trigger for pupil misbehaviour seems to be encountering learning difficulties that threaten the pupil's self-esteem. This often takes the form of being asked to undertake academic work that the pupil finds difficult and is having little success with. It is not surprising, therefore, that much misbehaviour is linked with low educational attainment. In such circumstances, the pupil is often caught in a double-bind. By trying to do the work, the pupil risks frustration and further failure. By opting out of making an effort, the pupil will inevitably become bored, incur teacher displeasure and find lessons increasingly hard to bear. Disruptive behaviour and truancy, which result from such a double-bind are, in a sense, a plea for help.

Second only to learning difficulties as a trigger for misbehaviour is boredom. There is little doubt that pupils find many lessons boring. This may be because the content is of little interest, because the learning activities are too passive, or because the manner of presentation fails to sustain attention and interest. Reacting to boredom by misbehaving is not just restricted to low-attaining pupils, but occurs throughout the ability range. Indeed, for gifted children, boredom with lessons may be a major problem and precipitate disruptive behaviour.

Robertson (1996) has argued that when considering the causes of misbehaviour it is useful to identify what the motive (or pay-off) for the pupil might be. He has identified four such common pay-offs:

- Attention seeking.
- Causing excitement.
- Malicious teasing.
- Avoiding work.

It is important to recognise that all pupil misbehaviour serves underlying psychological needs. Only by taking account of these needs can the explanation of such misbehaviour be established. A misdiagnosis may mean that certain action by a teacher aimed to discourage misbehaviour can be counter-productive. For example, reprimanding a pupil who is attention seeking, or who is trying to establish his or her social standing as a leader within an anti-school sub-group, may actually lead to the misbehaviour occurring again, unless the pupil perceives that the consequences threatened in the reprimand outweigh the pay-offs.

How you develop your approach to dealing with pupil misbehaviour is likely to be influenced by your beliefs about how best to address the underlying causes of pupil behaviour. Wolfgang (2004) has argued that there are three main approaches to dealing with misbehaviour, each based on a particular set of beliefs about discipline:

- A *non-interventionist* (relationship–listening) approach based on viewing the pupil as inherently good, who needs compassionate and empathetic support to behave well when they transgress.

- An *interactionist* (confronting–contracting) approach based on viewing the pupil's misbehaviour as a result of an inability to manage their behaviour in response to the pressures of classroom life – here the teacher interacts with pupils to share goals and standards and to 'socialise' pupils into self-regulating their behaviour better.

- An *interventionist* (rules and consequences) approach based on viewing good behaviour as being the result of pupils having a clear understanding of classroom rules and the consequences (rewards/punishments).

Wolfgang argues that whilst most teachers will make use of all three approaches, their behaviour is often dominated by one of these. A number of researchers have highlighted the need, at times, to tailor how one deals with pupil misbehaviour to what one knows about the particular pupil – a discipline strategy that may be effective with one pupil in a particular set of circumstances may not be effective with another pupil. For example, Lewis (2008) has highlighted how one can categorise pupils into four different types (A, B, C or D) on the basis of their misbehaviour, ranging from those who are generally positively motivated towards the work, are confident in their ability and who occasionally engage in low-level misbehaviour (category A pupils), to those pupils who are poorly motivated, have a negative academic self-concept and engage in repeated and more intrusive misbehaviour (category D). Lewis' approach seeks to help teachers to match their discipline techniques to the type of pupil and gradually move pupils in category D to C, those in C to B, and those in B to A, which he refers to as a 'developmental management' approach.

Whilst it is clearly impossible for a teacher to deal with every problem in an individualistic way, after teaching a class for a while it does become evident how certain approaches work better with particular pupils, and if a particular pupil's misbehaviour becomes persistent, an individualist approach then needs to be considered.

Pre-empting misbehaviour

The adage 'prevention is better than cure' applies with particular force to dealing with misbehaviour. Almost all discussions of misbehaviour make reference to the qualities of effective teaching that sustain pupils' engagement in the learning activities in hand. The skill of pre-empting misbehaviour resides in vigilance plus action. Vigilance involves the teacher monitoring the pupils' behaviour (in terms of attentiveness and receptiveness) and the learning activities (in terms of their appropriateness). The teacher should regularly scan the classroom and walk around to check pupils' progress. Action refers to what the teacher does to sustain pupils' academic engagement in the learning experience whenever it appears to be slipping. Such action includes giving academic help to anyone having problems, making changes in presentation (altering the pace of the lesson, moving on to another task, or asking questions) and exerting discipline and control (moving nearer to a pupil involved in non-task-related talking, establishing eye contact, or issuing a reprimand).

In addition to vigilance and action, a crucial aspect of pre-empting misbehaviour lies in establishing clear rules and expectations regarding classroom behaviour. Trying to adopt and enforce a long list of explicitly stated classroom rules will be cumbersome. Overall, the best approach seems to be to highlight just a few general rules, such as those discussed in the last chapter, and then to allow specific instances of transgression to mark out the boundaries. A typical practical list of basic classroom rules would be the following:

- Orderly and punctual entry into the classroom.
- No talking when the teacher talks or when a pupil is answering a question.
- Work sensibly.
- No chewing or wearing of unauthorised clothing.
- No unauthorised movement or making unacceptable noise.
- Put hand up for attention.
- Orderly exit.

Studies have shown that experienced teachers are very clear about the classroom rules they expect to be followed when they first meet their new classes at the start of an academic year, and are quick to take action to ensure compliance so that their expectations become firmly established as routine norms for the class. In contrast, student teachers tend to be much less certain about establishing classroom rules with a new class and are much less certain or consistent in taking action when transgressions occur.

Pre-empting misbehaviour is made much easier if the teacher's authority and expectations can be quickly established and accepted. There is a general consensus that during the first few weeks with a new class, the teacher's behaviour should be firm and serious, in order to establish a climate that is purposeful and task-oriented. Thereafter, a move towards the more human and relaxed side of teacher–pupil relations needs to develop. The advice 'Don't smile until Christmas' attempts to highlight the importance of the initial relations between teacher and pupils being based on teacher authority rather than friendliness. It is far easier to establish this firm and serious role at the outset, than to try to adopt this later if an initially too-friendly approach has led to problems. On the other hand, however, if the initial emphasis on authority at the outset is too severe and not tempered with humanity, it may be difficult to establish a positive relationship later.

Finally, one needs to anticipate problems. This may mean making sure that certain pupils do not sit together or sit at the back of the classroom, that a pupil who has missed previous work is given something to do immediately whilst the rest of the class are introduced to more advanced work, or that clear instructions are given regarding behaviour while disruption is likely (e.g. allowing only one pupil from each group to collect apparatus).

Reprimands and punishments

Most pupil misbehaviour is either pre-empted or dealt with so quickly (for example, by use of eye contact), that a casual observer might easily fail to notice any such action by the teacher. However, there are many occasions when the teacher is required to take more formal and overt action to deal with misbehaviour, and a number of studies have explored these different strategies. For example, Kyriacou *et al.* (2007) asked student teachers to rate the effectiveness of 14 strategies for dealing with pupil misbehaviour. These are listed below in order of their perceived effectiveness:

- Establish clear and consistent school and classroom rules about the behaviours that are acceptable and that are unacceptable.
- Speak to the pupil in a firm and assertive manner.
- Make sure all pupils are given work to do as soon as possible that will keep them occupied.
- Try to get the pupil reengaged in doing their schoolwork with as little fuss as possible.
- Have a conversation with the pupil after the lesson in which you try to counsel the pupil towards understanding why doing the work and not misbehaving is in their best interests.
- Use your authoritative presence to guide the pupil towards reengaging in the work.
- Investigate the misbehaviour in a sympathetic and non-threatening manner.
- Issue a quiet reprimand about the misbehaviour that other pupils do not overhear.
- Have a conversation with the pupil after the lesson in which you issue a firm warning to the pupil not to misbehave again.
- Issue the pupil with a sanction (e.g. a detention).
- Threaten to punish the pupil (e.g. with a detention) if the misbehaviour persists.
- Threaten to involve a more senior member of staff if the misbehaviour persists.
- Give pupils easier work to ensure that they are kept occupied.
- Issue a loud and public reprimand to the pupil about the misbehaviour.

A number of studies have also focused on pupils' views concerning their preferences regarding teachers' classroom control procedures (Evertson and Weinstein, 2006). In general, pupils favour teachers who display the following five qualities:

- *Calmness:* teachers remain calm when reprimanding pupils and do not shout, thus minimising embarrassment.
- *Rule clarity and reasonableness:* rules are made clear, reasons for sanctions are stated and based on ensuring that learning is not disrupted.
- *Appropriate punishment:* avoiding the use of extreme punishments and punishments unrelated to the misbehaviour.
- *Fairness:* fair warning and correct identification of misbehaving pupil.
- *Acceptance of responsibility:* teachers accept responsibility to maintain a sound learning atmosphere.

Before turning our attention to reprimands and punishments, it is worth reiterating the importance of coupling such actions with encouragement and support of desirable behaviour (through praise, merit awards and the satisfaction of work well done). This is often sufficient on its own to direct pupils' behaviour in the intended direction. Certainly, an emphasis on reprimands and punishments as the basis for maintaining order and control is likely to undermine the quality of the working relationship between teacher and pupils.

A reprimand refers to a communication by the teacher to a pupil (which can be verbal or non-verbal) indicating disapproval of the pupil's misbehaviour. Such action can range from a stern stare to a threat of punishment. Punishment refers to the formal administering of an unpleasant action designed to punish the misbehaviour. Such action can range from moving a pupil to a seat at the front of the classroom to exclusion from the school. The distinction between reprimand and punishment is often very blurred, since some actions, for example a fierce telling off at the end of a lesson, appear to be a mixture of both. In essence, however, a reprimand embodies a warning aimed to stop the misbehaviour and prevent its future reoccurrence. A punishment embodies a statement that the misbehaviour is so serious that formal action is required, which is intended to be unpleasant in order to emphasis the gravity of the situation. Such formal action has one or more of three main aims:

- *Retribution:* the idea that justice requires that bad acts are followed by morally deserved punishment.
- *Deterrence:* the punishment is intended to put off the pupil or other pupils from similar misbehaviour in the future through fear of the consequences.
- *Rehabilitation:* the punishment is intended to assist the pupil in understanding the moral wrongdoing of the misbehaviour and desiring not to repeat it again.

The role of punishment within the behavioural psychology of classroom management will be dealt with later in this chapter.

A number of qualities have been highlighted that increase the effectiveness of reprimands, and these are described in Table 8.1. As has been argued earlier, the most effective use of reprimands lies in pre-empting misbehaviour. They form a second line of defence, coming after the use of effective teaching and before the third and final

---

The following actions increase the likelihood that a reprimand will be effective in dealing with pupil misbehaviour.

Target correctly. The pupil being reprimanded has been correctly indentified as the pupil instigating or engaged in the misbehaviour, a particular danger here is failing to identify the first pupil who engaged in the misbehaviour, or identifying a pupil who simply reacted to another's provocation.

Be firm. A verbal reprimand should be clear and firm; its tone and content should not suggest pleading for cooperation or imply damage limitation (e.g. 'Let's get some decent work done for the last ten minutes'); the tone should be authoritative and induce compliance.

Build on rapport and mutual respect. The teacher's disapproval should matter to the pupil; hence a statement of disapproval will carry significant weight. On some occasions indicating anger by a loud verbal rebuke or a livid expression may be appropriate, but such displays should occur sparingly, and a teacher should not habitually shout at pupils or lose his or her temper.

Emphasise the positive. Reprimands should emphasise what pupils should be doing rather than complain about what they are doing; thus 'Pay attention' is better than 'Stop looking out of the window'; 'You can talk quietly, but only with your neighbour' is better than 'There is too much noise in here.'

Follow through psychologically. When a reprimand is given, it should be accompanied by the appropriate non-verbal cues, such as eye contact; after the reprimand is given, a momentary prolonging of eye contact together with a slight pause before continuing the lesson increases the force of the exchange.

Avoid confrontations. Do not force pupils into a situation where an emotional and heated exchange results; where such a situation seems to be likely, postpone the exchange by asking the pupil to stay behind at the end of the lesson, and quickly resume the lesson in order to curtail the exchange.

Criticise the behaviour, not the pupil. Criticism of the behaviour and not the pupil allows the pupil to dissociate themselves from the act, and emphasises that the teacher disapproves of the misbehaviour and not the pupil.

Use private rather than public reprimands. This minimises the tendency for reprimands to disrupt the flow of the lesson and causes less embarrassment to pupils as well as less likelihood of a confrontation. Such private reprimands might include a quite word, eye contact, physical proximity, and asking a question in a context where being asked implied a reprimand.

Be pre-emptive. Reprimands aimed at pre-empting misbehaviour are more effective than those which follow only after repeated or extended misbehaviour.

State rules and rationale. A reprimand can usefully consist of a statement of the rule being transgressed, together with an explanation of why the rule is required for the benefit of teaching and learning (e.g. 'Please put up your hand and wait until I ask you to answer so I can give everyone a fair chance to speak and we can hear what is said').

Avoid making hostile remarks. Hostile and deprecating remarks should be avoided; once a pupil feels personally disliked, disaffection and alienation may quickly follow. Sarcasm and ridicule are often felt by pupils to be an abuse of authority and can seriously undermine rapport and mutual respect, to the detriment of the classroom climate.

Avoid unfair comparisons. Pupils are particularly sensitive to reprimands that involve stereotyping, labelling or comparisons with other pupils (such as high-attaining pupils or family members who are or have been pupils), which describe their behaviour as typical or disappointing in terms of the teacher's expectations (e.g. 'Your sister's work was much better than this', 'Just because this is set 3 doesn't mean you don't have to pay attention').

Be consistent. Reprimands should be consistently applied to pupils so that they are able to establish what behaviour will be dealt with; pupils resent inconsistency both in terms of whether certain misbehaviour is reprimanded and in terms of the severity of the reprimand.

Avoid idle threats. Avoid reprimands which explicitly threaten certain consequences; when it is necessary to make such threats they should be carried out, and consequently threats which will not be carried out must not be made.

Avoid reprimanding the whole class. Having to reprimand the whole class is very serious, and implies that the teacher has been unable to stem the tide of individual acts of misbehaviour; the need for such reprimands may occur from time to time, such as when the noise level has crescendoed whilst the teacher was out of the room, or when a group of pupils collude to subvert the teacher's authority by surreptitiously tapping under desks.

Make an example. Occasionally a public reprimand to an individual is necessary; this tends to be when the teacher needs to convey to the whole class with particular force the seriousness of the transgression, or when the teacher feels that his or her authority needs to be displayed publicly, such as when the misbehaviour itself can be seen by pupils to be a public challenge or test of the teacher. Indeed, making an example is commonly used by some teachers during their first few lessons with a new class to establish their authority; making an example of pupils should be done sparingly or it will quickly lose its impact and may also start to undermine teacher–pupil rapport and mutual respect; reprimands are more effective when targeted at individuals rather than at the class or at some imaginary pupil at the teacher's feet or in mid-air; this may mean selecting one particular pupil as an example after fair warning has been given to the whole class.

Table 8.1 *Effective reprimands*

line of defence, punishment. Perhaps the most difficult judgement required of teachers is to know what level and type of reprimands will be most effective for a particular class or pupil. A balance needs to be struck between establishing authority and control to sustain the necessary discipline, and the coercion of reluctant learners. Reprimands are only effective in establishing a sound classroom climate if they are used sparingly to complement effective teaching. Frequent use of verbal reprimands is likely to be regarded by pupils as nagging. This further emphasises the need to employ private and non-verbal reprimands whenever possible.

Many criticisms have been levelled against the use of punishments. These include:

- They foster an inappropriate model for human relationships.
- They foster anxiety and resentment.
- They have a short-lived 'initial shock' effect.
- They encourage pupils to develop strategies to avoid getting caught.
- They do not promote good behaviour directly, but simply serve to inhibit or suppress misbehaviour.
- They do not deal with the causes of the misbehaviour.
- They focus attention on the misbehaviour.

These criticisms need to be borne in mind to emphasise the fact that punishment is not a panacea for discipline problems. Rather they must be regarded as part of a package of strategies that a teacher needs to use, and in some ways are best considered to be damage-limitation measures. In effect, having to use a punishment implies that the foremost strategies of effective teaching plus use of counselling and reprimands have not managed to sustain the desired pupil behaviour. Before making use of punishments it is also extremely important to make use of investigation and counselling techniques to see if there is an underlying problem causing the misbehaviour. The pupil must be given an opportunity to explain his or her misbehaviour. Too quick a jump from reprimands to punishments can often be unfair and inappropriate. Reasoning with the pupil should always be attempted with pupils once a cause for concern has developed. Sometimes that may need to involve discussion with other teachers in order to get a fuller picture of the pupil's behaviour in the school or possible explanations for their misbehaviour.

Nevertheless, punishments are a necessary part of maintaining discipline in schools. It would be nice if schools were so effective in setting up learning experiences that accommodated the needs of pupils that punishments were totally unnecessary. Indeed, most teachers will have taught a class for a whole year during which it was not necessary to punish a single pupil. However, there are occasions when punishment becomes necessary, when the teacher's use of reasoning and reprimands have not been sufficient to prevent or curtail certain misbehaviour, and the teacher decides that unless punishment is administered, the misbehaviour is likely to reoccur and become more widespread.

The vast majority of incidents leading to punishment involve a clash of wills between the teacher and pupil in which the pupil is deemed to have refused to accept the teacher's authority. Typically, in such incidents, the expectations of the teacher were clear, but despite this the pupil misbehaved. Indeed, it is persistent misbehaviour, following repeated reprimands, or a direct challenge to a teacher's authority (such as a refusal to undertake the work in hand or verbal abuse), that precipitates punishment. An alternative to punishment in such circumstances is to defer dealing with the matter until the end of the lesson, when an investigative interview, which seeks to explore the reasons for the misbehaviour, can take place (see later in this chapter).

Some teachers occasionally use punishments to emphasise their authority without due warning or use of reprimands. While some incidents, such as fighting between pupils, may be punished immediately, it is wisest and most effective to use punishments very sparingly and only as a last resort.

Unfortunately, there are some schools where challenges to authority occur so often that the use of punishments is frequent and widespread. In such schools, teachers sometimes appear to be fighting a rear-guard action to maintain a satisfactory level of discipline, in circumstances where many of the pupils have become alienated and disaffected, and where frequent use of punishments foster increasing resentment, truancy and, in turn, exclusions.

As well as punishments given when the teacher is exerting authority, some punishments are given in order to encourage sound moral and social behaviour (e.g. for bullying, cheating and lying) and acceptable study habits (e.g. for untidy work and lack of effort). In such cases, the teacher's authority may not be challenged in a direct way, and the teacher's prime concern is to act in the pupils' best interests. A major danger here involves not identifying accurately the nature and cause of the problem. To punish lying when the pupil was simply too scared to tell the truth, or to punish lack of effort that resulted from a learning difficulty, is not only inappropriate but may do immense harm. All punishments must be linked with a pastoral concern if the counter-productive consequences are to be minimised.

The main qualities that increase the effectiveness of punishments are described in Table 8.2.

The following qualities increase the likelihood that a punishment will be effective in dealing with pupil misbehaviour; in addition, the points made in relation to effective reprimands (in Table 8.1) also apply to effective punishments.

Judicious use. Punishments should be used sparingly, and in the vast majority of cases only after other ways of dealing with the misbehaviour (such as changes in teaching strategies, counselling and reprimands) have been tried.

Timing. Punishments should be given as soon after the offence as possible; if there is a long delay, the link should be re-established at the time given.

Tone. Punishments should not be given as a result of a teacher losing his or her temper, rather, it should be an expression of just and severe disapproval of the misbehaviour, and given because it is in the interest of the pupil and the class as a whole.

Fitting the crime. The type and severity of the punishment should fit the offence.

Due process. Fair warning and consistency must be applied; in addition, pupils should be given an opportunity to defend their behaviour, and encouraged to understand and accept why the punishment is just, deserved and appropriate.

Relating to school policy. The punishment must relate to the overall policy of the school towards discipline.

Aversiveness. The punishment must actually be unpleasant for the pupil; some pupils may not mind in the least being sent out of the room, or may gain status in the eyes of their peers if given a detention; consequently the punishment should be of a type that ensures its aversiveness and minimises any possible factors which might weaken its effectiveness.

Table 8.2   *Effective punishments*

As well as considering the qualities shown in Table 8.2, there are also a number of pros and cons regarding the use of particular types of punishments:

- *Detention.* This is perhaps the most educationally sound of all the different punishments. Its main strengths are that it allows time for penitence (both leading up to and during the detention); its formal nature adds weight to its sense of being a form of justice administered by the school as a whole; it can also be linked to record keeping concerning the pupil's conduct, thereby involving pastoral concerns. Its main disadvantages are that it occurs some time after the incident (usually at least a day later); it is time consuming for the teachers if they have to take it; and it may precipitate further problems (e.g. if the pupil fails to attend the detention or misbehaves during it). The content of the detention may vary. The pupil may simply be required to sit in silence, or may be given a task, such as to writing an essay on why the misbehaviour was reprehensible, writing out lines, or doing a piece of work. A particular problem is to ensure that the unpleasant nature of the detention does not result in intense resentment that undermines the working relationship between teacher and pupil.

- *Extra work.* The main strength of this punishment is that it can take place in the pupil's own time; to ensure its unpleasantness, teachers may set a mindless task, such as writing lines. Its weakness lies in its inherent patronising quality and its demonstration of the teacher's authority in forcing a pupil to undertake a mindless task. It is important to note here that setting extra work *as a punishment* should not be confused with requiring that work missed or not completed in a lesson or for homework should be done. Normal coursework is not a punishment, and requiring coursework to be done must be justified to the pupil on different grounds.

- *Loss of privileges.* This can range from moving a noisy pupil to sit alone, so that he or she cannot talk to anyone, to preventing a pupil going on a school outing. The main advantage is that this can be quite upsetting to the pupil. The main disadvantage is that it can easily be seen as vindictive and unfair.

- *Exclusion from the class.* This emphasises a feeling that the misbehaviour is unacceptable to the class community and is largely based on ostracism being unpleasant. Requiring a pupil to remain in the corridor may pose other problems (e.g. they may disappear or keep looking through a window), and as a result in many schools misbehaving pupils are sent to a specific location where another teacher takes charge. A variation used in some primary schools is to exclude the pupil within the classroom, by making the pupil sit in the 'naughty chair' in the corner of the room. Its main disadvantage is that for some pupils such exclusion is not particularly unpleasant, although it may be demeaning and thereby lead to resentment.

- *Informing significant others.* Informing or involving others, such as the headteacher or the pupil's parents is, for most pupils, very punishing. Its main drawback is the danger of provoking alienation.

- *Verbal intimidation.* A really severe talking to, whether by the teacher or by a senior colleague, can be considered a punishment rather than a reprimand, if its essential aim is to be extremely unpleasant for the pupil. Its main strength lies in its unpleasantness and the fact that it can be administered quickly (although this should be in private). Its main disadvantage is that it can easily provoke a confrontation, which could become very bitter and serious in its consequences.

- *Symbolic punishments.* The most common example of this is the giving of bad conduct marks. These can be totalled up and a stated number automatically results in a detention, which may be recorded on school reports. This has the advantage of offering the teacher a somewhat mild punishment, although some systems can be administratively clumsy.

● *Exclusion from school*. This is the ultimate sanction, which can mark a point of no return. Certain behaviours, such as violence and drug abuse, are so serious that the severest form of disapproval needs to be exercised, also taking account of the need to protect other pupils. In other cases, the history of misbehaviour has been so extensive that a short period of exclusion is the last resort, aimed to help the pupil reflect on the seriousness of the situation. For some, the return to school after exclusion may be successful. For others, and for those permanently excluded, it proves to be a point where disaffection and alienation are complete, and some other provision, such as transfer to another mainstream school or to a special school, needs to be made.

It will be clear from the consideration of the pros and cons of using punishment, that using punishments effectively is no easy matter and may even be counter-productive. By and large, pupils likely to misbehave persistently, despite reprimands, are those for whom punishments are least likely to be effective. In schools where misbehaviour is relatively infrequent, the use of punishments such as detentions, appears to have the required effect. In schools where misbehaviour occurs often, the frequent use of punishment seems to have much less effect. Overall, the main message is that teachers should strive, as far as possible, to minimise the occurrence of circumstances where punishment is required as a last resort, and to ensure that other options are fully utilised first. Perhaps the single most important aspect of punishment, is that if it is threatened then it must be applied. If pupils are made clear of the circumstances in which punishment will be applied, and that such application is sure and consistent, then the use of reprimands is much more likely to be sufficient.

It is interesting to note here, that the teacher's use of discipline strategies in a manner perceived to be 'aggressive' is widely regarded as ineffective. For example, a study by Lewis *et al.* (2005) of teachers and pupils in three national settings (Australia, China and Israel) found that 'teacher aggression' as a means of dealing with pupil misbehaviour (as evidenced by yelling angrily at pupils, deliberately embarrassing pupils, keeping in the whole class, and making sarcastic comments) was associated with greater pupil misbehaviour in all three national settings. Lewis *et al.* concluded that effective discipline needed to be based on establishing goodwill with pupils and the problem with teacher aggression was that it was likely to destroy such goodwill.

Finally, two aspects of reprimands and punishments are of crucial importance. First, the necessity to avoid confrontations, and second, their relationship to pastoral care and school policy towards discipline. These will now be considered.

Dealing with confrontations

One of the most unpleasant and distressing situations that can occur in the classroom is a heated and emotional confrontation between a teacher and pupil. The ability to avoid such confrontations or to deal with one that develops is crucial to the effective management of discipline. As was noted in the previous chapter, the effective exercise of authority involves the teacher being able to impose his or her will over pupils when such authority is challenged. In the vast majority of cases, this does not pose any problems. However, on some occasions the manner in which the authority is exercised, together with the psychological state of the pupil, leads to a confrontation. The most successful teachers seem to have a sixth sense that warns them early on in an exchange that a confrontation could develop. They are then able to use of variety of social skills and techniques, including humour, to alter the tone of the exchange and to give both the teacher and the pupil a face-saving solution to the incident.

Overall, there would appear to be four main aspects of a teacher's control style that may provoke a confrontation:

- *Physical or verbal intimidation*, such as poking a finger at a pupil's face, and making hostile remarks.
- *Public embarrassment*, which includes the use of sarcasm and ridicule, or attempting to make a pupil lose face in front of the class.
- *Losing one's temper* with a pupil.
- *Irritating behaviour*, i.e. behaving in a way that the pupil finds intensely irritating.

The first three aspects are to a large extent within the teacher's control, but the fourth can be very unpredictable, particularly as the teacher's behaviour may be regarded as quite innocuous in normal circumstances, and only provokes a confrontation because of the pupil's reactive psychological state. A teacher can often pick up subtle cues from a pupil's state of agitation that all is not well, but occasionally there are no warning signs. In such circumstances, the main danger is that the teacher will react inappropriately. Once a full-blown confrontation has begun, it is extremely difficult to regain control, particularly as the event may develop very quickly. The heightened emotional state engendered can then easily lead to further misunderstanding on both sides.

The first task in a confrontation is to remain calm. One way of doing this is to adopt a mental strategy of detachment, or counting to ten, or asking oneself why one feels angry. If, in the midst of a heated exchange, the teacher can switch to a calm and relaxed tone, there is a good chance that the exchange can be toned down. The second task is to offer the pupil an escape route. Backing off does not mean a loss of authority. The two main escape routes are to defer action to the end of the lesson or to arrange immediate exclusion from the class (which may involve a colleague collecting the pupil).

It is certainly important to bear in mind that many pupils are emotionally immature and lack the social skills necessary to avoid a confrontation. It thus behoves teachers to use their maturity and skill to defuse such situations. It is all too easy to regard extreme challenges to authority as a personal attack, when they are really a reaction by the pupils to circumstances he or she is unable to cope with.

Studies of teacher–pupil conflicts indicate that the key to a teacher's ability to deal with confrontation lies in his or her interpersonal skills (Evertson and Weinstein, 2006). Attempts to develop such abilities in teachers need to focus not so much on the actual discipline techniques they use, but rather on developing their power to recognise the nature of the confrontation they are engaged in and to be able to select the most appropriate course of action to resolve the confrontation satisfactorily rather than reacting in a stereotyped way. Of particular importance is the teacher's ability to negotiate and compromise, rather than to see a conflict situation as needing an 'I win – You lose' resolution. Indeed, the ideal solution is one in which both the teacher and pupil recognise each other's position and needs and can adopt a course of action in which both sets of needs are accommodated in return for important concessions. In addition, teachers need to be able to match the strategy they adopt to the context. No one strategy will always be best, and it is the teacher's sensitivity to the situation and the pupil that enables such conflicts to be managed effectively.

Pastoral care and school policy

Dealing with pupil misbehaviour is an important aspect of the classroom teacher's pastoral responsibility. A difficulty facing teachers in exercising discipline is that they sometimes have to decide between a course of action that will be effective in maintaining discipline for the class as a whole, and another course of action that more closely meets the personal needs of the misbehaving pupil. This conflict of interests is particularly acute when the method of dealing with the misbehaviour is publicly visible and a charge of unfair and inconsistent treatment may be levelled against the teacher if a special allowance appears to be made. In practice, however, this is not as problematic as one might expect, largely because both the offending pupil and the rest of the class are very much aware of such concerns, and are able to understand and tolerate a degree of differential treatment as long as it appears to be justified by the circumstances.

The teacher's pastoral care responsibility places an emphasis on the need for the teacher to ascertain the reasons for a pupil's misbehaviour, and to come to some mutual understanding with the pupil regarding its unacceptability in terms of the teacher's, the pupil's and the class's best interests. This goes beyond simply demarcating as clearly as possible what behaviour is unacceptable. It requires the teacher to help the pupil come to an informed understanding of the concern and an intention to behave as desired in future. Such counselling is of fundamental importance to dealing with misbehaviour. A teacher who relies simply on a mixture of reprimands and punishments is unlikely to establish this pastoral care element in the pupil's educational development. Moreover, counselling enables the teacher to explore whether there are any problems facing the pupil (for example, particular learning difficulties or home circumstances), which require attention.

It is argued here that such counselling is generally more important and effective as a means of dealing with misbehaviour than recourse to punishments. This is certainly the case if the development of the pupil's ability to understand and accept responsibility for his or her behaviour is to be given priority. Punishment does have a role to play, but it is more effective if allied to counselling rather than applied as a further line of defence when reprimands have been insufficient. Although in the infant school years pupils are clearly less able to reflect on their misbehaviour, it is still the case that such counselling provides an essential and complementary adjunct to the use of reprimands. Indeed, given the importance of the child's personal and social development in the early years of schooling, the case for counselling carries as much force then as it does in the later years of schooling.

A number of qualities and strategies may be adopted to increase the effectiveness of talking to a pupil (at the end of a lesson, or at some other time) about the misbehaviour that has occurred. The following five qualities are particularly important for effective counselling:

- *Establishing trust*. The conversation should take place in a context of trust, rapport and mutual respect.
- *Privacy*. It should take place in private.
- *Care*. The teacher should display a caring and concerned attitude towards the pupil, rather than a threatening and intimidating one.

- *Encouraging reflection.* Pupils should be encouraged to evaluate their misbehaviour and the undesirable consequences that may follow if such misbehaviour continues, including a lack of educational progress and punishments. It is important here for the pupil to do most of the talking and not the teacher.

- *Achieving a positive resolution.* The pupil should agree to behave in a more desirable way in future, and accept that doing so is in their own best interests.

This is not, of course, to argue that such counselling should constitute the teacher's response to every incident of misbehaviour, or that recourse to punishments should only take place if such counselling has occurred first. There are many occasions when the shared understanding and rapport between teacher and pupils makes such formalised counselling unnecessary and an inefficient use of the teacher's time. Furthermore, as was noted earlier, talking to a pupil at the end of a lesson can also serve other purposes, such as giving a severe reprimand. What is being argued here, however, is that on many occasions counselling is the most effective and appropriate course of action.

Nevertheless, two major problems need to be considered here. First, the time pressures on teachers may lead to the exchange being superficial and cursory. Second, pupils may lack sincerity in cooperating with the teacher. Indeed, some pupils are often over-ready to agree to whatever the teacher requires, but with no real intention of complying in practice. Some other pupils may be openly hostile to agreeing to any future change in their behaviour and see it as a mark of victory if they can leave a meeting with a teacher without having had any concessions drawn from them. In circumstances where a meeting with a pupil has not been satisfactory, it is important to call upon the support of colleagues, normally the pastoral staff, in order to formalise the school's concern. In doing so, it is important for all involved that this is not perceived as being a result of the teacher not being able to deal with the pupil, but rather as a reflection of the need for a broader approach to consider the pupil's circumstances. The pastoral care staff involved, including the form teacher and head of year or house, should in the first instance be seen to be acting to support the teacher rather than to be taking over. This is no mean task, as some teachers see the main role of the pastoral head as that of taking over and sorting out pupils who pose unacceptable problems. From the pastoral head's perspective, however, there are occasions where part of the problem seems to reside with the classroom teaching, and a major task in resolving the problem rests in getting the classroom teacher to adopt an approach to deal with the pupil that mitigates future misbehaviour occurring. Over the years the degree of partnership between pastoral care staff and the classroom teacher has become much more evident, and where a pupil's behaviour has led to a cause for concern, a coordinated approach to deal with the problem is commonly adopted. Indeed, many schools have developed what has been termed a *whole-school approach to discipline.* This is marked by three essential features:

- Clear agreement among all staff in the school regarding the standards of behaviour expected of pupils, and the procedures to be followed where there is a cause for concern.

- A recognition that all staff must act consistently and as a team in line with the agreed school policy, and must collaborate and be mutually supportive in addressing how best to deal with discipline problems.

- The adoption of a set of actions that the school can take, including, for example, the use of praise in the classroom or a merit system for good work and good behaviour and the use of aspects of the school's personal and social education programme, which aim to positively promote good behaviour rather than simply react when poor behaviour occurs.

Four school practices in particular have markedly increased as a means of dealing with misbehaviour. The first is the use of a short-term period of formal monitoring, usually lasting a week, during which a pupil's behaviour is commented upon by the teacher at the end of each lesson in the secondary school, or each half-day in the primary school. This is sometimes referred to as being 'put on report'. The pupil then discusses the report with the pastoral care head at the end of the period of monitoring. Such monitoring acts as a focus for the pupil to try and maintain a sustained period of acceptable behaviour, and the subsequent discussion can then feed into what future action is required. In many schools such monitoring is usefully coupled with the involvement of the pupil's parents and soliciting their support. Placing pupils on report is a very widespread practice, but its effectiveness is largely dependent on the counselling skills of the pastoral care head together with the pastoral care head's ability to alter the circumstances that primarily gave rise to the problem (such as failure to cope with academic demands, bullying another pupil, or drug abuse). This may often involve colleagues and those outside the school, such as social workers, educational psychologists and the pupil's parents.

A second major development has been the growing readiness to communicate with and involve parents when a pupil's behaviour is giving rise for serious concern. Good communication between the school and parents is essential if there is to be a sound partnership between the two. The increasing involvement of parents in the school's concerns is a healthy and desirable trend. Nevertheless, many schools have an ambivalent attitude towards such involvement, in part because it may imply some failure in the school's ability to deal effectively with the pupil, and in part because the pupil can resent such an involvement. It is important for the teacher and pastoral staff to carefully prepare the ground so that when the parents are involved, they can be given a full picture of the nature of the school's concern. In addition, it is desirable to indicate to the pupil why the parents are to be involved so that this does not come as a surprise.

The third major development has been the increasing use of 'contracting', in which pupils agree to behave better over a set period on the understanding that some type of reward or recognition of this will follow. Such contracting is most effective when pupils are helped to appreciate that the improved behaviour required will be in their best interests and where the rewards are designed to help the pupil to carry out their intention to behave as agreed, rather than acting as the sole motive for the improved behaviour. The use of a written contract signed by both parties has proved to be helpful. The type of reward offered must be tailored to each individual pupil. Examples include arranging extra swimming sessions, spending an afternoon in the art room, helping to run the school tuck shop, the award of a merit certificate for improved behaviour, or being bought an ice cream after school. Except in extreme cases, the reward primarily acts as a psychological support to encourage the pupil to carry out his or her intention to behave, rather than as an end in itself. The effectiveness of the contract depends on five key qualities:

- Good teacher–pupil rapport.
- Establishing in pupils a sincere intention to improve their behaviour.
- Explicit and appropriate targeting of the specific behaviour that needs to be improved.
- Taking account of any underlying problems or circumstances, particularly any learning difficulties.
- Identifying a suitable reward.

The fourth major development has been the increasing use of onsite and offsite centres for dealing with disruptive pupils, often linked with temporary and permanent exclusions, as was noted earlier in this chapter. Studies of the effectiveness of such centres indicates that pupils often adjust well in them, as shown by regular attendance and establishing a healthy rapport with staff at the centre. However, arranging a return to mainstream schooling is rarely successful, and the academic progress made in centres like these is often poor. The marked increase in the use of such centres linked with exclusions poses a major problem for the effective education of many pupils.

Studies of strategies for dealing with disaffected pupils (Munn et al., 2000; Riley and Rustique-Forrester, 2002) indicate that effective strategies can be grouped together into three main areas:

- Measures taken to carefully monitor attendance.
- Measures taken to provide direct support for pupils having emotional, social and/or behavioural problems.
- Measures taken to offer an alternative learning environment and/or curriculum experience.

Central to the success of these strategies was the adoption of effective whole-school policies and the provision of high-quality pastoral care.

Hallam and Rogers (2008) has also outlined a number of innovative strategies that can help improve pupils' behaviour, which include the involvement of parents and improving home–school relationships, offering alternative curricula, and supporting at-risk pupils through the involvement of outside agencies.

The central point of this discussion of pastoral care and school policy in relation to dealing with misbehaviour is that the classroom teacher's effectiveness in dealing with misbehaviour cannot be considered separately from the strategies and policy adopted in the school as a whole. Studies that have sought to compare the effectiveness of different schools in dealing with misbehaviour have employed a range of outcome measures, including misbehaviour in the classroom, truancy, rates of exclusion and juvenile delinquency. Such studies are notoriously difficult to conduct, particularly because they need to take account of the intake characteristics of pupils into the school (e.g. social class, ethnic composition, previous history of misbehaviour) if fair comparisons are to be made. Nevertheless, when such intake differences are controlled for, it does appear that the quality of pastoral care offered in the school is a major factor in contributing to greater relative effectiveness in promoting good behaviour within a school. An important aspect of this is the status accorded in the school to the views of the pastoral care heads in not only helping pupils to adjust to the demands of the school, but also in influencing how the school can adapt its demands, where possible and appropriate, to accommodate the pupils' needs more effectively. As such, the status and influence of the pastoral care heads within a school seems to be crucial in promoting good behaviour and dealing effectively with misbehaviour.

Behaviour modification

Behaviour modification refers to the use of principles derived from behavioural psychology to bring about improved behaviour in the classroom. In its purest form, behaviour modification draws upon the principles of operant conditioning as outlined by Skinner (see chapter 3). This is based on the notion that behaviour that is followed by reward is reinforced and as such is more likely to occur in the same circumstances in the future, whereas behaviour that is not rewarded (i.e. is ignored or punished) is less likely to occur. A number of writers have outlined how such principles may be used in the classroom (e.g. Canter and Canter, 2001; Long, 2000; Porter, 2006). It is interesting to note, however, that terms such as 'positive teaching' or 'the behavioural approach' seem to be commonly used to combat some of the prejudice attached to the term 'behaviour modification'.

The use of behaviour modification in the classroom usually involves a period in which the level of some desirable and undesirable behaviours are recorded (e.g. amount of time spent out of seat, amount of time spent working, number of times pupil disrupts another pupil). These are termed the 'target behaviours'. Sometimes the programme is directed at improving the behaviour of one particular pupil, whilst on other occasions it is intended to improve the behaviour of the whole class. In both cases, a treatment phase is then implemented in which instances of the desirable behaviours by the target pupil (or pupils) are systematically rewarded (e.g. by use of praise, or award of tokens to be redeemed later for sweets or other rewards), and instances of undesirable behaviours are ignored (ignoring is generally used rather than punishments). Once behaviour has improved, the level of frequency of the rewards is gradually reduced. Finally, a post-treatment phase is used to monitor the level of the desirable and undesirable behaviours occurring in order to verify whether the treatment has been successful and also to help establish what level of reward needs to employed in future to maintain the desirable behaviours. The key to behaviour modification in the classroom thus lies in following:

- careful monitoring of the target behaviours
- systematic and consist reward of the desirable behaviours
- ignoring undesirable behaviours.

The use of behaviour modification contrasts with most teachers' approach to discipline, which tends to concentrate on reprimanding and punishing undesirable behaviours and rarely comment on or explicitly reward good behaviour. The idea of ignoring undesirable behaviour would be regarded by most teachers as suspect and unworkable.

'Behaviourists' argue, however, that much misbehaviour is simply a form of attention-seeking, and as such, by ignoring such misbehaviour, pupils quickly switch to the behaviour that gains the teachers' attention (i.e. through praise if they cannot get it through being reprimanded). Studies of the use of this approach in both primary and secondary schools have shown that it is very effective in dealing with whole-class discipline and with the behaviour of particular targeted pupils.

One major feature of its use in schools is that the pupils are often told explicitly in a prior discussion of the need to engage in the desirable behaviours and agree to the type of rewards that will follow sustained desirable behaviours. The desirable behaviours may be stated in terms of adherence to classroom rules such as the following:

- We stay in our seats whilst working.
- We get on with our work quietly.
- We try not to interrupt.

The pupils are thus well aware that they are being monitored and what rewards will follow. Indeed, this is often set up as a type of game and in some cases groups of pupils sitting at different desks in the classroom may compete with each other to see which group is best behaved and will get the best reward. In the group version of this, peer pressure is then used by pupils against a pupil in the group who starts misbehaving. In many respects, such schemes are very similar to the notion of 'contracting' discussed earlier, except that in the behaviour-modification approach the use of recording and rewarding is more systematic.

Criticism of the behaviour-modification approach can be categorised in five main areas. The first is that it is very time consuming to apply, so it tends to be used in cases where there is a favourable teacher–pupil ratio or where the teacher's concern is so great that the effort involved is worthwhile. The second criticism is that the strategy of ignoring misbehaviour to promote its extinction can pose very real problems. It may create some ambiguity in the classroom regarding the normal expectations for behaviour. The third criticism is that the 'shaping' of pupils' behaviour is in a sense anti-educational. The essence of discipline involves educating pupils to accept responsibility for their actions and to freely accept the teacher's authority as legitimate. It can be argued that such self-control needs to be based on rational understanding and not inculcated as a habit. While this criticism has some force, and reflects a commonly held view among teachers, the increasing use of contracting has enabled many behaviour-modification schemes to adopt a more explicit educational role. The fourth criticism is that behaviour modification focuses on the pupils' misbehaviour and neglects to assess its underlying causes. Although in principle this is the case, in practice almost all teachers will attempt to examine the causes of the misbehaviour before adopting a programme of behaviour modification. In such cases, behaviour modification is employed as part of a total package of action intended to facilitate educational adjustment, and not as an isolated activity narrowly utilised. The fifth criticism is that the systematic use of rewards, including praise, is somewhat cold-blooded and insincere, and as such is not compatible with establishing discipline based on mutual respect and rapport. The importance of a sound teacher–pupil relationship cannot be over-estimated. If such a relationship does not exist, behaviour-modification schemes may have only limited success. Such mutual respect and rapport demands that teachers act with sensitivity and intuition in their dealings with pupils, and this may well be the reason for many teachers feeling uncomfortable when operating a behaviour-modification scheme, despite acknowledging the scheme's effectiveness in promoting the desired behaviour.

The behaviour-modification perspective explicitly requires the teacher to consider the desired behaviour that is to be fostered and the undesirable behaviour that is to be extinguished, and in doing this, to consider how the consequences for the pupil of behaving in these ways may increase or decrease the occurrence of such behaviour. Such analysis enables the teacher to consider a number of aspects of how discipline and authority are exercised in the classroom, and to identify a strategy that will more effectively bring about the intended changes in pupil behaviour. In general, teachers have not widely adopted behaviour-modification strategies. Nevertheless, many do operate such schemes and many more have adapted some of the principles underlying behaviour modification in their own practice. Given the five main criticisms described above, it is unlikely that the use of behaviour-modification programmes will ever be employed by the majority of teachers in the classroom, and the case for its more widespread use still needs to be made. The strategies outlined in the other sections of this chapter are the ones primarily advocated by the author, but there is, nevertheless, a role for the use of behaviour-modification schemes in certain circumstances.

Summary

It will be evident from the discussion of dealing with pupil misbehaviour that the key task facing teachers is to minimise its occurrence in the first place. Once pupil misbehaviour has occurred, the teacher's recourse to reprimands, punishments and counselling must involve the careful and sensitive selection of an appropriate course of action that maximises the chance that future misbehaviour will not occur. At the same time it attempts to ensure that this course of action does not undermine the mutual respect and rapport upon which a sound working relationship needs to be based. The emphasis in this chapter has been on the use of pre-empting skills, counselling, and the use of reprimands, together with the judicious use of punishments. There are no panaceas here and each method of dealing with misbehaviour has its strengths and weaknesses. An attempt has been made to indicate those qualities that will increase the likelihood of a course of action being effective, but in the final analysis most seem to depend on the quality of the teacher–pupil relationship as discussed in the previous chapter and as indicated in this chapter. Of paramount importance in such a relationship is that teachers convey that they genuinely care about pupils' educational progress and general wellbeing. It is for this reason that the teacher's pastoral care role has been considered in both this and the previous chapter.

Discussion questions

1 What are the main causes of pupil misbehaviour?
2 How can teachers pre-empt the occurrence of pupil misbehaviour?
3 How can reprimands and punishments be used to good effect?
4 What key skills are involved in effective counselling?
5 What features should be included in an effective whole-school policy for good discipline?
6 What are the strengths and weaknesses of the behavioural approach towards discipline?

Further reading

Cowley, S. (2006). *Getting the Buggers to Behave*, 3rd edn. London: Continuum. This is an awful title that sends the wrong message, but the book provides a very good thoughtful and practical consideration of strategies for dealing with pupil misbehaviour, whilst leaving the final decision about what to do with the reader.

Hallam, S. and Rogers, L. (2008). *Improving Behaviour and Attendance at School*. Maidenhead: Open University Press. This book presents an excellent analysis of how to improve pupil behaviour and attendance by looking at the issues confronting teachers in the wider context of out-of-classroom factors, and highlights a number of useful strategies and approaches that teachers and schools can adopt.

Lewis, R. (2008). *The Developmental Management Approach to Classroom Behaviour: Responding to Individual Needs*. Victoria, Australia: ACER Press. This book illustrates how disciplinary techniques can be more effective if the teacher takes careful account of the type of pupil and the nature of the misbehaviour.

Porter, L. (2006). *Behaviour in Schools*, 2nd edn. Maidenhead: Open University Press. A useful account of different ways of looking at the nature and causes of pupil misbehaviour and their implications for how to promote good behaviour.

Rogers, B. (2006). *Classroom Behaviour: A Practical Guide to Effective Teaching, Behaviour Management and Colleague Support*, 2nd edn. London: Paul Chapman. An excellent guide to dealing with pupil misbehaviour.

9   Appraising practice

Objective

To consider how best to deal with three key professional concerns: the school curriculum, teacher appraisal and teacher stress.

This chapter addresses the three most pressing professional concerns challenging teachers. The first is to develop the school curriculum so that it meets as fully as possible the educational aspirations held for it. The second is to develop systems of teacher appraisal that will foster more effective in-service professional development. The third is to develop ways in which the levels of stress experienced by teachers can be reduced. Day *et al.* (2007) have described how teachers' careers go through various phases in which they review their current practices, renew their enthusiasm for teaching, and consider how best to develop the work they undertake as teachers. One of the challenges facing teachers is the ability to continually revisit their sense of professional identity and effectiveness in a positive and constructive manner – a quality that Day *et al.* refer to as 'resilience'. Elsewhere Day (2004) highlights the important role played by teachers sustaining a sense of 'passion for teaching' as evidenced by their continued enthusiasm and commitment towards their work as teachers. These ideas of resilience and passion also apply to schools as a whole in as far as all schools need to sustain a positive attitude towards their own improvement and development in order to meet the demands made upon them (Brighouse and Woods, 2008). A major benefit for teachers of this is that the variety of their work as a teacher means that there are many opportunities to develop new interests and new aspects to one's work.

The curriculum

The broadest definition of the curriculum is that it covers all the learning experiences set up by a school to achieve specified educational objectives (Kelly, 2004). An analysis of the school curriculum thus needs to explore four key elements of the curriculum:

- Educational aims and objectives.
- Content.
- Teaching methods.
- Outcomes and assessment practices.

As was noted in chapter 3, this needs to include consideration of both the formal curriculum (embodied primarily in the subjects and topics taught) and the hidden curriculum (the messages conveyed to pupils from their experiences of school).

It is sometimes argued that discussion of effective teaching too readily accepts the current school curriculum as its starting point, focusing on how teachers can be as effective as possible within the school's curriculum, thereby failing to address how pupils' educational progress can be better fostered by certain curriculum changes. It is essential for the development of effective teaching in schools that teachers retain a critical stance towards the existing curriculum at any given moment in time, since it is in doing so that the continued reform of the curriculum for the better is maintained. Indeed, introducing and coping with changes in their classroom practice is a key feature of teachers' ability to maintain effectiveness. At the same time it needs to be borne in mind that frequent curriculum change can be dysfunctional as teachers need a period of stability in working with a change to develop its effectiveness. As such, curriculum development in schools needs to ensure that any changes are carefully introduced and followed by a period of stability in which the change can be established and delivered effectively.

Since the mid-1970s, the debate about the school curriculum has been fierce. This can be traced back to the 'Great Debate' concerning the school curriculum launched by the Labour Government in 1976, which, through a series of conferences, addressed four main topics of concern (DES, 1977; Lewis, 2006):

- The curriculum.
- The assessment of standards.
- The education and training of teachers.
- The school and working life.

These four areas have remained on the agenda ever since, and have been the subject of continuing debate and several major reforms. The debate about the nature and content of the school curriculum has led to much discussion about the content of the aims and content of the school curriculum. The view set out by the DES in *Better Schools* (DES, 1985), listed the purposes of learning at school as:

- to help pupils develop lively, enquiring minds, the ability to question and argue rationally and to apply themselves to tasks, and physical skills
- to help pupils to acquire understanding, knowledge and skills relevant to adult life and employment in a fast-changing world
- to help pupils to use language and number effectively
- to help pupils to develop personal moral values, respect for religious values, and tolerance of other races, religions, and ways of life
- to help pupils to understand the world in which they live, and the interdependence of individuals, groups and nations
- to help pupils to appreciate human achievements and aspirations.

The verb 'to help' used at the start of each statement is significant. It reflects a trend towards seeing the teacher's role as one of setting up learning experiences for pupils, as opposed to the more directive tone of the verb 'to teach'. This shift in emphasis is probably the single most important trend in the curriculum, and we shall return to it later. Also of particular significance is the emphasis given here to the preparation for adult life and employment. This will be a second major issue, which we shall return to later.

In its discussion of curriculum design, the HMI (1985) famously listed nine *areas of learning and experience* as:

- aesthetic and creative
- human and social
- linguistic and literary
- mathematical
- moral
- physical
- scientific
- spiritual
- technological.

The HMI made an important distinction between these nine areas of learning and experience on the one hand, and four *elements of learning*, namely knowledge, concepts, skills and attitudes, on the other hand, which need to be fostered within each of these areas. In addition, the HMI listed other areas of study, not necessarily contained within subjects, which the school curriculum needs to cover, such as environmental education, health education and information technology. The HMI also advocated that the curriculum should possess four key characteristics:

- *Breadth*. It should engage pupils adequately in all nine areas of learning and experience and with the four elements of learning associated with them.
- *Balance*. Each area of learning and experience and each element of learning should be given appropriate attention in relation to each other and to the whole curriculum.
- *Relevance*. The curriculum must be perceived by pupils to meet their present and future needs. What is taught and learnt should be worth learning.
- *Differentiation*. The curriculum must allow for differences between pupils in their abilities and other characteristics.

Despite all the discussion that has taken place regarding the school curriculum since the mid-1980s, the framework developed by the HMI then remains sound, and clearly formed the basis for the introduction of the National Curriculum, which was established in the Education Reform Act 1988. In that Act, the aims of the school curriculum were outlined as follows:

- To promote the spiritual, moral, cultural, mental and physical development of pupils at the school and of society.
- To prepare such pupils for the opportunities, responsibilities and experiences of adult life.

The Act also listed those subjects that would constitute the National Curriculum in primary and secondary schools (namely, mathematics, English, science, history, geography, technology, music, art and physical education, together with a modern foreign language in secondary schools) and the establishment of a programme of study based on attainment targets for each of these subjects. Citizenship education was added to the National Curriculum in 2002.

Many curriculum innovations are as much about changes in teaching methods and assessment as they are about change in content. Whilst the introduction of the National Curriculum was very much seen in terms of being a debate about content, in fact the publication of the attainment targets for each subject was also accompanied by 'non-statutory' guidance, which included advice on effective teaching methods. An analysis of this advice highlighted 10 features of effective teaching that were advocated (Kyria-cou and Wilkins, 1993):

- Teachers should make use of a variety of teaching methods.
- There should be use of investigative, inquiry and problem-solving activities.
- Learning activities should involve pupils communicating their ideas to others.
- Use should be made of both independent work and collaborative small group work tasks.
- Pupils should evaluate their own work and the work of others.
- Use should be made of a variety of learning materials, such as books, videos and information technology packages.
- Use should be made of direct teaching methods, most importantly question and answer.
- Learning should take place in different contexts, such as at home, in the community, during fieldwork, and in visits.
- Pupils' work should be presented in a variety of ways.
- Learning activities should help pupils to develop positive attitudes about the subject and about themselves as learners, and also desirable personal qualities such as perseverance.

In many respects this list represented a push towards the more *active learning* end of the continuum of teaching styles as opposed to a very traditional, didactic, teacher-centred, exposition-based approach to teaching. The notion of active learning has received a great deal of attention over the years. Active learning typically refers to activities such as small group work, role play, project work, problem-solving investiga-tions, and computer-assisted learning tasks, where a high degree of control over the learning process is given to pupils (Kyriacou, 2007; Watkins *et al.*, 2007). Advocates of active learning argue that it generates a high level of pupil involvement in the task, through which pupils learn more effectively compared with more didactic teaching methods. In addition, active learning promotes the development of a range of impor-tant learning skills, such as those involved in collaborating with others, and taking responsibility for organising one's own work.

In contrast, there are also many writers who advocate that teacher-centred approaches are generally more effective. In particular, an approach usually referred to as direct teaching has been widely cited as promoting higher levels of pupil attainment. Direct teaching essentially consists of lessons that follow five main stages:

- The teacher sets clear goals for the lesson.
- The teacher teaches through exposition of what is to be learnt.
- The teacher asks questions to check pupil understanding.
- There is a period of supervised practice.
- The teacher assesses pupils' work to check that the goals have been achieved.

Reports by the DfES and Ofsted in the 1980s and 1990s on how the National Curricu-lum has been implemented in schools since its introduction in 1979, indicated that the earlier advice, with its tendency towards promoting active learning, was gradually toned down in order to give more prominence towards direct teaching, with particular emphasis on the importance of using whole-class teaching methods. However, the guidance given to schools on teaching methods more recently in the form of the

National Strategies concerning pedagogy advocates a more flexible 'mixed-methods' approach to teaching and learning in schools, which is linked to the notion of personalised learning and the *Every Child Matters* agenda (DfES, 2003b,c, 2004a,b, 2005a,b, 2007). Indeed, in the review of mathematics teaching in primary schools for the DCSF (the Williams Report, 2008) the review group responded to its remit to identify 'the most effective pedagogy' by arguing that 'effective pedagogical practice is not confined to any single approach. Rather, it stems from a principled selection from a wide repertoire of techniques and organisational arrangements designed to match teaching to the developing learner' (p64).

A number of writers (e.g. Alexander, 2008b; Mortimore, 1999) have noted that in most European countries the term 'pedagogy' is frequently used to refer to the theory and practice of education, whereas in the UK (e.g. DfES, 2004b, 2007) this term tends to be used in the narrower sense of referring to teaching methods. A recent development has been the increasing use by some researchers in the UK of the term 'social pedagogy' (Kyriacou *et al.*, 2009).

Social pedagogy refers to a concern for the personal development, social education and general wellbeing of the child as advanced by adults acting alongside or in place of parents in a range of educational and social care settings (e.g. preschool play groups, residential care homes, youth clubs). At the heart of social pedagogy is the exercise by these adults of adopting a parenting/caring role in meeting the needs of the 'whole child'. In schools, the notion of social pedagogy overlaps with the notion of pastoral care.

Petrie *et al.* (2006) note that most aspects of the *Every Child Matters* agenda accord with the perspectives involved in social pedagogy, and research on social pedagogy is thus ideally placed to inform how effective teaching in schools can help deliver the *Every Child Matters* agenda.

The Qualifications and Curriculum Authority (QCA) has also been reviewing the aims of the National Curriculum in the context of a continuing concern that too many pupils fail to be engaged and inspired by their experience of schooling (QCA, 2005). The QCA (2007) has put forward the following aims for the Secondary National Curriculum. The curriculum should enable all young people to become:

- successful learners who enjoy learning, make progress and achieve
- confident individuals who are able to live safe, healthy and fulfilling lives
- responsible citizens who make a positive contribution to society.

Clearly, the debate about which teaching methods should be used to deliver whatever is to be taught in schools is a continually ongoing process. In considering the curriculum, there are four major challenges facing teachers. These are described below.

1 Improving the learning process

As noted earlier, the most significant change in schools over the years has been the shift towards seeing the teacher's role as one of setting up learning experiences in which pupils are active and have a marked degree of control over the work they undertake. This change can be characterised as a move away from a passive acquisition of knowledge (based on teacher presentation, exposition and demonstration) towards activities that enable pupils to develop intellectual and social skills involved in learning, and which thereby foster greater self-confidence across the full ability range, and the development of skills that will be useful beyond the subject matter in hand.

The best argument for this approach is that of the Education for Capability movement (see Burgess, 1986), which outlines the need for the school curriculum to make use of the following ways of working:

- *Active learning:* pupils learning through the practical activity of doing and through applying to their own experiences their knowledge and skills.
- *Problem solving:* pupils being encouraged to identify problems and find their own solutions to them.
- *Creativity:* pupils discovering and developing their creative abilities by doing, making and organising.
- *Communication:* pupils being encouraged to share with others their work, ideas and problems.
- *Cooperation:* pupils learning to get on with others by working in groups and teams of different sizes.
- *Negotiation:* pupils negotiating their work programme with teachers to meet their personal learning needs.
- *Assessment:* pupils receiving frequent and appropriate recognition of their achievements and experiences as recorded and assessed by themselves and others.

Developments along these lines have occurred both within the traditional school curriculum subjects as well as through cross-curricular, inter-disciplinary and extra-curricular activities.

Many of these ideas have been taken forward in attempts to reform the school curriculum, such as the Nuffield Review of what should constitute a *Curriculum for the 21st Century* (Pring, 2007).

Another important area of development has been the attempt to match learning activities to pupils' *learning styles* in order to maximise the effectiveness of the teaching. Learning style refers to a pupil's preferred general approach towards learning. It includes such aspects as pupils' preferences for particular types of learning activities and tasks, the strategies they tend to use for learning and their preferences regarding the physical and social characteristics of the learning situation (Pritchard, 2009; Woolfolk *et al.*, 2008). A particularly interesting distinction made is that between 'deep learning' (wanting to really understand the topic in depth), 'surface learning' (wanting to get a broad overview of the topic) and 'strategic learning' (wanting to be able to perform well in only those bits of the topic likely to be assessed). Whilst it is important for teachers to be aware that pupils differ in their learning styles, it is also important that teachers help pupils to develop the skills to learn effectively in their non-preferred learning styles.

The challenge of improving the learning process is an ongoing one. Views of the learning processes that are of the greatest educational value will continue to be redefined in the light of changing educational priorities. In the context of effective teaching, maintaining attentiveness, receptiveness and appropriateness is likely to be facilitated if the learning processes involved enable pupils to be more active in the learning experience. As such, the shift towards more active learning in schools appears to make good psychological as well as good educational sense. However, a sensible approach to effective teaching needs to involve a mix of teaching methods (both active learning and didactic teaching) as this ensures that pupils who have strong preferences for certain activities are helped to develop the skills involved in learning effectively when other non-preferred activities are used, and at the same time ensures that no pupil is offered an unrelenting diet of what is for them their non-preferred approach to learning.

2 Getting the curriculum right

All schools need to make decisions about the formal content of the curriculum as embodied in the school timetable, together with the content to be covered within each element of the timetable. Some countries have adopted a fairly relaxed approach to the school curriculum in terms of what is centrally prescribed by the national government or by the regional authority. In contrast, some countries have adopted a national curriculum that tightly prescribes what is taught, and how much time should be spent on each subject (and even specific topic areas). However, even in the context of a national curriculum, schools still have to make many important curriculum choices.

The OECD (1994) identified four major themes relating to the future of the school curriculum. These were:

- *The opportunity for all to learn.* It is important that all pupils have equal opportunities in terms of education provision. It is not acceptable that some pupils are badly served by the quality of the schools that exist in their particular area, whilst pupils in another area have access to a higher quality of education. In addition, there needs to be greater prominence given to lifelong education by strengthening the educational provision available for adults.

- *Critical transitions.* More attention needs to be given to the continuity of education as pupils move from one school to another (e.g. from nursery to primary, from primary to secondary, and from secondary to tertiary). Such transitions often result in problems of coherence in the education experience for pupils, and can lead to disaffection and drop-out.

- *Decision-making.* There needs to be a constructive and healthy dialogue between all those who have a stake in the education system (e.g. pupils, parents, teachers, employers, politicians). Proper account needs to be taken of the different views of the school curriculum held by such groups, particularly in the context of living in a pluralistic democratic society.

- *Areas of knowledge and experience.* The school curriculum needs to be continually monitored and adapted to meet the needs of society. In doing so it needs to take account of shifts in the areas of knowledge and experience deemed important, ranging from developments in school subject knowledge, to wider international issues about the world in which we live.

One of the major problems facing teachers is that the pace of change in society is often difficult to cope with. Such changes have a marked impact on both the content of the curriculum, as new knowledge is developed, and on teaching methods, most particularly in relation to the use of information technology. This requires teachers to continually develop their expertise, if the quality of the teaching involved in delivering curriculum change is to be maintained. This is by no means easy and the successful management of curriculum innovation is one of the key skills teachers must have if their teaching is to be effective.

Nevertheless, the task of continually improving the curriculum so that it can retain its meaningfulness and relevance for each new generation of pupils is paramount. What is evident is that as society changes ever more quickly, the need for schools to keep pace becomes ever more complex.

3 Preparing pupils for adult and working life

One of the major developments in the school curriculum over the years has been the increasing emphasis in secondary schools on courses and experiences explicitly aimed to prepare pupils for adult and working lives. Under this umbrella can be included courses of personal and social education and development, work experience and courses leading to vocational and prevocational qualifications. This emphasis may be contrasted with the traditional, liberal/humanist concern with developing pupils' cognitive and intellectual understanding.

There is little doubt that much of the impetus for this development stems from social and economic concerns. High levels of youth unemployment and the demands of employers for increasingly well-qualified school leavers, has led to calls for more vocational and prevocational education and training. The movement, often referred to as 'vocationalism', has been most targeted at 14–19 year olds.

Whatever the arguments for and against vocationalism in schools (Matheson, 2008; Pring, 1995; Sewell and Newman, 2006), the development of courses with a vocational focus within the school curriculum has often involved the use a variety of teaching methods, including small group work, experiential learning, and independent learning, all of which have had a major influence on the movement towards more active learning in the rest of the school curriculum, and which, to my mind, has been very beneficial.

However, the school curriculum needs to do more than prepare pupils for working lives. It also needs to prepare them for adult life as a whole. This includes a need for a whole range of other areas and skills to be covered. These include areas such as:

- personal finance
- career choice and planning
- health and wellbeing
- sustainable development.

The skills include:

- communication skills
- numeracy skills
- study and learning skills
- problem-solving skills
- personal and social skills
- ICT skills.

This wider challenge for the curriculum, to prepare pupils for adult and working life, is so large that if it were to be properly met there would be little time left for the teaching of traditional areas of knowledge and understanding. As such, the selection of what the school needs to address under this heading requires continuous review to ensure that the whole curriculum remains both manageable and deals with what is most essential.

4 Developing new forms of assessment

Changes in the school curriculum need to go hand in hand with changes in assessment practices if such developments are to be successful. Indeed, implementing new assessment practices often acts as a useful device for producing changes in teaching and learning.

One of the criticisms about examination performance is that it reduces a pupil's attainment to a single grade. This often tells us little about that pupil's strengths and weaknesses, or about their approach to work. In addition, examination results tend to dominate all other forms of attainment. The point has frequently been made that examination results alone do not give others (such as parents, employers, careers advisers or course tutors for further study) a full enough picture of the pupil. To address this problem, a number of assessment practices have been used that give a much broader picture of a pupils' achievement in each subject area and also records other areas of success (both in and out of school) attained during the school years. As a result, the nature and format of school reports have become much more detailed and informative.

As the demands and expectations concerning assessments develop, so assessment practices will continue to change. From the point of view of effective teaching, what is of key importance is that the teaching takes proper account of what is to be assessed and the method of assessment. As the type of assessment used in schools increases in variety, there is a real danger that the first time some pupils have to cope with a particular form of assessment is when it is being used to grade something of importance. All pupils will benefit immensely from feedback on how they have approached an assessment task and the criteria used in the assessment. The more frequently they have such experiences, the more likely it is that their performance on such assessment tasks will be enhanced.

Unfortunately there is a real problem with assessment based on coursework, as much of the work done is not subject to proper control and some pupils are able to gain help and advice from, for example, older brothers or sisters who have completed a similar course in previous years, that undoubtedly can improve the quality of what they produce. In addition, some pupils can find it very difficult to know when to stop and will produce mounds of work far longer than what is required, and sometimes not of a quality that enhances the grade beyond what they would have been awarded for a shorter submission.

The increasing variety of assessment practices has undoubtedly helped to enhance the quality of educational experience in schools, particularly through allowing for independent work, negotiated activities and an opportunity to show what one can do rather than be tested on what one does not know. Were it not for the competitive aspect that surrounds assessment and the importance of high grades for a pupil's future options, a much more relaxed view could be taken of the imperfections involved.

Teacher appraisal

One of the most significant developments in schools has been the introduction of formal and systematic schemes of teacher appraisal (Jones *et al.*, 2006; Middlewood and Cardno, 2001).

Self-appraisal and critical reflection by teachers on their own teaching is an important aspect of their ability to continue to improve and develop the quality of their teaching (Dymoke and Harrison, 2008; Pollard *et al.*, 2008). Pollard *et al.* (2008) describe 'reflective teaching' as the adoption by teachers of constant self-appraisal in which they monitor, evaluate and revise their own practice in a cyclical manner. Pollard *et al.* argue that adopting this stance requires an open-minded willingness to look at aims and consequences, to engage with colleagues and externally developed frameworks, and to consider different sources of evidence.

Whilst self-appraisal is often conducted in a somewhat informal and intuitive basis, a number of attempts have been made to use self-evaluation forms or checklists, either adopted by the teacher on his or her own initiative, or introduced as part of a whole-school self-evaluation programme. Typical questions asked in such self-appraisal are:

- Do I plan my lessons well, with clear aims and a suitable lesson content and structure?
- Do I prepare the materials needed for the lesson, such as worksheets and apparatus, in good time?
- Are my explanations and instructions clear and pitched at the right level for pupils to understand?
- Do I distribute questions around the classroom well and use both open and closed questions?
- Do I use a variety of learning activities?
- Are my lessons suitable for the range of ability of the pupils I teach (able, average and less able)?
- Do I maintain a level of control and order that is conducive for learning to occur?
- Do I monitor pupils' learning closely during the lesson and give help to those having difficulties?
- Do I mark work, including homework, thoroughly, constructively and in good time?
- Do I have a good relationship with pupils based on mutual respect and rapport?
- Is my subject expertise fine for the work I do?

In addition, many teachers have evaluated their own teaching by collecting research data on their own performance. This has often been referred to as *teacher action research* (Costello, 2003; Koshy, 2005). Such action research involves the teacher in working through a cycle comprising four stages. In the first stage, the teacher needs to clarify the nature of their concern about some aspect of their own classroom practice. This may, for example, deal with aspects such as their use of questions, the quality of pupils' written work, their relationship with pupils, the curriculum materials adopted, or perhaps the methods of assessment they use. Once the problem has been clarified, the second stage involves the teacher in designing a solution to the problem. The third stage involves implementing the solution through some change in their classroom practice. The final stage involves evaluating whether the action taken has resulted in an improvement. Each stage of this cycle can involve data collection, such as talking to colleagues and pupils, using questionnaires and collecting observation data by recording lessons or being observed by a colleague. The teacher can also make use of wider reading, consultations with advisers, examination of information databases concerning developments in other schools, and indeed visits to other schools to talk to teachers and observe practice there. In addition, this cycle can be repeated by adapting and modifying the solution until the teacher is satisfied with the level of improvement achieved.

Formal systems of teacher appraisal, or performance review/management, involve being appraised by a colleague. There are three main purposes underlying teacher appraisal:

- *Managerial.* It is argued that regular teacher appraisal enables the headteacher to monitor more effectively the extent to which teachers are carrying out their professional duties (teaching, administrative, and other), to identify any problems that have managerial implications, and to consider the potential role of particular teachers in any future developments within the school.

- *Public accountability*. This aspect of teacher appraisal focuses on establishing a means by which central government, local government, and school governing bodies, can satisfy themselves that teachers are effectively carrying out their duties. Much of the impetus here stems from the belief in some quarters that there are teachers who are ineffective and who will be more likely to improve or be removed if a formal system of appraisal is in operation.

- *Professional development*. This involves two strands. The first concerns the use of appraisal as a means by which teachers can improve and develop their skills in order to meet their current duties more effectively and take on further duties or responsibilities in the future. The second concerns fostering career development that will enhance promotion opportunities. Whilst these two strands are often complementary, they need not necessarily be so.

Teacher appraisal schemes are in use in many countries. Studies of such schemes have highlighted several problems and issues involved. First, there is a real tension between using a scheme to enhance professional development, and using it to formally evaluate the teacher's competence with the possibility, in extreme cases of poor teaching, that this could lead to dismissal. This has often been referred to as a tension between *formative assessment* (designed to help foster teacher development) and *summative assessment* (designed to be used as a basis for decisions about pay, promotion or competence). Second, its operation can be time consuming and expensive to resource. Third, any attempt to link teacher performance with merit pay or some other type of reward for outstanding work can be harmful and divisive in its effects.

A fully fledged scheme of teacher appraisal needs to comprise seven main stages:

- *Initial meeting*. Here the appraiser outlines the purpose of the appraisal scheme and how it will operate, and ensures that the teacher has all the appropriate documentation that relates to the scheme.

- *A self-appraisal stage*. In this stage the teacher is asked to reflect on his or her own performance and professional development concerns. This would normally be in response to a written checklist or form and will produce a written response that is given to the appraiser.

- *Setting the agenda*. This takes the form of a meeting at which the agenda for the appraisal interview is agreed. In addition, the lessons to be observed and any particular points of focus for the classroom observations are agreed.

- *Classroom observation*. Notes are made during lesson observations, which are to be used as a basis for providing useful feedback to the teacher concerning their classroom practice. There should also be a brief meeting after each lesson to discuss how it went and any issues it raises.

- *An appraisal interview*. This takes the form of a review meeting at which the teacher's all-round contribution to the school and his or her professional development are discussed. In particular, targets and objectives are agreed that are intended to contribute to the teacher's improved effectiveness and professional development.

- *Producing a written statement*. A written record of the appraisal is produced and agreed, which includes a note of the targets set.

- *A follow-up review*. At this meeting the extent to which the targets have been met and any other action points that were agreed at the appraisal interview are discussed.

Studies of teacher appraisal (or performance review/management) indicate that many teachers feel they have benefited from appraisal in a number of ways (Jones *et al.*, 2006; Wragg *et al.*, 1996). The following six comments are typical:

- It enables teachers to be told that their work was valued.
- Positive feedback is reassuring and can boost confidence.
- It enables teachers to review their career to date and get advice from a senior colleague on how their career might develop further.
- The teacher can get useful feedback and advice on aspects of their classroom practice.
- It offers an opportunity to talk through their worries with a senior colleague.
- The targets set and agreed can act as something positive to aim for and achieve.

However a number of teachers have voiced concerns about appraisal, typically in relation to the time and expense involved, and suspicions about the fairness of the information gathered about them and the use to which it will be put.

In the context of effective teaching, the appraisal of classroom teaching is of particular interest. In many schemes, a particular focus has been selected for the classroom observation part of the appraisal. For example, a teacher might ask an appraiser to look at the way they use questions in the classroom, or the way they differentiate the work to meet the needs of pupils of differing ability. In effect, the appraiser is being used as a consultant in the service of the teacher. This form of appraisal, in which the onus is on the teacher to make good use of appraisal, rather than to see it as something judgemental that is done to them, seems to lie at the heart of the tone adopted in the more successful examples of its operation. Overall, there appear to be five main purposes advocated for classroom observations:

- It enables an appraiser to encourage, support and assist the appraisee to think about their current and future classroom practice.
- It provides an opportunity for the appraiser and appraisee to share ideas about classroom practice.
- It enables the appraiser to offer advice, guidance and support concerning any particular concerns, problems or shortcomings that could usefully be addressed.
- It enables the appraiser to act as an extra pair of eyes to provide the appraisee with some useful data about specific aspects of the lesson.
- It enables the appraiser to make a judgement and evaluation about the quality of the appraisee's teaching.

Effective classroom observation for appraisal can be carried out in a number of different ways. Some appraisers make use of observation schedules or checklists, whilst others prefer to simply record what goes on in a more impressionistic way. Some appraisers simply sit at the back of the room and make notes, whilst others circulate around the room and may even participate in the teaching. Of particular importance is that the teacher has confidence in the views of the appraiser. The appraiser's main task is to share ideas with the teacher being observed in a way that will be helpful to the teacher. Many teachers have reported on how classroom observation has helped them think about and change their classroom practice. The most common examples of such changes reported by teachers who have been appraised are:

- better meeting the needs of the less able
- better meeting the needs of the more able
- asking more open-ended questions
- better pacing of lessons
- better mix of activities
- better allocation of time for activities
- better use of resources
- better handling of transitions between activities
- budgeting more time within lessons for individual attention
- trying out new materials and methods
- better planning
- better record keeping.

In addition, a number of teachers have reported on how being an appraiser has helped them because observing colleagues and talking to them about their teaching has given them insights about their own classroom practice.

Despite these positive features of appraisal, the task of being an appraiser is not an easy one. Indeed, the area of appraisal in which appraisers felt they had the least level of expertise was in the conduct of the classroom observations and how to use such observations so that it was of real benefit to the teacher being appraised. In addition, being an appraiser requires a high level of social skill in handling the sensitivities that can arise, particularly if the teacher is anxious, as is usually the case, and if there are areas of concern that need to be aired. This involves establishing as non-threatening a context for the appraisal as possible, and maintaining a helpful and constructive stance throughout the process.

As well as schemes of teacher appraisal, most countries also operate a system of formal inspection, which includes classroom observation. Preparing for such an inspection often produces a great deal of anxiety. However, it does force teachers and schools to consider the quality of education the school provides, and to measure these against any published criteria that they know the school inspectors will be using in making their assessments. The handbooks produced by Ofsted (e.g. Ofsted, 1995, 2003) for use by school inspectors, for example, gives details of key features to be used in arriving at a judgement concerning the quality of teaching observed in lessons. These features include the extent to which teachers:

- have a secure knowledge and understanding of the subjects or areas they teach
- set high expectations so as to challenge pupils and deepen their knowledge and understanding
- plan effectively
- employ methods and organisational strategies that match curricular objectives and the needs of all pupils
- manage pupils well and achieve high standards of discipline
- use time and resources effectively
- assess pupils' work thoroughly and constructively, and use assessments to inform teaching
- use homework effectively to reinforce and/or extend what is learned in school.

In addition, when observing lessons, Ofsted inspectors pay particular attention to the following features:

- Lessons should be purposeful.
- Lessons should give pupils the opportunity to be creative.
- Lessons should match pupils' abilities.
- Lessons should be interesting, relevant and challenging.
- Lessons should involve a variety of learning activities.

Whilst school inspections in the UK are a quite separate exercise from teacher appraisal, there is little doubt that the published criteria used in school inspections to judge the quality of teaching will have an influence on the type of features that may be highlighted by appraisers when conducting a classroom observation as part of the appraisal process. As a result, there is a danger that teacher appraisal may come to take the form of an inspection that the school conducts on itself, rather than an opportunity for genuine dialogue and the sharing of ideas among colleagues aimed at fostering professional development. It is also likely that the list of standards developed by the TDA in 2008 (TDA, 2008), which covers the quality of teaching expected of practitioners at different stages of their teaching career (the QTS standards; the core standards; the post-threshold standards; the excellent teacher standards; and the advanced skills teacher standards), will also colour the features of classroom practice that appraisers will wish to focus on.

Another issue concerning appraisal is how best to meet the professional needs of the teacher that have been identified during the appraisal process. For example, if teachers feel they need to update their subject knowledge or develop new classroom teaching skills, in-service support needs to be made available for this to happen. There is a danger that regular appraisal can simply serve to highlight needs that cannot be met. As such, an effective scheme must be resourced properly to ensure that such teacher development needs can be addressed in a satisfactory manner.

Finally, it is important to note that the teacher's professional development is also influenced by the school climate. Those teachers working is a school where they feel their attempts to develop their skills is encouraged and supported by colleagues are more likely to thrive. In addition, the opportunity to take part in a 'learning community' of teachers, in which teachers' reflections on their efforts to explore and improve their classroom practice are shared, is also very beneficial. A case study by Ahuja (2007), for example, of a 'successful' high school operating in a challenging urban setting, identified teamwork, capability development, and a sense of collective efficacy, as major factors underpinning the school's 'excellence in urban pedagogy'. Interestingly, however, the study noted there was no key to effective pedagogy but, rather, there was an eagerness among the teachers to learn to improve their own practice and to make extra efforts in meeting pupils' needs.

Teacher stress

Occupational stress among schoolteachers (teacher stress) has over the years become a major area of discussion and concern (Kyriacou, 2000; Troman and Woods, 2001). Teacher stress may be defined as the experience by teachers of unpleasant emotions, such as tension, frustration, anxiety, anger and depression, resulting from aspects of their work as teachers. The increasing awareness of teacher stress stems in part from a concern that many good teachers leave the profession because of stress, in part from the mounting evidence that prolonged occupational stress can precipitate both mental and physical ill-health, and in part because of indications that experiencing stress may well undermine teachers' classroom effectiveness.

In addressing the question of why teachers experience stress, the key element appears to be teachers' perception of their circumstances as threatening. This perception is based on three key aspects of the situation:

- That important demands are being made upon them.
- That they may be unable to meet these demands.
- That failure to meet these demands will damage their mental or physical wellbeing.

One of the puzzling features of teacher stress is why teachers in very similar circumstances differ so much in the level and sources of stress they experience. This is, however, in large measure explained by the fact that the process of experiencing stress is heavily dependent on how teachers view their circumstances. For one teacher it may be having to deal with a difficult pupil, whilst for another it comes from the pressure of preparing lessons. Clearly, teachers will also differ in terms of how important they perceive certain demands to be and how much it matters to themselves or to others whether these demands are met.

Teachers also differ in the extent to which they feel they have control over the situation they are faced with. For example, if one is suffering from having to do a great deal of marking, it makes a big difference if one has the power to allocate some of the marking to a colleague. Any situation that couples a high level of important demands with little power to control the flow of demands or how they can be met, is likely to cause a very high level of stress.

Studies of teacher stress (Kyriacou, 2000; Troman and Woods, 2001) have indicated that the type of teachers most prone to stress are those who have a naturally neurotic disposition, who tend to have unrealistically high expectations for their own work and for the work of others, and who generally feel that they lack control over important things that happen to them in their lives. In contrast, stress-resistant teachers tend to have a very realistic set of expectations about their work, a philosophical approach concerning what can be done and how well it can be done, and a positive attitude towards their ability to be successful in dealing with problems through their own actions.

Studies exploring the extent of teacher stress have tended to rely heavily on questionnaire surveys using a self-report measure of the experience of stress. My own studies, for example, have involved a series of questionnaire surveys of teachers in secondary schools. One of the questions asked teachers to respond to the question 'In general, how stressful do you find being a teacher?' using a five-point scale labelled 'not at all stressful', 'mildly stressful', 'moderately stressful', 'very stressful' and 'extremely stressful' (Kyriacou, 2000). Overall, about 25 per cent of the school teachers used the categories of 'very' and 'extremely' stressful. Other studies, conducted in primary and secondary schools, using a similar method, have revealed similar results. Compared with other professional groups, teachers appear to be one of the highest in terms of the overall level of occupational stress they report. Despite this, the overall level of stress-related physical and mental ill-health among teachers seems to be no higher than average, and it may well be that the regular school holidays between terms mitigates the effects of stress on ill-health.

Overall, studies of teacher stress indicate that there are seven major categories of sources of stress:

- Poor pupil behaviour, ranging from low levels of motivation to outright indiscipline.
- Time pressure and work overload.
- Poor school ethos, including poor relationships with the headteacher and between colleagues.
- Poor working conditions, including a lack of resources and poor physical features of the building used.
- Poor prospects concerning pay, promotion and career development.
- Over-demanding performance targets.
- Coping with change.

Discussion of teacher stress often refers to pupil misbehaviour as a major source of stress. This is particularly the case for studies of student teachers. For example, a study by Chaplain (2008) of 262 secondary PGCE student teachers found that 'controlling pupil behaviour' and 'pupils with behaviour problems' received the highest overall rating as a source of stress on a 20-item survey instrument.

One interesting finding arising from studies of teacher stress is that it is pupils with poor attitudes and low motivation that is often reported as causing teachers the most stress rather than outright indiscipline *per se*. In the study by Chaplain, looking at student teachers, the item 'motivating disinterested pupils' received the fifth highest overall rating as a source of stress. The reason for this is that dealing with such low-level and less-intense forms of misbehaviour is a more insidious and day-to-day feature of typical classroom life in many schools. The degree of mental effort, alertness and vigilance involved in trying to chivvy and coerce pupils towards working at a reasonable pace and level in large measure accounts for the sense of being emotionally drained at the end of a school day far more than does having to deal with the occasional instance of overt misbehaviour. At the same time, this sense of emotional exhaustion can in turn make the teacher more vulnerable to other sources of stress, both at school and at home.

Heavy workload and time pressure is also a major source of stress. Part of the problem here lies in the fact that a teacher has to cope with a wide variety of tasks, related to both their classroom teaching role and wider duties. These demands are often crammed together during intense periods of time when far more needs to be done than there is time available. This is made worse by the fact that many demands are unpredictable (for example, a parent arriving unannounced or a pupil having an epileptic fit) but may require much time and sensitivity to be handled appropriately.

The area of school climate, ethos and relationships with colleagues is also extremely important, because teachers at a school need to operate as a mutually supportive community. Where relationships between teachers have deteriorated, this can becoming a major source of anxiety. Poor working conditions often cause problems because difficulties, such as a lack of resources, simply serve to frustrate the teacher in performing as they would like. Concerns over pay, promotion and career development can be particularly acute during the middle years of a teaching career when teachers often go through a period of reflection concerning their aspirations and come to terms with the extent to which the lifestyle they have established matches up to what they had hoped for.

Finally, dealing with change poses many problems for teachers. Change often makes demands that require new skills to be developed in a short of period of time, often with inadequate support. Change often also means having to leave behind the security of tried and tested routines and practice. At the same time, change may carry with it a hint that previous practice was unsatisfactory (hence the need for change), which can make dealing with the change feel threatening and upsetting.

In considering these six areas as the major sources of stress, it is very important to note that each individual teacher has their own personal and unique profile of sources of stress. The above seven areas are the most commonly reported areas of stress. However, for an individual teacher, their own major source of stress may come from a completely different aspect of their situation. In addition, an individual's stress profile is likely to change as their career progresses, and they have to deal with new demands and new circumstances.

As well as looking at the sources of stress facing teachers, many studies have also explored the coping actions teachers take to deal with stress. A coping action can be defined as an action that a teacher takes to reduce their experience of stress. Such coping actions fall into two main categories: *direct action techniques* and *palliative techniques*. The former refers to actions that can be taken to identify the source of stress and then deal with it so that the source of stress no longer exists. The latter refers to things that a teacher can do to reduce the emotional and physical feelings associated with the experience of stress.

By and large direct action techniques are the best ways of dealing with stress. This involves identifying the source of stress (e.g. a misbehaving pupil, problems arising from a lack of time to mark books properly, worries about the curriculum materials being used), and then doing something positive that will resolve the situation satisfactorily (e.g. referring the pupil to the head of pastoral care, setting aside more time for marking, modifying the curriculum materials). Of course, not every source of stress can be easily dealt with by appropriate action, and a teacher may need to try more than one solution to a problem. However, it is surprising how often teachers allow a concern to fester before they take action. In many cases, the action is successful and the source of stress simply disappears. The reason why direct action is the best approach is that it offers the chance to deal effectively with the source of stress.

In contrast, palliative techniques do not deal with the source of stress, but rather deal with reducing the emotional experience of stress. This can be done in two main ways. The first is to use *mental strategies*, and the second approach is to use *physical strategies*. In the case of the former, the most important of these is to keep things in perspective. Often during the school day, it is easy to allow minor problems to assume far greater status as a worry than they warrant. The ability to stand back and reflect on the situation more objectively can be very effective. Another important mental strategy is to see the humour in the situation. When one is confronted with a pupil who is insolent, it is easy to get angry. The ability to maintain calmness can be enhanced by becoming aware of how many situations have a comical aspect to them. Another mental strategy is to employ a form of emotional distancing from the situation, although this technique needs to be used carefully as it can sometimes induce a sense of denial. Denial can lead to the teacher feeling that certain incidents are not serious and do not need to be dealt with or are simply not happening, such as when a teacher becomes happy to accept a high level of pupil misbehaviour as unproblematic.

Physical strategies involve things a person can do that helps the body maintain a level of relaxation, or helps it to reduce the feelings of tension and anxiety that have built up. Common physical techniques involve having a hot bath as soon as one arrives home, or listening to some relaxing music, or engaging in physical exercise such as playing squash. Another useful technique is to do something one enjoys such as going out for a meal, or having enjoyable hobbies and pastimes such as rambling or singing. Some courses aimed at helping teachers to cope with stress involve relaxation training, based on breathing exercises and developing the ability to sense when muscles are getting tense and being able to relax them.

In a study I carried out looking at teachers' coping actions (Kyriacou, 2000), the following were the ten most frequently reported coping actions:

- Try to keep things in perspective.
- Try to avoid confrontations.
- Try to relax after work.
- Try to take some immediate action on the basis of your present understanding of the situation.
- Think objectively about the situation and keep your feelings under control.
- Stand back and rationalise the situation.
- Try to nip potential sources of stress in the bud.
- Try to reassure yourself everything is going to work out all right.
- Don't let the problem go until you have solved it or reconciled it satisfactorily.
- Make sure people are aware you are doing your best.

An analysis of these responses indicated that the coping actions reported by the teachers formed three main groups. The first involved actions based on expressing feelings to others and seeking their social support. The second involved a careful consideration of the situation followed by taking appropriate action. The third involved actions based on thinking about pleasurable activities in the future. Studies of teachers' coping actions indicate two things of importance. First, that an atmosphere of social support from colleagues at the school plays an important part in helping teachers to cope with stress. Second, that having a healthy home life with other interests can also make a teacher better able to deal with stress arising at school.

A number of writers and reports have addressed the issue of how stress levels in schools can be reduced. Action that needs to be taken to reduce levels of teacher stress in schools falls into three main categories:

- *What the teacher can do.* This includes developing skills to deal with the demands of school life as effectively as possible. As well as the skills involved in effective classroom teaching, these also include developing sound time-management and organisation skills, and the social skills involved in dealing with others, both pupils and colleagues. Teachers also need to develop a range of coping skills (both direct action and palliative) to deal with those sources of stress that do occur. In addition, teachers need to have interests outside school, as this can make them feel more resilient and less vulnerable when facing the trials and tribulations of life at work.

- *What senior school management can do.* This includes adopting organisational practices that remove unnecessary sources of stress and reduce others. For example, ensuring that important deadlines, such as those for writing school reports, do not coincide with other important activities such as a parents' evening. Another important aspect of the school's role is to ensure that a mutually supportive climate exists in which teachers can identify problems that occur and discuss how they can be dealt with. The school's role is also important in terms of ensuring that good communication occurs, so that teachers are fully informed of changes and developments, and the reasons for them, and can prepare for these in good time.

- *What the government can do.* There is a duty on governments and local authorities to ensure that any changes that they introduce are carefully thought through and are introduced over a sensible period of time. In addition, they need to ensure that there are teachers in place with the necessary skills and resources to implement these changes successfully. Governments and local authorities also need to continually promote the status of teaching as a profession so that teachers feel valued for the work they do, and are provided with the level of resources needed to meet the demands made on them.

In the context of effective teaching, teacher stress raises a number of concerns and issues. First, it needs to be borne in mind that many teachers who experience high levels of stress are also very effective as teachers in the classroom. Indeed, it is sometimes their high standards and commitment that make them vulnerable to stress. This raises a dilemma, in that it may be desirable for the teacher's own health to strive less hard to be so effective. In part, this is probably the case. All teachers should attempt to be as effective as possible, but if the standards they set for themselves are excessively high, there is a real danger that over a long period they may succumb to stress-related ill-health, or a general state of exhaustion, widely referred to as 'burnout' (Kyriacou, 2000). To prevent this, such teachers need to either moderate their standards to a more realistically achievable level or to ensure they use an effective set of coping actions (most notably, that they do not become easily upset when their aims are thwarted, but are able to put things in perspective and maintain a healthy and well-balanced emotional state).

In addition, for some teachers the experience of stress does indeed undermine their effectiveness. This may occur directly, such as when the experience of stress in the classroom impairs their ability to think coherently about their lesson organisation or instructions, or to sustain the sense of generosity of spirit and goodwill towards others required for maintaining a positive rapport with pupils. It may also occur indirectly, through a reduction in their general morale and commitment towards teaching, resulting in less well-planned lessons and less enthusiasm being displayed while teaching. It is imperative for such teachers to be helped to diagnose the nature of their problems and to receive appropriate support and guidance to enable them to regain and sustain their effectiveness.

Finally, it needs to be borne in mind that teaching is a demanding profession and, if teachers are to be helped to give of their best, they will need the appropriate level of support to do so. This support includes both professional development and school resources. In the light of the two professional concerns outlined earlier in this chapter, it is clear that teachers will have to cope with many challenges and changes throughout their working lives, and if these are not to involve much unnecessary stress, they will require sensible planning and support.

Summary

It is evident from the three professional concerns discussed in this chapter that teachers face a number of important challenges, which they must meet if they are to sustain the effectiveness of their teaching. It is also clear that teachers cannot do this successfully if they act as isolated individuals, relying only on their own resources and professional commitment. Rather, what is required is teamwork involving all aspects of the education service, which will foster, facilitate and support the activity of teaching. Such effective teamwork requires an appropriate ethos and infrastructure, both at a micro-level (in terms of the school's internal organisational and managerial practices) and at a macro-level (in terms of the partnership between teachers, parents, and local and central government). Great strides have been made over the years to increase the quality of learning experiences offered to pupils. If effective teamwork can be established and maintained in the face of the challenges that need to be met, then such progress will continue. Therein lies the major challenge and hope facing effective teaching for the future.

Discussion questions

1 What do you feel education should be about?
2 What types of learning activities would you like to see used more in schools?
3 What would a school timetable look like in your ideal school?
4 In what ways can teacher appraisal lead to school improvement?
5 How can teachers best cope with the demands of school life?
6 How can teachers develop and improve their classroom practice?

Further reading

Alexander, R. J. (2008). *Essays on Pedagogy*. Abingdon: Routledge. This book provides a thought-provoking analysis of teaching and learning located within a rich characterisation of the notion of pedagogy, which informs our understanding of what makes teaching an educative process and offers of an insightful and authoritative critique of pertinent research, policy and practice.

Brighouse, T. and Woods, D. (2008). *What Makes a Good School Now?* London: Network Continuum. A thought-provoking book that looks at effective teaching in the context of the wider picture concerning how schools can meet the challenge of improving in order to provide a high-quality education in an ever-changing world.

Jones, J., Jenkin, M. and Lord, S. (2006). *Developing Effective Teacher Performance*. London: Paul Chapman. This book looks at the ways in which professional development activities can enhance the effectiveness of teachers' classroom practice.

Kyriacou, C. (2000). *Stress-busting for Teachers*. Cheltenham: Nelson Thornes. This book deals with the nature of teacher stress and the strategies and techniques that can be used to deal with the experience of stress.

Pollard, A. with Anderson, J., Maddock, M., Swaffield, S., Warin, J. and Warwick, P. (2008). *Reflective Teaching: Evidence-informed Professional Practice*, 3rd edn. London: Continuum. This book provides a comprehensive overview of reflective teaching regarding the key aspects of classroom practice; the book includes numerous 'reflective activities' and provides a number of useful summaries with extensive links to further reading.

10 Conclusions

Having completed our analysis of effective teaching, what conclusions can we draw? First, that in discussing effective teaching, we need to be clear about what type of educational outcomes the teacher is trying to foster and how far the learning experience, set up to achieve these outcomes, takes account of the context for that experience. Setting up an effective learning experience to foster recall of a poem for 8-year-olds may be very different from setting up one to foster hypothesis-forming in a science lesson for 15-year-olds.

Our second conclusion is that a consideration of the psychological basis of pupil learning provides a very helpful focal point in order to explore the effectiveness of a learning experience. In essence, it draws attention to the importance of eliciting and maintaining:

- pupils' *attentiveness*, ensuring that the pupils are attending to the learning experience
- pupils' *receptiveness*, making sure that the pupils are motivated and willing to learn and respond to the experience
- *appropriateness*, setting up an experience that is appropriate for the desired learning outcomes.

Considering these three aspects of pupil learning forces one to see the learning experience from the pupil's perspective in exploring how to maximise its likely effectiveness.

Third, there are many different types of learning experiences, and there is now a recognition of the importance of making greater use of those experiences that involve pupils being more actively involved and having greater control. In part, this is a reflection of the greater emphasis being placed on those skills that are fostered in pupils when involved in more active learning experiences, such as developing communication skills, and the skills involved organising one's own work or collaborating with others.

Fourth, despite the complexity of teaching, when one takes account of the nature of pupil learning, the different types of learning activities, and the range of pupil differences, an agenda of important teaching qualities can be drawn up. These qualities, and how they relate to the key tasks of teaching, need to be considered and discussed. Doing so will enable us to separate out the holistic and complex nature of teaching into its constituent elements, and to consider the ways in which effective teaching can be fostered and maintained.

Fifth, effective teaching is bound up with, rather than separate from, sound relationships with pupils, which includes the strategies used to minimise and deal with pupil misbehaviour. More than any other, the notion of mutual respect and rapport between teacher and pupils serves to illustrate the important interplay between the cognitive and affective aspects of learning experiences.

In fostering effective teaching in schools, there is a need to recognise the challenges facing teachers. Without doubt, teachers regularly have to cope with many changes regarding the types of learning experiences to be offered and the educational outcomes to be fostered. Such changes require proper resources and support for teachers. This involves both the necessary physical resources in terms of equipment and materials, and the necessary education and training through in-service courses and other support activities. However, more than these, it requires the time for teachers to engage in the necessary planning and preparation. This means that schools need to create an organisational infrastructure to enable such time to be made available.

Effective teaching also requires teacher commitment towards being effective. All professionals who do their work well have a commitment towards doing so, and such teachers take professional pride in the quality of their work. This degree of commitment tends to call for an effort over and above that strictly required by the call of duty. To foster such commitment in schools two conditions need to be met. First, teachers need to feel that their work is worthwhile and that it is respected, valued and appreciated by senior colleagues in the school and by the community at large (parents, local and central government, and the media). Second, teachers need to feel part of a professional community in which the quality of their work is allied to the support necessary for professional development and enhancement. While many teachers already possess levels of commitment above and beyond the call of duty, if these two conditions are fully met, it would make a significant contribution to fostering more effective teaching.

Finally, the challenges and developments involving schools make teaching a very exciting profession. Many of these changes reflect a continuing attempt to make the educational benefits to pupils of learning experiences as meaningful, relevant and worthwhile as possible. They aim at the development of autonomous learners who value and can apply their education in their adult lives. If all those concerned with education (pupils, teachers, parents, and local and central government) can establish a mutually supportive sense of teamwork and cooperation, the learning experiences that we set up for pupils will truly live up to the name of education.

References

Ahuja, R. (2007). 'Towards an understanding of excellence in urban pedagogy: a portrait of a high school'. *Qualitative Report,* 12(1), 1–19.

Akiba, M., Le Tendre, G. K. and Scriber, J. P. (2007). 'Teacher quality, opportunity gap, and national achievements in 46 countries'. *Educational Researcher,* 36(7), 369–87.

Alderman, M. K. (2008). *Motivation for Achievement: Possibilities for Teaching and Learning* (3rd edition). London: Routledge.

Alexander, R. J. (2008a). *Towards Dialogic Teaching: Rethinking Classroom Talk* (4th edition). York: Dialogos.

Alexander, R. J. (2008b). *Essays on Pedagogy.* Abingdon: Routledge.

Anderson, J. R., Reder, L. M. and Simon, H. A. (1996). 'Situated learning and education.' *Educational Researcher*, 25(4), 5–11.

Aronson, J. (ed.) (2002). *Improving Academic Achievement: Impact of Psychological Factors on Education.* London: Academic Press.

Arthur, J., Grainger, T. and Wray, D. (eds) (2006). *Learning to Teach in the Primary School.* London: Routledge.

Ausubel, D. P. (2000). *The Acquisition and Retention of Knowledge: A Cognitive View.* Dordrecht: Kluwer.

Avramidis, E. (2006). 'Promoting inclusive education: from 'expertism' to sustainable inclusive practices'. In Webb, R. (ed.) *Changing Teaching and Learning in the Primary School* (pp103–14). Maidenhead: Open University Press.

Bandura, A. (1997). *Self-Efficacy: The Exercise of Control.* New York: Freeman.

Bartlett, S. and Burton, D. (2007). *Introduction to Education Studies* (2nd edition). London: Sage.

Bernstein, B. (ed.) (1971). *Class, Codes and Control: Volume 1: Theoretical Studies Towards a Sociology of Language.* London: Routledge and Kegan Paul.

Bills, L. and Brooks, V. (2007). 'Using differentiation to support learning'. In Brooks, V., Abbott, I. and Bills, L. (eds) *Preparing to Teach in Secondary Schools* (2nd edition) (pp74–87). Maidenhead: Open University Press.

Black, P., Harrison, C., Lee, C., Marshall, B. and Wiliam, D. (2003). *Assessment for Learning: Putting it into Practice.* Maidenhead: Open University Press.

Blair, M. (2001). *Why Pick on Me?: School Exclusion and Black Youth.* Stoke on Trent: Trentham Books.

Bloom, B. S., Engelhart, M., Furst, E., Hill, W. and Krathwohl, D. (1956). *Taxonomy of Educational Objectives: The Classification of Educational Goals, Handbook 1: Cognitive Domain.* New York: Longmans Green.

Borich, G. D. (2007). *Effective Teaching Methods: Research Based Practice* (6th edition). Englewood Cliffs: Prentice Hall.

Brighouse, T. and Woods, D. (2008). *What Makes a Good School Now?* London: Network Continuum.

British Educational Communications and Technology Agency (2007). *Teaching Interactively with Electronic Whiteboards in the Primary Phase*. Coventry: Becta.

British Educational Communications and Technology Agency (2008). *Getting Started with your Learning Platform: Advice for Schools*. Coventry: Becta.

Broadfoot, P. (2007). *An Introduction to Assessment*. London: Continuum.

Bruner, J. S. (2006). *In Search of Pedagogy: The Selected Works of Jerome S. Bruner*. Vols 1 and 2. London: Routledge.

Burgess, T. (ed.) (1986). *Education for Capability*. Windsor: NFER–Nelson.

Butt, G. (2008). *Lesson Planning* (3rd edition). London: Continuum.

Canter, L. and Canter, M. (2001). *Assertive Discipline: Positive Behavior Management for Today's Classroom* (3rd edition). Bloomington, Indiana: Solution Tree.

Cattell, R. B. (1931). 'The assessment of teaching ability'. *British Journal of Educational Psychology*, 1(1), 48–72.

Campbell, J., Kyriakides, L., Muijs, D. and Robinson, W. (2004). *Assessing Teacher Effectiveness: Developing a Differentiated Model*. London: RoutledgeFalmer.

Chaplain, R. P. (2003). *Teaching Without Disruption in the Primary School: A Model for Managing Pupil Behaviour*. London: RoutledgeFalmer.

Chaplain, R. P. (2008). 'Stress and psychological distress among trainee secondary teachers in England'. *Educational Psychology*, 28(2), 195–209.

Cheminais, R. (2006). *Every Child Matters: A Practical Guide for Teachers*. London: David Fulton.

Child, D. (2007). *Psychology and the Teacher* (8th edition). London: Continuum.

Coffey, S. (2007). 'Differentiation in theory and practice'. In Dillon, J. and Maguire, M. (eds) *Becoming a Teacher: Issues in Secondary Teaching* (3rd edition) (pp187–200). Maidenhead: Open University Press.

Colley, A. and Comber, C. (2003). 'School subject preferences: age and gender differences revisited'. *Educational Studies*, 29(1), 59–67.

Connolly, P. (2006). 'The effects of social class and ethnicity on gender differences in GCSE attainment: a secondary analysis of the Youth Cohort Study of England and Wales 1997–2001'. *British Educational Research Journal*, 32(1), 3–21.

Costello, P. (2003). *Action Research*. London: Continuum.

Courcier, I. (2007). 'Teachers' perceptions of personalised learning'. *Evaluation and Research in Education*, 20(2), 59–80.

Covington, M. V. (1998). *The Will to Learn: A Guide to Motivating Young People*. Cambridge: Cambridge University Press.

Cowley, S. (2006). *Getting the Buggers to Behave* (3rd edition). London: Continuum.

Creemers, B. P. M. and Kyriakides, L. (2008). *The Dynamics of Educational Effectiveness*. London: Routledge.

Crow, F. (2008). 'Learning for wellbeing: personal, social and health education and a changing curriculum'. *Pastoral Care in Education*, 26(1), 43–51.

Cullingford, C. (2003). *The Best Years of their Lives? Pupils' Experiences of School*. London: RoutledgeFalmer.

Day, C. (2004). *A Passion for Teaching*. London: RoutledgeFalmer.

Day, C., Sammons, P., Stobart, G., Kington, A. and Gu, Q. (2007). *Teachers Matter: Connecting Lives, Work and Effectiveness*. Maidenhead: Open University Press.

De Bono, E. (2004). *How to Have a Beautiful Mind*. London: Vermilion.

Deci, E. L. and Ryan, R. M. (2002). 'The paradox of achievement: the harder you push, the worse it gets'. In Aronson, J. (ed.) *Improving Academic Achievement: Impact of Psychological Factors on Education* (pp59–85). New York: Academic Press.

Department for Children, Schools and Families (2007a). *Effective Provision for Gifted and Talented Students in Secondary Education.* London: DCSF.

Department for Children, Schools and Families (2007b). *Social and Emotional Aspects of Learning (SEAL).* London: DCSF.

Department for Education and Skills (2003a). *EiC Primary Pilot, Guidance. The Identification of the Gifted and Talented.* London; DfES.

Department for Education and Skills (2003b). *Key Stage 3 National Strategy Key Messages: Pedagogy and Practice.* London: DfES.

Department for Education and Skills (2003c). *Excellence and Enjoyment: A Strategy for Primary Schools.* London: DfES.

Department for Education and Skills (2004a). *Every Child Matters: Change for Children in Schools.* London: DfES.

Department for Education and Skills (2004b). *Pedagogy and Practice: Teaching and Learning in Secondary Schools.* London: DfES.

Department for Education and Skills (2005a). *Higher Standards, Better Schools for All: More Choice for Parents and Pupils* (White Paper, Cmnd 6677). London: Stationery Office.

Department for Education and Skills (2005b). *Key Stage 3 National Strategy. Leading in Learning: Developing Thinking Skills at Key Stage 3. Handbook for Teachers.* London: DfES.

Department for Education and Skills (2007). *Primary and Secondary National Strategies: Pedagogy and Personalisation.* London: DfES.

Department of Education and Science (1977). *Educating Our Children: Four Subjects for Debate.* London: DES.

Department of Education and Science (1985). *Better Schools* (Government White Paper, Cmnd 9469). London: HMSO.

Department of Education and Science (1989). *National Curriculum: From Policy to Practice.* London: DES.

Dillon, J. (2007). 'Reflection, inspection and accountability'. In Dillon, J. and Maguire, M. (eds) *Becoming a Teacher: Issues in Secondary Teaching* (3rd edition) (pp98–111). Maidenhead: Open University Press.

Dweck, C. S. (2000). *Self-Theories: Their Role in Motivation, Personality and Development.* Philadelphia: Taylor and Francis.

Dweck, C. S. (2002). 'Messages that motivate: how praise molds students' beliefs, motivation and performance (in surprising ways)'. In Aronson, J. (ed.) *Improving Academic Achievement: Impact of Psychological Factors on Education* (pp37–60). London: Academic Press.

Dymoke, S. and Harrison, J. (eds) (2008). *Reflective Teaching and Learning: A Guide to Professional Issues for Beginning Secondary Teachers.* London: Sage.

Elliot, J. G., Hufton, N. R., Willis, W. and Illushin, L. (2005). *Motivation, Engagement and Educational Performance.* Basingstoke: Palgrave Macmillan.

Ellis, V. (ed.) (2007). *Learning and Teaching in Secondary Schools* (3rd edition). Exeter: Learning Matters.

Evans, L. (2007). *Inclusion.* London: Routledge.

Evertson, C. M. and Weinstein, C. S. (eds) (2006). *Handbook of Classroom Management: Research, Practice, and Contemporary Issues.* Mahwah, New Jersey: Lawrence Erlbaum.

Fautley, M. and Savage, J. (2008). *Assessment for Learning and Teaching in Secondary Schools.* Exeter: Learning Matters.

Fisher, R. (2008). *Teaching Thinking: Philosophical Enquiry in the Classroom* (3rd edition). London: Continuum.

Fox, R. (2005). *Teaching and Learning: Lessons from Psychology*. Oxford: Blackwell.

Fredricks, J. A., Blumenfeld, P. C. and Paris, A. H. (2004). 'School engagement: potential of the concept, state of evidence'. *Review of Educational Research*, 74(1), 59–109.

Gagné, R. M., Wager, W. W., Golas, K. C. and Keller, J. M. (2005). *Principles of Instructional Design* (5th edition). London: Wadsworth.

Galton, M. (2007). *Learning and Teaching in the Primary Classroom*. London: Sage.

Gardner, H. (2006). *Multiple Intelligences: New Horizons in Theory and Practice* (2nd edition). New York: Basic Books.

Gardner, J. (ed.) (2006). *Assessment and Learning*. London: Sage.

Gathercole, S. E. and Alloway, T. P. (2008). *Working Memory and Learning: A Guide for Teachers*. London: Sage.

Gillespie, H. (2006). *Unlocking Learning and Teaching with ICT: Identifying and Overcoming Barriers*. London: David Fulton.

Gillies, R. M. (2004). 'The effects of cooperative activities on junior high school students during small group learning'. *Learning and Instruction*, 14(2), 197–213.

Glanville, J. L. and Wildhagen, T. (2007). 'The measurement of school engagement: assessing dimensionality and measurement invariance across race and ethnicity'. *Educational and Psychological Measurement*, 67(6), 1019–41.

Good, T. and Brophy, J. (2003). *Looking in Classrooms* (9th edition). Boston: Pearson, Allyn and Bacon.

Goswami, U. (2008). *Cognitive Development: The Learning Brain*. Hove: Psychology Press.

Gronlund, N. E. and Tro, N. J. (2004). *Writing Instructional Objectives for Teaching and Assessment* (7th edition). Englewood Cliffs: Prentice Hall.

Gross, M. U. M. (2004). *Exceptionally Gifted Children* (2nd edition). London: RoutledgeFalmer.

Guy, P. (2006). *Study Skills: A Teaching Programme for Students in Schools and Colleges*. London: Paul Chapman.

Hallam, S. and Rogers, L. (2008). *Improving Behaviour and Attendance at School*. Maidenhead: Open University Press.

Hansen, A. (ed.) (2005). *Children's Errors in Mathematics: Understanding Common Misconceptions in Primary Schools*. Exeter: Learning Matters.

Hattie, J. (2008). *Visible Learning*. London: Routledge.

Haydn, T. (2007). *Managing Pupil Behaviour: Key Issues in Teaching and Learning*. London: Routledge.

Hayes, D. (2006). *Inspiring Primary Teaching: Insights into Excellent Primary Practice*. Exeter: Learning Matters.

Her Majesty's Inspectorate of Schools (HMI) (1985). *The Curriculum from 5 to 16* (HMI Series: Curriculum Matters, no. 2). London: HMSO.

Hewitt, D. (2008). *Understanding Effective Learning: Strategies for the Classroom*. London: McGraw Hill.

Jackson, C. (2006). *Lads and Ladettes in School: Gender and a Fear of Failure*. Maidenhead: Open University Press.

Jacques, K. and Hyland, R. (eds) (2007). *Professional Studies: Primary and Early Years* (3rd edition). Exeter: Learning Matters.

Jarvis, M. (2005). *The Psychology of Effective Learning and Teaching*. Cheltenham: Nelson Thornes.

Jones, J., Jenkin, M. and Lord, S. (2006). *Developing Effective Teacher Performance*. London: Paul Chapman.

Johnston, J. (2007). Differentiation. In Johnston, J., Halocha, J. and Chater, M. (eds) *Developing Teaching Skills in the Primary School* (pp99–118). Maidenhead: Open University Press.

Johnston, J., Halocha, J. and Chater, M. (2007). *Developing Teaching Skills in the Primary School*. Maidenhead: Open University Press.

Jordan, A., Carlile, O. and Stack, A. (2008). *Approaches to Learning: A Guide for Teachers*. Maidenhead: Open University Press.

Kellett, M. (2008). 'Special educational needs and inclusion in education: an historical overview'. In Matheson, D. (ed.) *An Introduction to the Study of Education* (3rd edition) (pp156–70). London: David Fulton.

Kelly, A. V. (2004). *The Curriculum: Theory and Practice* (5th edition). London: Sage.

Kerry, T. (2002). *Explaining and Questioning*. Cheltenham: Nelson Thornes.

Kerry, T. and Wilding, M. (2004). *Effective Classroom Teacher: Developing the Skills You Need in Today's Classroom*. London: Pearson.

Koshy, V. (2005). *Action Research for Improving Practice: A Practical Guide*. London: Paul Chapman.

Kounin, J. S. (1970). *Discipline and Group Management in Classrooms*. New York: Holt, Rinehart and Winston.

Kunter, M., Baumert, J. and Köller, O. (2007). 'Effective classroom management and the development of subject-related interest'. *Learning and Instruction*, 17(5), 494–509.

Kutnick, P. (2006). *Promoting Effective Groupwork in Primary Classrooms*. London: Routledge.

Kyriacou, C. (2000). *Stress-busting for Teachers*. Cheltenham: Nelson Thornes.

Kyriacou, C. (2003). *Helping Troubled Pupils*. Cheltenham: Nelson Thornes.

Kyriacou, C. (2007). *Essential Teaching Skills* (3rd edition). Cheltenham: Nelson Thornes.

Kyriacou, C. and Cheng, H. (1993). 'Student teachers' attitudes towards the humanistic approach to teaching and learning in schools'. *European Journal of Teacher Education*, 16(2), 163–168.

Kyriacou, C. and Kunc, R. (2007). 'Beginning teachers' expectations of teaching'. *Teaching and Teacher Education*, 23(8), 1246–1257.

Kyriacou, C. and McKelvey, J. (1985). 'An exploration of individual differences in 'effective' teaching'. *Educational Review*, 37(1), 13–17.

Kyriacou, C. and Wilkins, M. (1993). 'The impact of the National Curriculum on teaching methods at a secondary school'. *Educational Research*, 35(3), 270–276.

Kyriacou, C., Avramidis, E., Høie, H., Hultgren, Å. and Stephens, P. (2007). 'The development of student teachers' views on pupil misbehaviour during an initial teacher training programme in England and Norway'. *Journal of Education for Teaching*, 33(3), 293–307.

Kyriacou, C., Ellingsen, I.T., Stephens, P. and Sundaram, V. (2009). 'Social pedagogy and the teacher: England and Norway compared'. *Pedagogy, Culture and Society*, accepted for publication.

Leask, M. and Pachler, N. (eds) (2005). *Learning to Teach using ICT in the Secondary School: A Companion to School Experience* (2nd edition). London: Routledge.

Lewis, A. and Norwich, B. (eds) (2005). *Special Teaching for Special Children?: Pedagogies for Inclusion*. Maidenhead: Open University Press.

Lewis, M. (2006). 'The national context for the curriculum'. In Arthur, J., Grainger, T. and Wray, D. (eds) *Learning to Teaching in the Primary School* (pp173–183). London: Routledge.

Lewis, R. (2008). *The Developmental Management Approach to Classroom Behaviour: Responding to Individual Needs*. Victoria, Australia: ACER Press.

Lewis, R., Romi, S., Qui, X. and Katz, Y. J. (2005). 'Teachers' classroom discipline and student misbehaviour in Australia, China and Israel'. *Teaching and Teacher Education*, 21(6), 729–741.

Lindsay, G. (2007). 'Educational psychology and the effectiveness of inclusive education/mainstreaming'. *British Journal of Educational Psychology*, 77(1), 1–24.

Long, M. (2000). *The Psychology of Education*. London: RoutledgeFalmer.

Marsh, H. W. (2007). *Self-concept Theory, Measurement and Research into Practice: The Role of Self Concept in Educational Psychology*. Leicester: British Psychological Society.

Martin, J. (2008). 'Gender in education'. In Matheson, D. (ed.) *An Introduction to the Study of Education* (3rd edition) (pp126–141). London: David Fulton.

Maslow, A. H. (1987). *Motivation and Personality* (3rd edition). New York: Harper Collins.

Matheson, D. (2008). 'What is education?' In Matheson, D. (ed.) *An Introduction to the Study of Education* (3rd edition) (pp1–16). London: David Fulton.

Mercer, N. (1995). *The Guided Construction of Knowledge: Talk amongst Teachers and Learners*. Clevedon: Multilingual Matters.

Mercer, N. and Littleton, K. (2007). *Dialogue and the Development of Children's Thinking: A Sociocultural Approach*. London: Routledge.

Mercer, N. and Sams, C. (2006). 'Teaching children how to use language to solve maths problems'. *Language and Education*, 20(6), 507–528.

Middlewood, D. and Cardno, C. E. M. (eds) (2001). *Managing Teacher Appraisal and Performance*. London: RoutledgeFalmer.

Mortimore, P. (ed.) (1999). *Understanding Pedagogy and its Impact on Learning*. London: Paul Chapman.

Muijs, D. and Reynolds, D. (2005). *Effective Teaching: Evidence and Practice* (2nd edition). London: Sage.

Munn, P. and Lloyd, G. (2005). 'Exclusion and excluded pupils'. *British Educational Research Journal*, 31(2), 205–221.

Munn, P., Lloyd, G. and Cullen, M. A. (2000). *Alternatives to Exclusion from School*. London: Paul Chapman.

Myhill, D., Jones, S. and Hopper, R. (2006). *Talking, Listening and Learning: Effective Talk in the Primary Classroom*. Maidenhead: Open University Press.

Myhill, D. and Warren, P. (2005). 'Scaffolds or straitjackets? Critical moments in classroom discourse'. *Educational Review*, 57(1), 55–69.

Oakley, A. (2002). 'Social science and evidence-based everything: the case of education'. *Educational Review*, 54(3), 277–286.

Office for Standards in Education (1995). *The Ofsted Handbook: Guidance and Resource Packs for the Inspection of Schools*. London: HMSO.

Office for Standards in Education (2002). *Good Teaching, Effective Departments: Findings from a HMI Survey of Subject Teaching in Secondary Schools, 2000/2001 (HMI Report 337)*. London: Ofsted.

Office for Standards in Education (2003). *Inspecting Schools: Handbook for Inspecting Secondary Schools (HMI 1360)* (2nd edition). London: Ofsted.

Office for Standards in Education (2004). *Special Educational Needs and Disability: Towards Inclusive Schools*. London: Ofsted.

Office for Standards in Education, Children's Services and Skills (2008a). *The Annual Report of Her Majesty's Chief Inspector of Education, Children's Services and Skills 2007/2008*. London: The Stationery Office.

Office for Standards in Education, Children's Services and Skills (2008b). *Sustaining Improvement: The Journey from Special Measures*. London: Ofsted.

Organisation for Economic Co-operation and Development (1994). *Quality in Teaching*. Paris: OECD.

Organisation for Economic Co-operation and Development (2007). *Education at a Glance*. Paris: OECD.

Ornstein, A. C. and Lasley, T. J. (2004). *Strategies for Effective Teaching* (4th edition). New York: McGraw-Hill.

Pavlov, I. P. (1927). *Conditioned Reflexes*. New York: Oxford University Press.

Petrie, P., Boddy, J., Cameron, C., Wigfall, V. and Simon, A. (2006). *Working with Children in Care: European Perspectives*. Maidenhead: Open University Press.

Petty, G. (2006). *Evidence Based Teaching: A Practical Approach*. Cheltenham: Nelson Thornes.

Piaget, J. (1972). *Psychology and Epistemology*. Harmondsworth: Penguin.

Piaget, J. and Inhelder, B. (1969). *The Psychology of the Child*. London: Routledge and Kegan Paul.

Pollard, A. and Triggs, P. with Broadfoot, P., McNess, E. and Osborn, M. (2000). *What Pupils Say: Changing Policy and Practice in Primary Education*. London: Continuum.

Pollard, A. with Anderson, J., Maddock, M., Swaffield, S., Warin, J. and Warwick, P. (2008). *Reflective Teaching: Evidence-informed Professional Practice* (3rd edition). London: Continuum.

Porter, L. (2006). *Behaviour in Schools* (2nd edition). Maidenhead: Open University Press.

Power, S., Edwards, T., Whitty, G. and Wigfall, V. (2003). *Education and Middle Class*. Buckingham: Open University Press.

Pring, R. A. (1995). *Closing the Gap: Liberal Education and Vocational Preparation*. London: Hodder and Stoughton.

Pring, R. A. (2007). 'The 14–19 curriculum: aims and values'. In Ellis. V. (ed.) *Learning and Teaching in Secondary Schools* (3rd edition) (pp124–33). Exeter: Learning Matters.

Pritchard, A. (2009). *Ways of Learning: Learning Theories and Learning Styles in the Classroom* (2nd edition). London: David Fulton.

Pye, J. (1988). *Invisible Children: Who are the Real Losers at School?* Oxford: Oxford University Press.

Qualifications and Curriculum Authority (2005). *Futures: Meeting the Challenge*. London: QCA.

Qualifications and Curriculum Authority (2007). *The New Secondary Curriculum*. London: QCA.

Richards, S. (2008). *The Way We See It*. Stoke on Trent: Trentham Books.

Riley, K. and Rustique-Forrester, E. (2002). *Working with Disaffected Students: Why Students Lose Interest in School and What We Can Do*. London: Paul Chapman.

Robertson, J. (1996). *Effective Classroom Control* (3rd edition). London: Hodder and Stoughton.

Rogers, B. (2006). *Classroom Behaviour: A Practical Guide to Effective Teaching, Behaviour Management and Colleague Support* (2nd edition). London: Paul Chapman.

Rogers, C. R. and Freiberg, H. J. (1994). *Freedom to Learn* (3rd edition). New York: Merrill.

Rosenthal, R. and Jacobson, L. (1968). *Pygmalion in the Classroom*. New York: Holt, Rinehart and Winston.

Rubie-Davies, C. M. (2007). 'Classroom interactions: exploring the practices of high- and low-expectation teachers'. *British Journal of Educational Psychology,* 77(2), 289–306.

Rudduck, J. and McIntyre, D. (2007). *Improving Learning through Consulting Pupils.* London: Routledge.

Schunk, D. H. (2008). *Learning Theories: An Educational Perspective* (5th edition). London: Pearson.

Schunk, D. H. and Zimmerman, B. J. (eds) (2008). *Motivation and Self-Regulated Learning: Theory, Research and Applications.* New York: Lawrence Erlbaum.

Sewell, K. and Newman, S. (2006). 'What is education?' In Sharp, J., Ward, S. and Hankin, L. (ed.) *Education Studies: An Issues-based Approach* (pp5–11). Exeter: Learning Matters.

Skinner, B. F. (1968). *The Technology of Teaching.* New York: Appleton Century Crofts.

Skowron, J. (2006). *Powerful Lesson Planning: Every Teacher's Guide to Effective Instruction* (2nd edition). London: Sage.

Slavin, R. E. (2006). *Educational Psychology: Theory and Practice* (8th edition). New York: Allyn and Bacon.

Slavin, R. E. (2008). 'Work works? Issues in synthesizing educational program evaluations'. *Educational Researcher,* 37(1), 5–14.

Smith, C. J. and Laslett, R. (1992). *Effective Classroom Management: A Teacher's Guide* (2nd edition). London: Routledge.

Smith, F., Hardman, F., Wall, K. and Mroz, M. (2004). 'Interactive whole class teaching in the National Literacy and Numeracy strategies'. *British Educational Research Journal,* 30(3), 395–411.

Smith, P. K., Cowie, H. and Blades, M. (2003). *Understanding Children's Development* (4th edition). Oxford: Blackwell.

Somekh, B. (2006). *Action Research: A Methodology for Change and Development.* Maidenhead: Open University Press.

Somekh, B. (2007). *Pedagogy and Learning with ICT: Researching the Art of Innovation.* London: Routledge.

Stanley, J. (2008). '"Race" and education'. In Matheson, D. (ed.) *An Introduction to the Study of Education* (3rd edition) (pp105–25). London: David Fulton.

Steer Report (2005). *Learning Behaviour: The Report of the Practitioners' Group on School Behaviour and Discipline.* London: DfES.

Stones, E. and Morris, S. (eds) (1972). *Teaching Practice: Problems and Perspectives.* London: Methuen.

Stronge, J. H. (2007). *Qualities of Effective Teachers* (2nd edition). Alexandria, Virginia: Association for Supervision and Curriculum Development.

Swann Report (1985). *Education for All.* London: HMSO.

Thornberg, R. (2008). 'School children's reasoning about school rules'. *Research Papers in Education,* 23(1), 37–52.

Tomlinson, S. (2008). *Race and Education: Policy and Politics in Britain.* Buckingham: Open University Press.

Training and Development Agency for Schools (2008). *Professional Standards for Teachers in England.* London: TDA.

Troman, G. and Woods, P. (2001). *Primary Teachers' Stress.* London: RoutledgeFalmer.

Tunnicliffe, C. (2008). *Teaching Gifted Children: Strategies, Activities and Resources.* London: Paul Chapman.

Vulliamy, G. and Webb, R. (2003). 'Reducing school exclusions: an evaluation of a multi-site development project'. *Oxford Review of Education,* 29(1), 33–49.

Vygotsky, L.S. (1962). *Thought and Language.* Cambridge, Massachusetts: MIT Press.

Walsh, J. A. and Settes, B. D. (2005). *Quality Questioning: Research–based Practice to Engage Every Learner.* London: Sage.

Warnock Report (1978). *Special Educational Needs.* London: HMSO.

Watkins, C. (2005). *Classrooms as Learning Communities: What's in it for Schools?* London: RoutledgeFalmer.

Watkins, C., Carnell, E. and Lodge, C. (2007). *Effective Learning in Classrooms.* London: Paul Chapman.

Webb, R. and Vulliamy, G. (2007). 'Changing classroom practice at Key Stage 2: the impact of New Labour's national strategies'. *Oxford Review of Education,* 33(5), 561–80.

Wheeler, S. (ed.) (2005). *Transforming Primary ICT.* Exeter: Learning Matters.

Wilen, W., Hutchinson, J. and Ishler, M. (2008). *Dynamics of Effective Secondary Teaching* (6th edition). New York: Pearson.

Williams Report (2008). *Independent Review of Mathematics Teaching in Early Years Settings and Primary Schools: Final Report.* London: DCSF.

Wolfgang, C. H. (2004). *Solving Discipline and Class Management Problems: Methods and Models for Today's Teachers* (6th edition). New York: Wiley.

Woolfolk, A. (2007). *Educational Psychology* (10th edition). Boston: Pearson.

Woolfolk, A., Hughes, M. and Walkup, V. (2008). *Psychology in Education.* London: Pearson.

Wortley, A. and Harrison, J. (2008). 'Pastoral care and tutorial roles'. In Dymoke, S. and Harrison, J. (eds) *Reflective Teaching and Learning: A Guide to Professional Issues for Beginning Secondary Teachers* (pp239–87). London: Sage.

Wragg, E. C. (2005). *The Art and Science of Teaching and Learning: The Selected Works of Ted Wragg.* London: RoutledgeFalmer.

Wragg, E. C. and Brown, G. (2001a). *Explaining in the Primary School* (2nd edition). London: RoutledgeFalmer.

Wragg, E. C. and Brown, G. (2001b). *Explaining in the Secondary Schools* (2nd edition). London: RoutledgeFalmer.

Wragg, E. C. and Brown, G. (2001c). *Questioning in the Primary School* (2nd edition). London: RoutledgeFalmer.

Wragg, E. C. and Brown, G. (2001d). *Questioning in the Secondary School* (2nd edition). London: RoutledgeFalmer.

Wragg, E. C., Wikeley, F. J., Wragg, C. M. and Haynes, G. S. (1996). *Teacher Appraisal Observed.* London: Routledge.

Wright, C., Weeks, D. and McGlaughin, A. (1999). *Race, Class and Gender in Exclusion from School: An Introduction for Teachers.* London: Taylor and Francis.

Wyness, M. (2008). 'Schooling and social class'. In Matheson, D. (2008). *An Introduction to the Study of Education* (2nd edition) (pp142–55). London: David Fulton.

Author index

Akiba, M. 78, 165
Alderman, M. K. 26, 61, 76, 165
Alexander, R. J. 44, 147, 162, 165
Alloway, T. P. 23, 168
Anderson, J. 32, 163, 171
Anderson, J. R. 32, 165
Aronson, J. 26, 165
Arthur, J. 145, 165
Ausubel, D. P. 21–23, 40, 165
Avramidis, E. 60, 74, 165, 169

Bandura, A. 18, 63, 165
Bartlett, S. 20, 165
Baumert, J. 169
Becta 54, 166
Bernstein, B. 66–67, 165
Bills, L. 60, 165
Black, P. 97, 98, 165
Blades, M. 172
Blair, M. 124, 165
Bloom, B. S. 21–22, 43, 165
Blumenfeld, P. C. 168
Boddy, J. 171
Borich, G. D. 9, 19, 40, 88, 165
Brighouse, T. 143, 162, 165
Broadfoot, P. 98, 166, 171
Brooks, V. 60, 166
Brophy, J. 12, 40, 42, 88, 168
Brown, G. 42, 43, 173
Bruner, J. S. 24, 166
Burgess, T. 148, 166

Burton, D. 20, 165
Butt, G. 86, 100, 166

Cameron, C. 171
Campbell, J. 101, 111, 119, 166
Canter, L. 27, 139, 166
Canter, M. 27, 139, 166
Cardno, C. E. M. 99, 151, 170
Carlile, O. 169
Carnell, E. 55, 173
Cattell, R. B. 7, 166
Chaplain, R. P. 101, 119, 158, 166
Chater, M. 169
Cheminais, R. 98, 115, 166
Cheng, H. 112, 169
Child, D. 26, 28, 31, 37, 166
Coffey, S. 60, 166
Colley, A. 68, 166
Comber, C. 68, 166
Connolly, P. 64, 166
Costello, P. 152, 166
Courcier, I. 98, 166
Covington, M. V. 63, 166
Cowie, H. 172
Cowley, S. 120, 141, 166
Creemers, B. P. M. 16, 19, 166
Crow, F. 115, 116, 166
Cullen, M. A. 170
Cullingford, C. 11, 35, 108, 166

Day, C. 143, 166
DCSF 58, 116, 147, 167
De Bono, E. 23, 166

Deci, E. L. 25, 166
DES 94, 144, 167
DfES 57, 98, 115, 146, 147, 167
Dillon, J. 99, 167
Dweck, C. S. 59, 63, 167
Dymoke, S. 151, 167

Edwards, T. 171
Ellingsen, I. T. 169
Elliot, J. G. 33, 167
Ellis, V. 56, 74, 76, 167
Engelhart, M. 165
Evans, L. 74, 76, 167
Evertson, C. M. 120, 121, 127, 134, 167

Fautley, M. 98, 166
Fisher, R. 31, 45, 166
Fox, R. 20, 37, 167
Fredricks, J. A. 28, 167
Freiberg, H. J. 52, 111, 170
Furst, E. 165

Gagné, R. M. 21–22, 168
Galton, M. 16, 19, 168
Gardner, H. 61, 168
Gardner, J. 97, 98, 100, 168
Gathercole, S. E. 23, 168
Gillespie, H. 95, 100, 168
Gillies, R. M. 51, 168
Glanville, J. L. 28, 168
Golas, K. C. 168
Good, T. 12, 40, 42, 88, 168
Goswami, U. 23, 30, 168
Grainger, T. 165
Gronlund, N. E. 94, 168

Subject index